Economic Mobility and the Rise of the Latin American Middle Class

Economic Mobility and the Rise of the Latin American Middle Class

Francisco H. G. Ferreira, Julian Messina,
Jamele Rigolini, Luis-Felipe López-Calva,
Maria Ana Lugo, and Renos Vakis

THE WORLD BANK
Washington, D.C.

ISBN (paper): 978-0-8213-9634-6
ISBN (electronic): 978-0-8213-9723-7
DOI: 10.1596/978-0-8213-9634-6

Cover design: Naylor Design

Library of Congress Cataloging-in-Publication Data
Ferreira, Francisco H. G.
  Economic mobility and the rise of the Latin American middle class / Francisco H.G. Ferreira [and five others].
    pages cm. — (World Bank Latin American and Caribbean studies)
  Includes bibliographical references.
  ISBN 978-0-8213-9634-6 — ISBN 978-0-8213-9723-7 (electronic)
1. Income—Latin America. 2. Middle class—Latin America. 3. Households—Economic aspects—Latin America. 4. Occupational mobility—Latin America. 5. Social mobility—Latin America. 6. Latin America—Economic conditions. I. World Bank. II. Title.
  HC130.I5F47 2012
  305.5'5098—dc23

2012041229

Contents

Boxes

Figures

Focus Notes

Tables

Foreword

After a decade marked by sustained economic growth—despite the 2008–09 global financial crisis—and declining inequality in many countries in Latin America and the Caribbean (LAC), it is time to take stock of the region's broad socio-economic trends. Moderate poverty fell from more than 40 percent in 2000 to less than 30 percent in 2010. This decline in poverty implies that 50 million Latin Americans escaped poverty over the decade. But which workers and households succeeded in leaving poverty, and which did not? What happened to those who left poverty behind? Did they all join the region's growing middle class? What are the implications for public policy?

To address these questions, *Economic Mobility and the Rise of the Latin American Middle Class* exploits a unique combination of data sources, ranging from multiple household surveys and student achievement tests to surveys of attitudes, opinions, and beliefs, to shed light on the social transformation going on in Latin America in this new millennium. It proposes a new definition of the middle class based on economic security and applies it to most countries in the region. The report also investigates economic mobility, both within and across generations, to understand the drivers of success in escaping poverty.

The result is a nuanced picture. On the one hand, in most countries in the region, while intergenerational mobility has improved, it remains limited: parents' education and income levels still substantially influence their children's outcomes, and this appears to be true to a greater extent than in other regions. On the other hand, mobility within generations has been significant. At least 40 percent of the region's households are estimated to have moved upward in "socio-economic class" between 1995 and 2010. Most of the poor that moved up did not go directly to the middle class but rather joined a group sandwiched between the poor and the middle class, which the report calls the vulnerable class and is now the largest class in the region.

Still, the Latin American middle class did grow and very substantially: from 100 million people in 2000 to around 150 million by the end of the last decade. The emerging middle class differs, of course, from country to country, but there are a number of common threads. Middle class entrants are more educated than those they have left behind. They are also more likely to live in urban areas and to work in formal sector jobs. Middle class women are more likely to have fewer children and to participate in the labor force than women in the poor or vulnerable groups.

This report will certainly stimulate the debate on the implications of these new trends—for the functioning of the economy, for policy priorities, and for the performance of democratic institutions. While LAC is now on the path to becoming a middle-income region, much remains to be done. Regional leaders will need to continue to devote considerable policy attention to the one-third of Latin Americans who remain poor, while seeking to promote the security and prosperity of those who are vulnerable.

Hasan Tuluy
Vice President
Latin America and the Caribbean Region

Acknowledgments

This report is dedicated to the memory of Gonzalo Llorente.

This report was prepared by a team led by Francisco H.G. Ferreira, Julian Messina, and Jamele Rigolini, and comprising Luis Felipe López-Calva, Maria Ana Lugo, and Renos Vakis. Important additional contributions were made by João Pedro Azevedo, Nancy Birdsall, Maurizio Bussolo, Guillermo Cruces, Markus Jäntti, Peter Lanjouw, Norman Loayza, Leonardo Lucchetti, Nora Lustig, Bill Maloney, Eduardo Ortiz, Harry Patrinos, Elizaveta Perova, Miguel Sánchez, Roby Senderowitsch, Florencia Torche, and Mariana Viollaz. The team was ably assisted by Manuel Fernández Sierra, Gonzalo Llorente, Nathaly Rivera Casanova, and Cynthia van der Werf. The work was conducted under the general guidance of Augusto de la Torre, LCR Chief Economist.

The team was fortunate to receive advice and guidance from four distinguished peer reviewers: François Bourguignon, Gary Fields, Philip Keefer and Ana Revenga, as well as from a panel of advisers comprising Nancy Birdsall, Louise Cord, and James Foster. While we are very grateful for the guidance received, these advisors and reviewers are not responsible for any remaining errors, omissions or interpretations. Additional insights from Barbara Bruns, Michael Crawford, Wendy Cunningham, Anna Fruttero, Rafael de Hoyos, and Alex Solis are gratefully acknowledged.

We are also grateful to the individuals and organizations that hosted a series of consultations undertaken in the spring 2011, including (but not restricted to) Leonardo Gasparini (CEDLAS), Alejandro Gaviria (Universidad de los Andes), Miguel Jaramillo (GRADE), Eduardo Lora (IDB), Patricio Meller (CIEPLAN), Marcelo Neri (CPS-FGV), Rafael Rofman (World Bank), Isidro Soloaga (El Colegio de México), and Miguel Székely (Instituto Tecnológico de Monterrey). Thanks are also due to our hosts at the Institute for Economic Analysis (IAE), Barcelona, where a mid-term conference was held: Joan Maria Estebán, Ada Ferrer-i-Carbonnel and Xavi Ramos. The team would like to acknowledge financial support from the Government of Spain, under the SFLAC program. Book design, editing, and production were coordinated by the World Bank's Office of the Publisher, under the supervision of Patricia Katayama, Nora Ridolfi, and Dina Towbin.

Last but not least, we thank Ruth Delgado, Erika Bazan Lavanda, and Jacqueline Larrabure Rivero for unfailing administrative support.

Abbreviations

CCT	conditional cash transfer
ELTI	mobility as equalizer of long-term incomes
ESCS	economic, social, and cultural status (PISA index)
GDP	gross domestic product
GIC	growth incidence curve
IMD	directional income movement
IMND	nondirectional income movement
km	kilometer(s)
MOI	mobility as origin independence
OECD	Organisation for Economic Co-operation and Development
PISA	Program for International Student Assessment
PM	positional movement
PPP	purchasing power parity
SEDLAC	Socioeconomic Database for Latin America and the Caribbean (by the Centro de Estudios Distributivos, Laborales y Sociales [CEDLAS] of the Universidad de la Plata in Argentina, and the World Bank)
SERCE	Second Regional Comparative and Explanatory Study
SM	share movement
USAID	U.S. Agency for International Development
WDI	*World Development Indicators*

Overview

After decades of stagnation, the size of the middle class in Latin America and the Caribbean recently expanded by 50 percent—from 103 million people in 2003 to 152 million (or 30 percent of the continent's population) in 2009. Over the same period, as household incomes grew and inequality edged downward in most countries, the proportion of people in poverty fell markedly: from 44 percent to 30 percent. As a result, the middle class and the poor now account for roughly the same share of Latin America's population. This is in stark contrast to the situation prevailing (for a long period) until about 10 years ago, when the share of the poor hovered around 2.5 times that of the middle class. This study investigates the nature, determinants, and possible consequences of this remarkable process of social transformation. (See figures O.1 and O.2.)

Such large changes in the size and composition of social classes must, by definition, imply substantial economic mobility of some form. A large number of people who were poor in the late 1990s are now no longer poor. Others who were not yet middle class have now joined its ranks. But social and economic mobility does not mean the same thing to different people or in different contexts.

This report discusses the relevant concepts and documents the facts about mobility in Latin America and the Caribbean over the past two decades, both within and between generations. In addition, it investigates the rise of the Latin American middle class over the past 10–15 years and explores the size, nature, and composition of this pivotal new social group. More speculatively, it also asks how the rising middle class may reshape the region's social contract.

A middle-income region on the way to becoming a middle-class region

Defining the middle class is not a trivial matter, and the choices depend on the perspective of the researcher. Sociologists and political scientists, for instance, usually define the middle class in terms of education (for example, above secondary), occupation (typically white collar), or asset ownership (including the ownership of basic consumer durables or a house). Economists, by contrast, tend to focus on income levels. This study adopts an economic perspective but, to arrive at a more robust—less arbitrary—definition, it anchors the income-based definition on the crucial notion of economic security (that is, a low probability of falling back into poverty). The thresholds chosen for per capita income and economic security arise from the analysis of Latin American data and are therefore broadly applicable to middle-income countries.

The study applies this definition of the middle class consistently across a comprehensive, Latin America-wide set of household surveys. It presents a profile of the new middle class in the region, highlighting both objective characteristics—including demographics, education, and occupation—and subjective values and beliefs. It also asks how this middle class interacts with economic and social policy, both in terms of the past policies that helped shape its growth and in terms of what its views, opinions, and rising political weight might mean for future policy choices. Because policy choices and the growth of the middle class are jointly determined, the study often documents correlations. Only where special data circumstances permit are causal effects between policies and income movements inferred.

The concept of economic security is central to our approach because a defining feature of middle-class status is a certain degree of economic stability and resilience to shocks. We adopt a probability of falling into poverty over a five-year interval of 10 percent (approximately the average in countries such as Argentina, Colombia, and Costa Rica) as the maximum level of insecurity that may reasonably be borne by a household that is considered middle class. To map such a probability to a household income range, we ask—in those countries for which the right kinds of data are available—which income levels are typically associated with that level of insecurity. This exercise yields an income threshold of US$10 per day, at purchasing power parity (PPP) exchange rates, as our lower-bound *per capita* household income for the middle class.[1] The upper income threshold for the middle class is set at US$50 per capita per day, based primarily on survey data considerations. According to these thresholds, a family of four would be considered middle class if its *annual* household income ranged between US$14,600 and US$73,000.

Although US$10 per day (or US$3,650 per person per year) may not sound like a particularly demanding requirement for a family to be considered middle class, this income level corresponds to the 68th percentile of the Latin American income distribution in 2009. In other words, according to our definition, 68 percent of the region's population—over two-thirds—lived below middle-class income standards in 2009. Not all of these people were poor, of course. If we use US$4 per day as a moderate poverty line for the region, as typically done by the World Bank, these 68.0 percent are split into 30.5 percent of the population living in poverty (US$0–US$4 per day) and 37.5 percent living between poverty and the middle class (US$4–US$10 per day). This second group is a segment of the population that is at risk of falling into poverty, with an estimated probability greater than 10 percent.

Above the vulnerable segment, about 30 percent of the Latin American population are in the middle class (US$10–US$50 per day) and some 2 percent are in the upper-income class (living on more than US$50 per day), to whom we will refer interchangeably as the rich or the elite. Figure O.1, which draws on harmonized household surveys from 15 countries in Latin America and the Caribbean (accounting for 86 percent of the region's population and representing 500 million people) depicts the continent-wide income distribution and indicates the three key per capita income thresholds in our analysis: the poverty line at US$4 per day, the lower bound for the middle class at US$10 per day, and its upper bound at US$50 per day.[2]

Figure O.1 illustrates one of the key results from this study: if one adopts a middle class definition based on the notion of economic security—and validated by self-perceptions—as well as a standard moderate poverty line, then there are four, not three, classes in Latin America and the Caribbean. Sandwiched between the poor and the middle class, there lies a large group of people who appear to make ends meet well enough so as not to be counted among the poor but who do not enjoy the economic security that would be

FIGURE O.1 The distribution of income in Latin America and the Caribbean, 2009

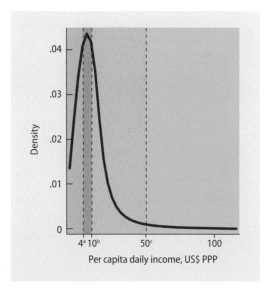

Source: Authors' calculations on data from SEDLAC (Socio-Economic Database for Latin America and the Caribbean).
Note: PPP = purchasing power parity. Countries include Argentina, Bolivia (2008), Brazil, Chile, Colombia, Costa Rica, the Dominican Republic, Ecuador, El Salvador, Honduras, Mexico (2010), Panama, Paraguay, Peru, and Uruguay.
a. US$4 = moderate Latin American and Caribbean poverty line.
b. US$10 = lower bound of Latin American middle class.
c. US$50 = upper bound of Latin American middle class.

required for membership in the middle class. One might have called this group by various names, such as the near-poor or the lower middle class. Because, by virtue of our definition of the middle class, these are households with a relatively high probability of experiencing spells of poverty in the future, we call them "the vulnerable."

As shown in figure O.1, this vulnerable class includes the modal Latin American household—the household whose income is observed with the highest frequency in the distribution. And as shown in figure O.2, it is now the largest social class in the region, accounting for 38 percent of the population. As poverty fell and the middle class rose—to about 30 percent of the population each during the past decade—the most common Latin American family is in a state of vulnerability.

Yet there is no question that the dynamics illustrated by figure O.2 are, on the whole, very encouraging. Being a continent where the vulnerable are the largest segment of the

population is much less attractive than being a middle-class continent, but it is clearly much better than being a predominantly poor continent. Moreover, the current situation in the region is as recent as it is unprecedented—it is the result of a process of social transformation that began around 2003, in which upward social mobility took place at a remarkable pace. Before 2005, as figure O.2 shows, poverty was still the most prevalent condition in our four-way classification.

In an almost mechanical sense, this transformation reflects both economic growth and declining inequality in Latin America and the Caribbean over the period. Gross domestic product (GDP) per capita grew at an annual rate of 2.2 percent between 2000 and 2010 and somewhat faster over the crucial 2003–09 period. Although these are not East Asian growth rates, they represent a substantial improvement over the region's own past growth performance: negative 0.2 percent per year in the 1980s and positive 1.2 percent in the 1990s. And whereas in those earlier

FIGURE O.2 Trends in middle class, vulnerability, and poverty in Latin America and the Caribbean, 1995–2009

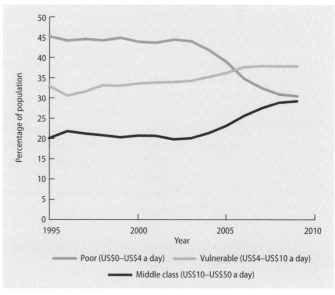

Source: Authors' calculations on data from SEDLAC (Socio-Economic Database for Latin America and the Caribbean).
Note: PPP = purchasing power parity. Covered countries include Argentina, Bolivia, Brazil, Chile, Colombia, Costa Rica, the Dominican Republic, El Salvador, Ecuador, Guatemala, Honduras, Mexico, Nicaragua, Panama, Paraguay, Peru, Uruguay, and República Bolivariana de Venezuela. Poverty lines and incomes are expressed in 2005 US$ PPP per day.

FIGURE O.3   **The growth and redistribution components of middle-class growth in Latin America and the Caribbean, 1995–2010**

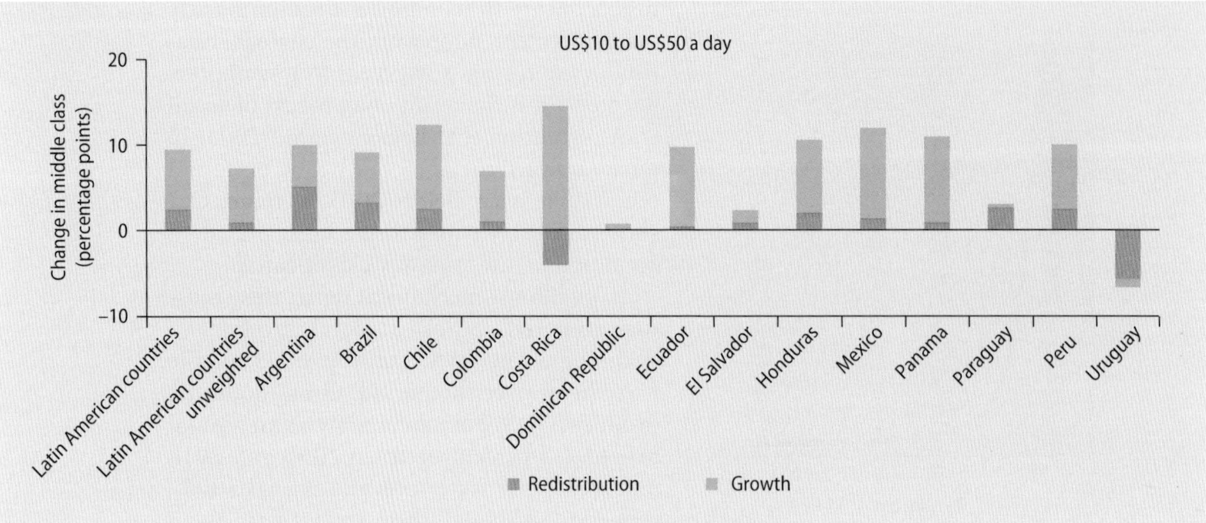

Source: Azevedo and Sanfelice (2012) based on SEDLAC (Socio-Economic Database for Latin America and the Caribbean) data.
Note: PPP = purchasing power parity. Middle-class per capita income is expressed in 2005 US$ PPP per day.

decades inequality was either stable or rising, the 2000s saw declining income disparities in 12 of the 15 countries for which data are available (as further discussed in chapter 1).

Both of these factors—higher incomes and less income inequality—contributed to poverty reduction *and* the growth in the middle class. Statistically, however, economic growth (growth in average per capita income) played a much larger role, accounting for 66 percent of the reduction in poverty and 74 percent of the rise of the middle class in the 2000s (with the remainder, in each case, associated with changes in inequality). Yet, as figure O.3 illustrates, the average hides significant intercountry variation within Latin America in these decompositions: in Argentina and Brazil, for example, falling income inequality contributed substantially to the expansion of the middle class.[3]

Within generations, remarkable upward mobility

In a deeper sense, the rise of the region's middle class also reflects substantial upward economic mobility. The growth in mean incomes and the changes in inequality over the past

15 years or so—which are used to account for middle-class growth in figure O.3—are themselves aggregate statistics that simply summarize changes in well-being for individuals and families. Behind these accounting decompositions are real individual trajectories, which generally imply significant churning in the distribution of incomes. In any given year, some households earn more than before while others earn less. Behind the net changes in the size of each socioeconomic class depicted in figure O.2, there are larger gross flows, with many households moving up while others move down.

To shed light on these dynamics, we adopt a measure of economic mobility within generations (intragenerational mobility) that summarizes (*directional*) income movement. Put simply, this measure of directional income movement captures the average growth rate in household-specific incomes.[4] This mobility index, which is well known in the scholarly literature, can be decomposed into "gainers" and "losers" as well as by the original social class of each household. This decomposition allows various versions of the measure to be expressed in terms of *transition matrices*, such as in table O.1. Considering that data

TABLE O.1   Intragenerational mobility in Latin America over the past 15 years, circa 1995–2010

(percentage of population)

		Destination (c. 2010)			
		Poor	**Vulnerable**	**Middle class**	**Total**
	Poor	22.5	21.0	2.2	45.7
Origin (c.1995)	**Vulnerable**	0.9	14.3	18.2	33.4
	Middle class	0.1	0.5	20.3	20.9
Total		23.4	35.9	40.7	100.0

Source: Authors' calculations on data from SEDLAC (Socio-Economic Database for Latin America and the Caribbean).

Note: "Poor" = individuals with a daily per capita income lower than US$4. "Vulnerable" = individuals with a daily per capita income of US$4–US$10. "Middle class" = individuals with a daily per capita income higher than US$10. Poverty lines and incomes are expressed in 2005 US$ PPP per day. PPP = purchasing power parity. The table shows lower-bound mobility estimates. Results are weighted averages for 18 Latin American and Caribbean countries using country-specific population estimates of the last available period (as detailed further in the notes to table 4.1, chapter 4). The bottom row does not match the numbers used above for describing figure O.1 because of sample differences in both countries and years. In addition, table O.1 conflates the middle class and elite into a single class.

following the same individuals (that is, panel data) for long time spans are rarely available in the region, directional income mobility was estimated using synthetic panels, and we report here conservative (that is, lower-bound) measures of mobility.[5]

Table O.1 provides a summary of economic mobility within generations between circa 1995 and circa 2010 for Latin America as a whole. The data are representative of 18 countries in the region. Each cell gives the proportion of the overall population that started out in the "origin" row of socioeconomic class in 1995 and ended up in the "destination" column of class in 2010. For example, the first row tells us that, of the 45.7 percent of the population who were poor in 1995, fewer than half (22.5 percent) were still poor in 2010, while the rest mainly moved up to become vulnerable (21.0 percent) and, to a substantially lesser extent, jumped directly to the middle class (2.2 percent). Analogously, of the 33.4 percent of the population who started out as vulnerable in 1995, more than half (18.2 percent) moved up and joined the middle class.[6]

Table O.1 reveals an impressive degree of income mobility in Latin America. The population shares along the main diagonal represent the "stayers": people whose income movement over this period, upward or downward, was insufficient for them to cross a class threshold. Because these shares add up to 57.1 percent, we can conclude that *at least 43.0 percent of all Latin Americans changed*

social classes between the mid-1990s and the end of the 2000s, and most of this movement was upward. In fact, only 2 percent of the population experienced a downward class transition, (although this is also a lower bound).

As one might expect, most class movement was gradual: most of the "climbers" moved either from poverty to vulnerability or from vulnerability to the middle class; few made the jump directly from poverty to the middle class during these 15 years. Rags-to-riches stories capture the imagination precisely because they are, in reality, rather rare—even in a high-mobility context such as Latin America in the 2000s.

Naturally, these average statistics once again hide considerable variation, both within and across countries. The extent of economic mobility captured by our measure of directional income movement was much higher in Brazil and Chile, for example, than in Guatemala or Paraguay. There was also variation in terms of where in the distribution the mobility was taking place, often associated with the initial level of the country's income per capita: whereas most mobility in Ecuador and Peru came from the originally poor, in Argentina and Uruguay—countries with a higher initial per capita income—most of it was accounted for by the originally vulnerable.

Within most Latin American countries, households were more likely to experience upward mobility if the household head had more years of schooling in the initial year. Movements into the middle class, in particular, were much likelier for people who had some tertiary education. Being employed in the formal sector and living in an urban area were also good predictors of upward mobility. Migration from rural to urban areas was also associated with greater prospects of upward movement, and more so for movements out of poverty than for transitions into the middle class.

Across Latin American and Caribbean countries, there was a clear association between faster GDP growth and higher income mobility—not surprising in light of our earlier comments on economic growth as the principal driver of middle-class growth. Overall economic mobility was also correlated with public health and education spending. Interestingly, mobility was not found to be correlated with total social protection expenditures, but when one disaggregates those expenditures by type, mobility turned out to be associated with measures of targeted, progressive social protection programs, including conditional cash transfers. Although the extent of mobility into the middle class was positively correlated with increases in female labor force participation, this was not true of mobility out of poverty. All of these are, of course, purely descriptive correlations. On the basis of the evidence presented in the report, the variables in question should not be interpreted as *causes* of mobility.

Across generations, mobility remains low

The above evidence does *not* imply that Latin America is a high-mobility society in every sense of the word. As noted earlier, mobility has different meanings in different contexts, and one important such meaning—particularly in an intergenerational context—is that of "origin independence." A measure of mobility as origin independence reaches its maximum when information on the original, or initial, period is useless in predicting terminal (or final) position. The measure

decreases as the correlation between initial and final positions increases. In the present context, origin *dependence* would refer to the extent to which the family and socioeconomic conditions into which a person is born determine his or her future income and socioeconomic class. A higher measure of origin *independence* implies higher intergenerational mobility.

As this discussion suggests, when the concept of mobility as origin independence is applied to an intergenerational context, it is closely related to the concept of equality of opportunity. Equality of opportunity is now predominantly understood to refer to a hypothetical situation in which predetermined circumstances—such as race, gender, birthplace, or family background—have no effect on people's life achievements. Perfect mobility in an origin-independence sense means the same thing when one looks only at a single circumstance variable, such as parental schooling.[7]

The main message of this report in this respect is that, sadly, despite substantial upward income movements within generations, intergenerational mobility remains limited in Latin America. Because data on parental incomes for today's working adults are impossible to obtain (and difficult to estimate) for most countries in the region, most of our analysis of intergenerational mobility—or lack thereof—relies on educational attainment (as measured by years of schooling) and educational achievement (as measured by standardized test scores). In particular, we ask to what extent the education of a person's parents appears to determine the person's own level of educational attainment (or achievement). One way to make that comparison across countries is to consider the effect of one standard deviation in parental years of schooling on the years of schooling of the children. By this metric, as figure O.4 illustrates, there is much greater intergenerational persistence—that is, much less mobility—in Latin American countries (such as Brazil, Ecuador, Panama, and Peru) than in most other countries—rich or poor—for which data are available.

FIGURE O.4   Association between parental education and children's years of schooling, selected countries

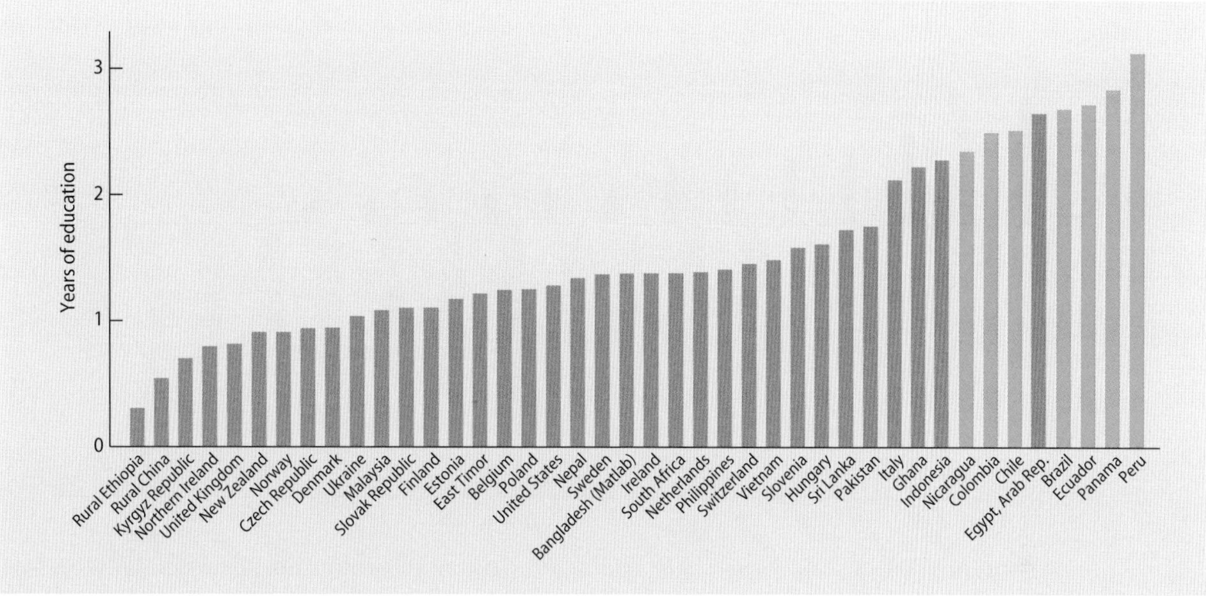

Source: Authors' calculations based on data from Hertz et al. 2007.
Note: Bars represent the impact of one standard deviation of parental years of schooling on the years of schooling of children. The impact is averaged across birth cohorts born between 1930 and 1980.

A similar, if slightly less stark, picture arises if one considers the effect of parental background (measured by an index of socioeconomic status) on student achievement, measured by standardized test scores in Program for International Student Assessment (PISA) exams, illustrated in figure O.5.[8] Most Latin American countries for which the relevant data are available also appear toward the right of the distribution of that impact estimate, suggesting that family background is a bigger determinant of student learning in Latin America than in other regions. But there is more variation in those estimates than in the attainment numbers shown in figure O.4: in Mexico, for example, parental background appears to be much less closely associated with PISA test scores than in other Latin American countries or in a number of nations in other regions. Crucially, however, most Latin American countries display not only lower intergenerational mobility in educational achievement but also very low *levels* of student learning—an unfortunate

FIGURE O.5   Relationship between average PISA test scores and intergenerational mobility across 65 countries, 2009

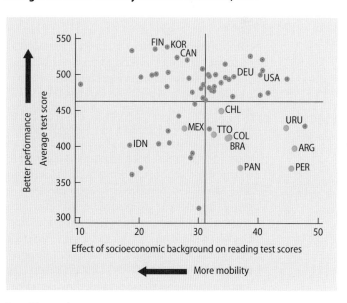

Source: PISA 2009 data.
Note: PISA = Program for International Student Assessment. The effect of socioeconomic background on reading test scores is calculated using the PISA index of economic, social, and cultural status. The horizontal line represents the average test score in the sample. The vertical line represents the average effect of socioeconomic background on scores in the sample.

FIGURE O.6   **Impact of parental background on children's educational gap at age 15 in Latin America, 1995–2009**

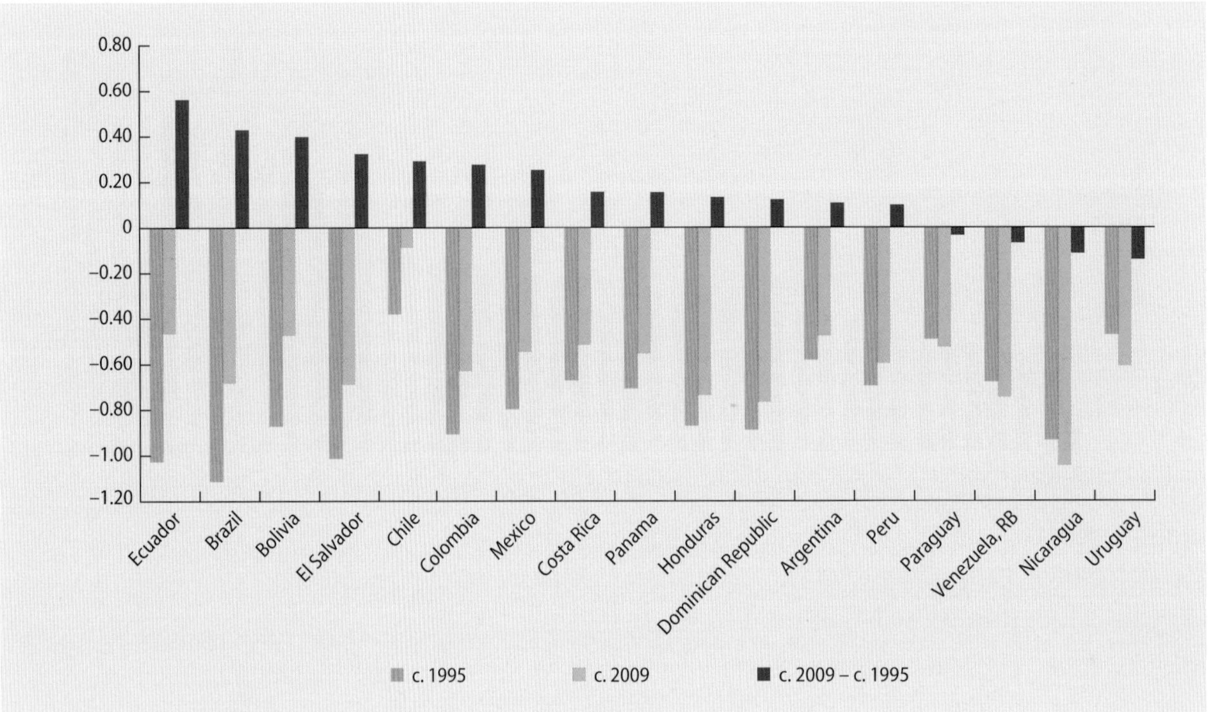

Source: Data from SEDLAC (Socio-Economic Database for Latin America and the Caribbean).
Note: "Educational gap" is defined as the difference between potential years of education at a given age and the years of completed education at that age. The green and orange bars represent the expected reduction in the schooling gap associated with one standard deviation of parental education in 1995 and 2009, respectively. The red bar is the difference between the two. Other covariates in the regression are children's gender, living in an urban area, and country fixed effects. The estimated effect of parental education on the educational gap is always statistically different from zero and so are the differences between 1995 and 2009.

combination that clearly leaves a great deal of scope for policy interventions in this area.

There is also some evidence on the mechanisms through which the intergenerational persistence of educational achievement occurs. In particular, it appears that *sorting*—the process whereby children from more-advantaged backgrounds concentrate in the same schools, from which those from less-privileged families are excluded—is a more important component of intergenerational immobility in Latin America than elsewhere. Sorting matters in Latin America because of the usual peer effects and because the schools attended by rich children are much better than those attended by the poor, in terms of their governance and accountability as well as their physical infrastructure and teaching quality. Of course, in addition, parental background also affects children's

cognitive outcomes through better nutrition, exposure to richer vocabulary, differences in cognitive stimulation, material resources at home, and so on.

There is some room for hope that these abysmally low levels of intergenerational mobility in Latin America—that is, high levels of inequality of opportunity—are beginning to change. Intergenerational mobility in educational *attainment* appears to have been rising over the past decade or so in most of the region. Figure O.6 shows estimates of the effect of one standard deviation of parental education on children's schooling gap (the difference between the highest grade a child could be attending under normal circumstances and the last or current grade actually attended) in 1995 and 2009. The red bars show that the differences are positive and substantial in most Latin American countries, suggesting a generally improving trend. While this is encouraging, the result is restricted to educational attainment. There is no clear evidence of similar improvements in educational achievement and, hence, no room for complacency.

How likely is it that these measures of (low) intergenerational educational mobility imply similarly limited mobility in incomes between generations? Although we did not conduct original analysis on intergenerational income transitions for this report, the scholarly literature suggests that Latin America is also a region of low intergenerational mobility in terms of income, and that this goes hand in hand with the region's (still) high levels of income inequality. This relationship is corroborated in figure O.7—which reproduces a well-known positive association: the higher the inequality of income (as measured by the Gini coefficient), the higher the intergenerational immobility.

In sum, the region's stubbornly low levels of intergenerational mobility stand in contrast to the recent sharp increase in intragenerational mobility. The overall picture of economic mobility in Latin America is therefore a mixed one. Mobility across generations—in the sense that personal outcomes are independent of family background and social origin—remains an elusive goal. In intergenerational terms, Latin America is not a mobile society, and the signs that it is becoming a little more mobile are tentative and so far limited to educational attainment. This picture is consistent with what is known about the high degree of inequality of opportunity that continues to characterize the region.

A snapshot of the Latin American middle class

What are the main characteristics of this emerging middle class? How similar is it across countries? Does it hold different views and opinions than other social groups? Our analysis suggests, perhaps surprisingly, that the rising Latin American middle class, while sharing some common objective features across the region, displays much less similarity

FIGURE O.7   Association between income inequality and intergenerational immobility

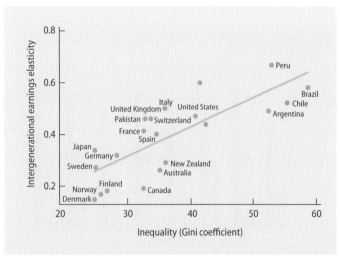

Source: Corak 2012.

in its subjective values and beliefs. Take first the common objective features: In all Latin American countries, the heads of middle-class households have substantially more years of schooling than those in the poor or vulnerable classes but fewer years than the rich (figure O.8). Middle-class households are also more urbanized than poorer groups. In addition, formal employment appears to be a distinctive sign of the middle class in Latin America; the middle-class worker is typically a formal employee rather than being self-employed, unemployed, or an employer. In contrast, the poor and vulnerable rely on self-employment (or suffer from unemployment) more often, while the rich are more frequently employers and, in some countries, self-employed.

In terms of sector of economic activity, middle-class workers are frequently found in the services sector, including health, education, and public services, but manufacturing jobs are more frequent among the middle class (and the vulnerable) than they are among the poor or the rich. There is no evidence that the middle class is overly dependent on—or employed by—the public sector. In most Latin American countries for which data exist, public sector employment was more frequent among the rich than among the

FIGURE O.8 **Average years of schooling (ages 25–65), selected Latin American countries, by income class, circa 2009**

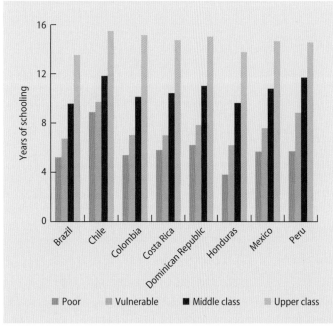

Source: Birdsall 2012.
Note: "Poor" = individuals with a per capita daily income lower than US$4. "Vulnerable" = individuals with a per capita daily income of US$4–US$10. "Middle class" = individuals with a per capita daily income of US$10–US$50. "Upper class" = individuals with a per capita daily income exceeding US$50. Poverty lines and incomes are expressed in 2005 US$ PPP per day. PPP= purchasing power parity.

middle class (although Mexico and Peru were exceptions). The public sector employed more than one-fourth of middle-class workers in only one country: Honduras. It would appear, therefore, that popular images of the middle class—as being made up of either intrepid entrepreneurs (who start their own small businesses and pull themselves up the ladder by their own shoestrings) or lazy bureaucrats (comfortably relying on a government paycheck)—are inaccurate. Typically, the Latin American middle-class worker is a reasonably educated service worker, formally employed by a private enterprise in an urban area.

Family dynamics and demographics provide, perhaps, the most interesting traits of the Latin American middle-class profile. Between 1992 and 2009, the average size of a middle-class household in Latin America fell from 3.3 to 2.9 individuals. This compares with populationwide averages of 4.1 and 3.4,

respectively. Middle-class households typically have fewer children as well as women who join the labor force more frequently: 73 percent of middle-class women ages 25–65 across Latin America are either employed or looking for work compared with a region-wide population average of 62 percent. Their children are typically in school: virtually all 6- to 12-year-old middle-class children attend school, as do roughly three-quarters of those who are 13–18.

In summary, although there are evidently variations in the middle-class profile across countries, the similarities dominate: the middle class presents a set of distinctive demographic and socioeconomic patterns that are present in almost every Latin American country. Would this mean that the middle class also systematically shares opinions and beliefs about society that are different from other groups? Our research suggests this not to be the case.

An analysis of middle-class values and beliefs using opinion surveys shows that country characteristics account for a much larger share of the variance in people's values than class membership. In particular, there is no strong evidence of any "middle-class exceptionalism" in terms of values and beliefs. To be sure, middle-class respondents are generally likelier than their poorer counterparts to trust their countries' institutions (including the government, political parties, and the police) and to report greater faith in the meritocracy of their societies, and they are less likely to perceive political violence as legitimate. But most of these associations simply reflect positive correlations with income and education rather than something to do specifically with middle-class status. And, on the whole, income and class status account for only a small share of the overall variance in values.

This contrasting reality may be simply described as follows: when it comes to socioeconomic and demographic characteristics, a middle-class person in Peru has more in common with a middle-class person in Mexico than with a poorer person in Peru; but when it comes to values and aspirations, the same middle-class person in Peru has more in common with a poor person in Peru than with a middle-class person in Mexico.

The middle class and the social contract

What, if any, are the implications of a rising middle class with these characteristics—urban, better educated, largely privately employed, and with beliefs and opinions broadly in line with those of their poorer and less-educated fellow citizens—for social and economic policy? In particular, is the growth of the Latin American middle class likely to spell any changes for the region's fragmented social contract?

A "social contract" may be broadly understood as the combination of implicit and explicit arrangements that determine what each group contributes to and receives from the state. In stylized terms, Latin America's social contract in the latter half of the 20th century was characterized by a small state, to which the elite (and the small middle class appended to it) contributed through low taxes, and from which they benefited largely through a "truncated" set of in-cash benefits such as retirement pensions, severance payments, and the like, for which only formal sector workers qualified.[9] Little was left for providing high-quality public services in the areas of education, health, infrastructure, and security, for example. Public services in these areas were therefore generally of low quality; while the vast majority of the (poor and vulnerable) population had no choice, the rich and the small middle class opted out and chose privately provided alternatives. The essence of this (implicit) contract was simple: the upper and middle classes were not asked to pay much and did not expect to receive much from public services either. The poor also paid little and received correspondingly little in terms of public benefits.

One manifestation of this social contract was a state that was typically small as well as skewed toward the provision of formal sector social security payments to the better-off. To this day, with the exception of Argentina and Brazil, the region is characterized by relatively low tax revenues overall. The average total tax revenue in 2010 was 20.4 percent of GDP in Latin America, versus 33.7 percent in the Organisation for Economic Co-operation and Development (OECD) countries, for example.[10] In addition, the composition of these tax revenues tended to be skewed toward indirect (sales) taxes and social security contributions, relative to income and property taxes, leading to a system that is not particularly progressive.

On the benefit side, the middle class (and the elite) participated disproportionately in the social security system (including old-age and disability pensions, unemployment protection, severance payments, and health insurance). But it tended to opt out of public education and health services, in particular. Instead, the upper and middle classes in Latin America often resorted to private alternatives to obtain these latter services. This tendency to opt out extended even to services where public provision should be the uncontested norm, such as electricity: in some Latin American countries, private ownership of electricity generators is still observed to rise with household income. The same applies for public security, with private security in closed condominiums not uncommon in a number of countries in the region.

This picture has not remained static, however. Over the past 10–20 years—and, in particular, following redemocratization processes in many Latin American countries—this political equilibrium has begun to shift, albeit gradually. The spread of noncontributory old-age pension and health insurance schemes and the growth of conditional cash transfers has meant that redistributive transfers from the state now reach the poor to an extent that was unheard of 20 years ago in most of the region. At the same time, in most countries in the region, the extension of cash benefits to the poor has not been matched by a return of the middle class to public health and education services. Latin America's "welfare state" may have become less "truncated," but its social contract remains fragmented.

It is natural to question whether Latin America will be able to continue its recent run of "growth with equity" (or at least with declining inequality) on the basis of such a fragmented contract, which inherently generates fewer opportunities for the bulk of the population. Whether in postwar Western Europe or postrevolutionary China, whether in the post-land-reform Republic of Korea or in the United States under the New Deal, socioeconomic progress has often required a combination of economic freedom and a sound foundation of public education, health, and infrastructure. It is almost certain that most countries in Latin America and the Caribbean will require additional reforms to their social contracts to enable their states to provide that foundation and sustain growth.

But can the rise of the middle class documented in this study facilitate these reforms? Or will it instead entrench the middle-class choice of private services and further reduce its willingness to contribute to the public purse to generate opportunities for those who remain poor? In a sense, as it evolves toward a more mature social structure, with a larger and more vocal middle class, Latin America stands at a crossroads: will it break (further) with the fragmented social contract it inherited from its colonial past and continue to pursue greater parity of opportunities, or will it embrace even more forcefully a perverse model where the middle class opts out and fends for itself?

This study does not answer those big questions. It merely poses them, because they follow naturally from the recent trends in economic mobility and the size of the middle class—trends that combine the good news of recent income growth and poverty reduction with the reality of limited mobility between generations and persistent inequality of opportunity. The study suggests, however, that the middle classes may not automatically become the much-hoped-for catalytic agent for reforms. Whether and how the new middle class will help strengthen the region's social contract

remains to be seen and will doubtless be the subject of much research in the future. Nevertheless, the report highlights three areas where reforms may help to gain the support of the middle class for a fairer and more legitimate social contract:

- *Incorporate the goal of equal opportunities more explicitly into public policy.* This is crucial for ensuring that the middle classes feel that they live in a society where effort pays and merit is rewarded instead of one that is rigged in favor of privileged groups. It is also crucial for broadening the access of those who remain poor or vulnerable to good jobs and stable sources of income. Although this effort will require reforms in a wide range of fields, this report emphasizes the need to improve the quality of public education, from the development of cognitive and social skills during early childhood all the way to better colleges and universities. Greater equality of opportunity would, in turn, enhance economic efficiency, thus helping address Latin America's persistent low-growth problem and improving the conditions for the region's private sector to generate better and more stable jobs for all classes.

- *Embark on a second generation of reforms to the social protection system, encompassing both social assistance and social insurance.* Although the aforementioned improvements in targeted social assistance during the past 10–15 years contributed much to the observed reductions in poverty and income inequality, their expansion has not been well integrated into the overall social protection system, and this has led to new challenges for both efficiency and fairness. Increasingly, the middle classes are asked to pay for services that are provided to others for free. A dual social protection system based on targeted assistance for the poor and (subsidized) insurance for the middle classes may also be poorly tailored to a large vulnerable population that is neither poor nor middle class and whose vulnerability will rise if the external environment becomes less favorable than in the past. The time is ripe for embarking on a second generation of social protection reforms, in which fragmentation will be overcome in ways that enhance fairness, solidarity, and inclusion.

- *Break the vicious cycle of low taxation and low quality of public services that leads the middle and upper classes to opt out.* Although there is some margin to improve the quality of public services within the current budget envelopes, it will be challenging to do so without strengthening the revenue base, which remains low practically everywhere except in Argentina and Brazil. Improving the perception of fairness in taxation and the redistributive effectiveness of public spending will be key to any successful reform. The middle classes will not buy into and contribute to an improved social contract if the goods that they value highly (such as civil rights protection, education, police, and health services) are deficiently supplied by the state and if they do not perceive that the rich contribute fairly to the social contract.

During most of the 2000s, Latin America's improved policy framework allowed many countries to take advantage of a benign external environment to begin an impressive transition toward a middle-class society. This has created enormous expectations, which risk turning into frustration if this transition stalls. But the region cannot count on the external environment remaining as friendly as in the recent past to achieve further social and economic gains. A much greater policy effort will thus be required to consolidate and deepen the process of upward mobility and to make it more resilient to potential adverse shocks. In the end, the onus will mainly rest on the shoulders of the political leaders and democratic institutions of the region: they face the challenge of overhauling its social contract.

Notes

1. This lower income threshold was independently validated by an alternative approach, based on self-perceptions of class membership, that was separately applied to five countries: Brazil, Chile, Colombia, Mexico, and Peru. Methodological details of both approaches are documented in chapter 2 of the main report and in references therein.

2. As is well known, the household surveys on which figure O.1 is based commonly suffer from compliance and reporting problems that render them unrepresentative of the top tail of the distribution. We are therefore circumspect in our analysis of the "rich" in our sample.

3. As detailed in chapter 5, these decompositions are for the 1995–2010 period.

4. Because each household's growth rate is given equal weight, the average of growth rates is not the same as the growth in the average income. The latter involves income weights, whereas the former uses population weights.

5. Our measure of directional mobility is applied to a set of "synthetic panels" constructed from the region's repeated cross-section household surveys. A key caveat is that the statistical procedures used to construct these synthetic panels can only generate upper- and lower-bound estimates of mobility rather than exact figures. Most of the analysis in this report relies on the lower-bound estimates, which yield a conservative picture of mobility *in either direction*. In our results, therefore, upward and downward mobility are *both* likely to be underestimated.

6. The bottom row does not match the numbers used above for describing figure O.1 because of sample differences in both countries and years. In addition, table O.1 conflates the middle class and elite into a single class. Despite sampling differences, though, the overall picture is consistent with the cross-section analysis described earlier.

7. The concepts of equality and inequality of opportunity are increasingly important to the World Bank's work in Latin America. See, for example, the *World Development Report 2006: Equity and Development* (World Bank 2006), the regional study on *Measuring Inequality of Opportunities in Latin America and the Caribbean* (Barros et al. 2009), and references in those two volumes.

8. The OECD's Program of International Student Assessment (PISA) produces a set of school-based surveys that administer identical cognitive achievement tests to samples of students across a number of countries, as well as collecting (reasonably) comparable information about the students' families and the schools they attend.

9. The capture of Latin America's social security systems by (largely better-off) formal sector workers, to the exclusion of most of the continent's poor, was described as a "truncated welfare state" in a previous regional report in this series, *Inequality in Latin America: Breaking with History?* (de Ferranti et al. 2004).

10. In 2010, Brazil's total tax revenues were 33.6 percent of GDP, whereas in Argentina the figure was 33.3 percent.

References

Azevedo, Joao P., and Viviane Sanfelice. 2012. "The Rise of the Middle Class in Latin America." Draft, World Bank, Washington, DC.

Barros, Ricardo, Francisco H. G. Ferreira, José Molinas, and Jaime Saavedra. 2009. *Measuring Inequality of Opportunities in Latin America and the Caribbean.* Washington, DC: World Bank.

Birdsall, Nancy. 2012. "A Note on the Middle Class in Latin America." Unpublished manuscript, Center for Global Development, Washington, DC.

Corak, Miles. Forthcoming. "Inequality from Generation to Generation: The United States in Comparison." In *The Economics of Inequality, Poverty and Discrimination in the 21st Century*, ed. Robert Rycroft. ABC-CLIO.

De Ferranti, David, Francisco H. G. Ferreira, Guillermo E. Perry, and Michael Walton. 2004. *Inequality in Latin America: Breaking with History?* Washington, DC: World Bank.

Hertz, Tom, Tamara Jayasundera, Patrizio Piraino, Sibel Selcuk, Nicole Smith, and Alina Verashchagina. 2007. "The Inheritance of Educational Inequality: International Comparisons and Fifty-Year Trends." *The B.E. Journal of Economic Analysis & Policy* 7 (2).

SEDLAC (Socio-Economic Database for Latin America and the Caribbean). 2011. Database of the Center for Distributive, Labor and Social Studies, Argentina, and World Bank, Washington, DC. http://sedlac.econo.unlp.edu.ar/eng/.

World Bank. 2006. *World Development Report 2006: Equity and Development.* Washington, DC: World Bank.

Introduction | 1

Isabel's life is nothing like those she likes to follow in the evening *telenovelas*. For one thing, she has been married for 20 years to the same man, Roberto. For another, she and her husband do not drive an imported car or live in a luxurious apartment with a sea view in Ipanema. Yet although she likes to dream about some of the glamorous aspects of life in a Brazilian soap opera, Isabel is conscious that her family—like her country—has not been doing badly of late.

Isabel, Roberto, and their only child, Patrícia, live in Presidente Prudente, a city of some 210,000 people that lies 580 kilometers (km) west of São Paulo, Brazil. They are real locals: both were born here, and Isabel's late father owned a small *padaria* (bakery) in one of the city's older residential neighborhoods. He used to say that the bakery's opening in 1952 was the fourth happiest day in his life: coming after only his wedding day and the birth dates of Isabel and her brother. Both of Isabel's parents had completed high school, and they encouraged her to attend a local college. The family never experienced poverty during her childhood.

At age 50, Isabel is a kindergarten teacher at a small, private day care center in her own neighborhood. Roberto is a sales manager at a local agricultural machinery store that sells combine harvesters, tractors, and other equipment to the sugar cane plantations that have boomed in western São Paulo state, supplying ethanol to the whole country. Together, they brought home US$4,380 per month in 2010 at purchasing power parity (PPP) exchange rates.[1] For the family of three, this translates into an annual income of US$52,560. It was enough to pay the fees for Patrícia's private school, from which she has just graduated. (At 18 years of age, she was accepted into São Paulo State University [UNESP], the excellent university based in her home town, to study veterinary sciences.) Although it would not occur to the family to think of their income in daily terms, their per capita daily income was US$48 at PPP—an income that places them near the top of what this volume will argue should be considered Latin America's middle class in 2010.

You don't have to go far to find rather different living standards. Fabiano and Irene live in the small town of Quatá, some 80 km east of Isabel's house. They have two children, Marisa and Ricardo. Unlike Isabel, Irene was not born in the state of São Paulo. She was born in 1971, in Santa Quitéria, in the state of Maranhão in the Brazilian Northeast. Her father had not finished primary school, and her mother had no formal schooling at all. They moved to western São Paulo state in the mid-1970s, when Irene was a little girl, as demand for agricultural labor rose in the booming Southeast. Here, Irene was sent to public school and completed all eight years of primary school. At age 39, she is a part-time waitress at a local snack bar. She does not have a *carteira de trabalho* (formal work papers) and earns just over US$200 per month.

Fabiano works as a farmhand at one of the region's large sugar cane *engenhos* (plantations). For most of his working life, he, too, was an informal worker and, when he started out, they still cut the cane by hand. He has since been taught to drive the tractors and operate other farm machinery and, in 2007, the plantation owners decided to regularize most of their labor force. Fabiano now earns two minimum wages and is entitled to paid holidays and a minimum pension.[2] Though the family made much less money in 1995, things have steadily improved since then. Marisa, now 15, attends the local public school, and the plan is that she will start secondary school next year—the first person ever to do so in her family. Putting together the two minimum wages plus Irene's income at the snack bar, the family earns US$730 per month, for an annual family income of US$8,760.

As Irene and Fabiano are instinctively aware, this is not enough to earn them a place in the new Brazilian middle class, of which they have recently been hearing more and more on the evening news. But when Irene thinks back to what she remembers of her childhood in Maranhão, with no electricity in the house and occasionally not enough food to go around for her and her three brothers and sisters, she acknowledges that things have improved. If her childhood in Maranhão—or, for that matter, those of some of her nephews and nieces who still live "up north" today—characterized poverty, then her own family is no longer poor. They are not quite middle-class yet, but they have escaped real poverty. The past few years have been good in Quatá. Fabiano is proud of his official labor papers, and Irene's tips have

gone up roughly in line with the international price of sugar (although she was probably too busy to notice the correlation).

Now that Marisa has promised to stay on at school next year, the only nagging worry that keeps Irene awake at night is the fear that her boss at the bar might one day choose to replace her with a younger, more energetic worker. The family's modest relative bliss would not survive such a shock. Vulnerability, rather than extreme poverty, is their bane nowadays. The waitress's family has a daily per capita income of US$6 at PPP—one-eighth that of Isabel (the kindergarten teacher) and her family but 50 percent more than the international per capita poverty line of US$4 per day that is often applied to Latin America and the Caribbean (World Bank 2011).

Although Irene cannot afford it, Isabel does have her nails done regularly, at a little manicure shop near the day care center. Sônia is her favorite manicurist, and they see each other often enough that Isabel knows her life story. Sônia was born in 1978 and graduated from high school at age 18. She had her only child, a boy named Pedro, shortly thereafter but was never married and raises him on her own. Pedro was named after his maternal grandfather, a construction worker who had worked hard all his life and whose meager earnings had been barely enough to support his four children and their stay-at-home mom.

With little child care available, times were tough for Sônia during her twenties. Leaving the boy with his grandmother, she worked mostly as a shop assistant, and the minimum wage she earned was just enough to keep her and her son above the poverty line. As Pedro grew older and enrolled in school, Sônia's hard work and dedication paid off. Noticing the number of new beauty parlors opening to serve the growing number of affluent ladies in Presidente Prudente, she took an evening course in manicure and pedicure and landed the job she currently holds. Between the small monthly contribution the courts force Pedro's father to pay and her earnings at the salon, Sônia takes home just over US$709 PPP per month, for a total annual family income of

US$9,490. Because hers is only a two-person family, this implies a daily per capita income of US$13—more than twice what waitress Irene and her family live on but just over a quarter of the equivalent figure for her client, Isabel. On the basis of these numbers, although Sônia was not middle-class in the late 1990s, she is now.

Latin American "climbers" and "stayers"

Although these three families are imaginary, they are also eminently plausible in the sense that their characteristics (incomes, family sizes, educational attainment levels, and occupations) are in line with "typical" families in their broad social groups.[3] Their stories were chosen to illustrate both the broad theme of this volume—the complex relationship between economic mobility and the rise of the Latin American middle class—and the nuances and apparent contradictions that surround that relationship.

All three families were better off in 2010 than their parents had been 30 to 40 years prior, but their family backgrounds still powerfully shape where they are today: one could scarcely imagine a child of Irene's parents living like Isabel and Roberto (the kindergarten teacher and sales manager) or vice versa. All three families have also experienced real income gains over the past decade, enabling the richer family (Isabel and Roberto) to stay comfortably atop the country's expanding middle class, and Sônia and her son to enter it from below. It has also seen Irene and Fabiano, the striving Quatá couple, cross that imaginary threshold (the poverty line) that separates the poor from the nonpoor. They did not jump miraculously from poverty into the middle class—a feat that, as we shall see, relatively few people across the continent have achieved. Instead, Fabiano and Irene now inhabit an intermediate group defined primarily by its vulnerability. They may not know it, but they are very close to the mode of the Latin American income distribution.

As this volume will show, these imaginary families living in western São Paulo state, in

southeastern Brazil, typify three of the four broad groups that account for the bulk of Latin America's population in terms of their economic mobility during the 2000s. Two broad groups of "climbers" are illustrated by the waitress-farmworker couple, who move from poverty to vulnerability, and by the manicurist and her son, who move from vulnerability to the middle class. The kindergarten teacher-sales manager couple and their daughter illustrate one of the two main groups of "stayers": those who remained in the middle class throughout the period. Finally, the fourth main broad family type, which we have not named, would have started out poor and stayed poor throughout the period. In a sense, this last, least-happy story is that of Irene's brothers and sisters who stayed up in Maranhão. Although still poor, even they would have had some progress to report. They would probably be receiving the "Bolsa Família" benefit now, a social welfare program reaching the less favored in Brazil, and outright hunger (not uncommon in their parents' day) would now be unlikely.

The three families also exemplify some of the themes that will recur throughout the volume: all three are very small families, by historical standards, but quite typical of their social groups in Brazil today.[4] Related to falling fertility and family size, and to rising levels of educational attainment, is a tale of increasing labor force participation among women: none of our three leading ladies chose to stay at home with their children, as Sônia's mother had. Occupational shifts (including a movement toward working with more capital and technology within agriculture) and growing access to formal employment have also been important. Even the link between these larger employment opportunities and local economic growth—possibly fueled in part by higher commodity prices—is not entirely fictional.

As these illustrative stories suggest, economic mobility and the resulting transformations in the size and composition of social classes are a complex set of subjects. There is change, both across generations and within them. There are thresholds defining the poor and the middle class. There are causes and correlates of various changes, both at a microeconomic household level and at a more aggregate level. And these changes may well have implications for the future.

Before we can make any headway in understanding these issues, we need to remind ourselves of the backdrop to the social change of the 2000s and state the precise questions that we seek to answer in this volume. That backdrop is the object of the next section. Finally, in "Pursuing the Questions," we summarize the main objectives of the report in terms of the questions we are about to ask.

The broad context

Economic growth in the Presidente Prudente area during 2000–10 led to better conditions in Fabiano's farm job and opened up new work opportunities for Sônia, the manicurist. It was one important reason why the past decade was good for our three families.

Moving from the illustrative to the statistical, the 2000s were also a good decade for Latin America more broadly. Despite the onset of the global financial crisis in late 2008, the continent's gross domestic product (GDP) per capita grew at an average rate of 2.2 percent per year between 2000 and 2010.[5] In six countries (including Argentina, the Dominican Republic, Panama, and Peru), annual growth rates in excess of 3 percent per capita per year accumulated throughout the period. Although this is by no means a stellar growth performance if compared with the likes of China (averaging 9.6 percent annual growth in the same period) and India (averaging 5.7 percent) or with that of the East Asian tigers in the 1990s, it represents a considerable improvement over the region's own average annual growth rates in the 1980s (–0.2 percent) and 1990s (1.2 percent). Figure 1.1 shows the distribution of annual GDP per capita growth rates for the 32 countries in the Latin America and Caribbean region, as well as the region's simple and population-weighted averages.

It is easy to forget the transformative power of compound economic growth to raise living

standards: by averaging 4.2 percent annual growth in per capita incomes, average GDP per person in Peru rose from US$5,543 PPP in 2000 to US$8,555 PPP in 2010. But in the 2000s, to sustained economic growth was added another—even rarer—achievement: in most Latin American countries for which data are available, income inequality fell. The Gini coefficient, one of the most commonly used measures of inequality, declined in 12 of the 15 countries reported in figure 1.2. These declines were all statistically significant, and their magnitude was not trivial: The average total decline between 2000 and 2010 in the 12 countries where inequality fell was 5 Gini points. Across all 15 countries for which data are available, the decline was 3.5 Gini points.

Inequality fell in the three largest economies in the region—Brazil, Mexico, and Argentina—by 5, 7, and 6 points of the Gini, respectively. As Barros et al. (2010) note for the case of Brazil, this process was the result of sustained German-like growth rates for the top tenth of the income distribution, combined with Chinese-like growth rates for the bottom tenth, over a 10-year period.[6] It is difficult to overstate the importance of this achievement: ever since household survey data became available in the 1970s (and, other data suggests, since long before), Latin America has been the world's most unequal region, rivaled only by certain countries in Sub-Saharan Africa.

That remains true today: apart from South Africa and Swaziland, all other countries with the 10 highest Gini coefficients available for 2008–10 in the *World Development Indicators* (WDI) database are in Latin America.[7] But whereas periods of stability and rising inequality had historically alternated, there is no record of a previous period of similarly broad-based and sustained *decline* in income disparities in the region. The same *WDI* database lists six Latin American countries among those with the 10 largest drops in the Gini coefficient between 2000 and 2010.[8] The picture of inequality dynamics in Latin America during 2000–10 evokes contradictory emotions: the levels remain unacceptably high, but the changes are undeniable and point in the right direction.

FIGURE 1.1   **Average annual per capita GDP growth in Latin America and the Caribbean, 2000–10**

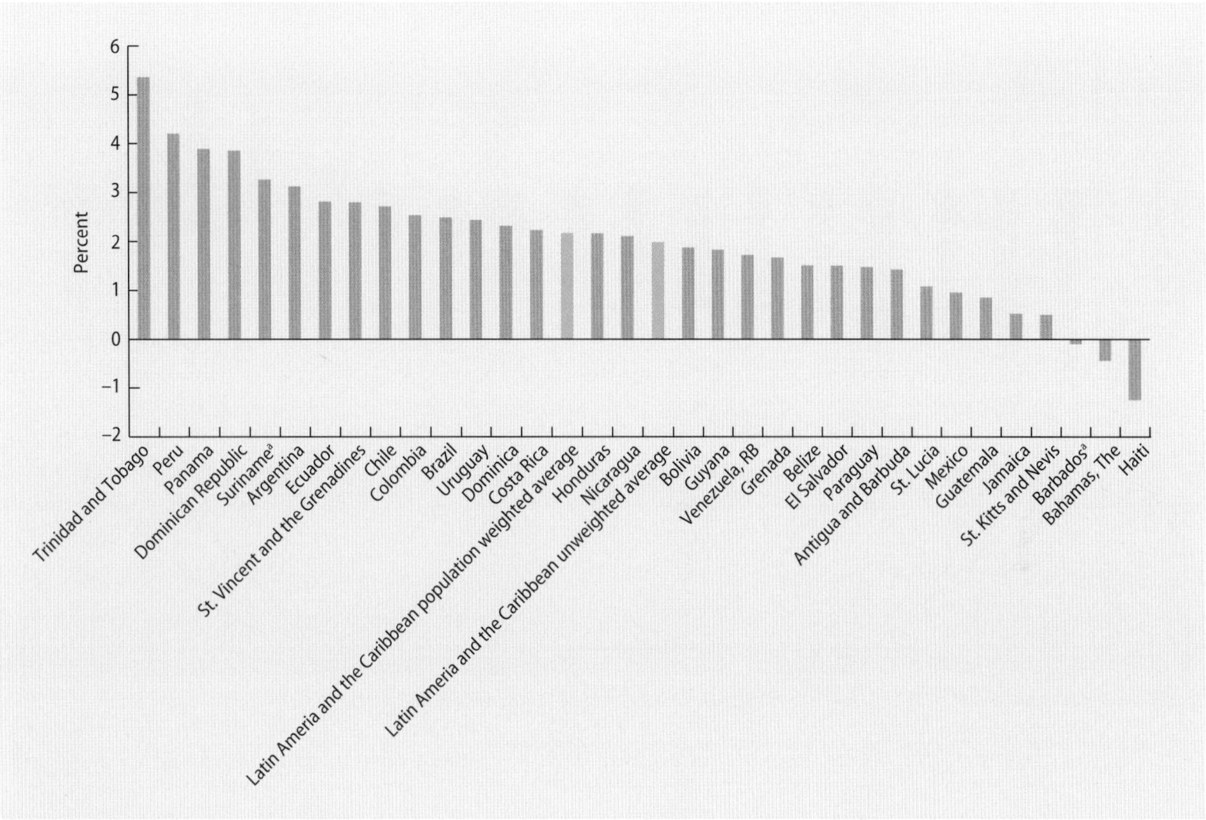

Source: World Development Indicators, World Bank.
Note: GDP measured using purchasing power parity exchange rates.
a. Fiscal year 2009.

Naturally, the combination of sustained (even if still largely unspectacular) economic growth with reductions in inequality resulted in substantial drops in absolute poverty. The incidence of moderate poverty in Latin America fell from 41.4 percent in 2000 to 28.0 percent in 2010 despite the global financial crisis in the last two years of the decade (World Bank 2011). This decline in poverty implies that 50 million fewer Latin Americans were living in poverty in 2010 than 10 years earlier.[9] If the comparison is made with 2003 instead, the decline in absolute numbers is even larger: 75 million.

This result contrasts with significantly worse performances during the previous two decades. In the lost decade of the 1980s, moderate poverty in Latin America rose substantially. Even the 1990s were marked largely by stagnation, with the poverty headcount ending the decade at 43 percent in 1999. There was something really different about the 2000s, and figure 1.3 clearly illustrates the structural break in Latin American poverty reduction trends around the turn of the millennium. The year 2003 stands out as a break in the series.

Pursuing the questions

When poverty is reduced by almost a third in 10 years—or by 13 percentage points of the population—it is likely that real social change is taking place. What is happening to all these people who are no longer officially poor? Have they all joined the emerging

FIGURE 1.2   Change in the Gini index, selected Latin American countries, 2000–10

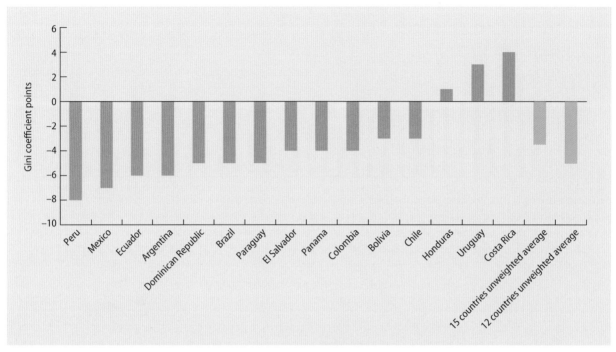

Source: Socio-Economic Database for Latin America and the Caribbean (SEDLAC), updating figure 1.2 in López-Calva and Lustig 2010.
Note: The Gini Index is a commonly used measure of inequality, and can be defined as half the relative mean difference. A Gini coefficient of zero expresses perfect equality (everyone has exactly the same income), whereas a Gini of one expresses maximal inequality (one person has all the income).

FIGURE 1.3   Moderate and extreme poverty in Latin America, 1995–2010

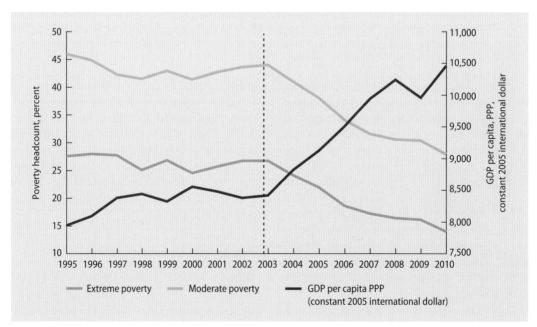

Source: World Bank 2011.
Note: GDP = gross domestic product. PPP = purchasing power parity.

Latin American middle class, of which one often hears? How does one define that middle class? Does it begin where poverty ends, at the poverty line of US$4 per day? Where does "middle class" end and the "elite" begin? Do these declines in poverty and inequality, combined with a growing middle class, mean that Latin America has become a more mobile set of societies? How can that mobility be properly measured, and what does it presage for the region's future?

This volume is motivated by those questions—questions about recent social change in Latin America in a context of reasonably paced growth, a decline in economic inequality, and the resulting poverty reduction and middle-class growth. In particular, we ask the following:

- Among the myriad concepts, domains, and measures of economic mobility available in the literature, which are most appropriate to gauge the extent of mobility in Latin America in the 2000s?
- Similarly, how is the middle class—a complex concept, treated differently by different disciplines and heterogeneously within them—best defined for this continent, and at this point in its history?
- When one looks *across* generations, how mobile is Latin America today? How important are one's parents in determining one's chances of success, even in these promising times? Is there any evidence of change in those patterns of intergenerational persistence?
- And how much mobility is there *within* individual lifetimes? Behind headline numbers for economic growth, falling poverty, and growing middle classes, individual Latin American families must be experiencing economic progress. Who are they? How many are moving across class barriers? How much vulnerability to reversals of fortune remains?
- Once agreement is reached on a definition of the middle class, how has it evolved over the past decade or so? How have its size and composition changed, and have these changes differed across countries? What

does the new Latin American middle class look like?
- Finally, what are the implications of these social changes—and of the rise of the middle class in particular—for Latin America's social contract in the future? Is there any evidence that the middle class holds special values or beliefs that may lead to greater stability, better policy making, and faster economic progress? Can it be anchored to a cohesive social contract, under which taxes are paid and quality public services demanded and provided, so that those who have been left behind retain a chance of completing their own journeys out of poverty?

The volume is structured around those six groups of questions. Chapter 2, "Economic Mobility and the Middle Class: Concepts and Measurement," addresses the conceptual issues and definitional questions. It discusses different concepts of mobility and different definitions of the middle class, and it lays out the arguments underpinning the choice of concepts and measures used in the subsequent chapters. Although chapter 2 is important for a full understanding of our approach, it is also somewhat dryer and more technical than the rest of the report, and some readers may prefer to skip it.

Chapter 3, "Mobility across Generations," reviews the evidence on intergenerational mobility in Latin America—some from the existing literature and some drawing on original work.

Chapter 4, "Mobility within Generations," relies on synthetic panel techniques to shed light on the extent of mobility—viewed primarily as income growth for individual households—within lifetimes. It pays particular attention to movements across classes: out of poverty, into the middle class, and in and out of the vulnerable group that lies between.

Chapter 5, "The Rising Latin American and Caribbean Middle Class," discusses quantitative trends in the size and composition of the Latin American middle class and presents its current profile.

Chapter 6, "The Middle Class and the Social Contract in Latin America," discusses some international evidence on the association between middle-class size and policy choices, and asks whether those associations are likely to hold in Latin America. Survey evidence on the values and beliefs held by individuals in different social groups is brought to bear, and the implications for the future of the region's social contract are examined.

Notes

1. If they were real people, Isabel and Roberto would naturally think of their income in Brazilian reais. However, because they are fictional characters in this technical volume about economic mobility and the middle class in Latin America, we use PPP dollars to compare incomes across space and time.
2. The Brazilian minimum wage was R$510.00 per month in 2010, equivalent to US$324.60 at purchasing power parity.
3. Most of these characteristics are further described in tables in chapters 4 and 5.
4. The families might be just a little larger in some other countries in the region.
5. These are population-weighted averages across the 30 Latin American and Caribbean countries shown in figure 1.1. GDP is measured in constant 2005 international dollars, at PPP exchange rates.
6. See also Ferreira, Leite, and Litchfield (2008) for an early account of declining inequality in Brazil.
7. They are Honduras (0.57); Bolivia and Colombia (0.56 each); Brazil (0.55); Chile, Panama, and Paraguay (0.52 each); and Costa Rica (0.51). Note that these are the latest numbers available for each country during 2008–10 and do not account for subsequent changes.
8. The other four countries in that list are Armenia, Côte d'Ivoire, Kazakhstan, and Moldova.
9. Moderate poverty is defined by comparing household income per capita with a poverty line of US$4 per day at PPP exchange rates. Extreme poverty, which is defined with respect to a poverty line of US$2.50 per day for Latin America, fell from 24.5 percent to 14.0 percent in the same period (see World Bank 2011).

References

Barros, Ricardo P., M. Carvalho, S. Franco, and R. Mendonça. 2010. "Markets, the State, and the Dynamics of Inequality in Brazil." In *Declining Inequality in Latin America: A Decade of Progress?*, ed. Luis F. López-Calva and Nora Lustig, 134–174. Washington, DC: Brookings Institution Press.

Ferreira, Francisco H. G., Phillippe Leite, and Julie Litchfield. 2008. "The Rise and Fall of Brazilian Inequality: 1981–2004." *Macroeconomic Dynamics* 12 (S2): 199–230.

López-Calva, Luis F., and Nora Lustig, eds. 2010. *Declining Inequality in Latin America: A Decade of Progress?* Washington, DC: Brookings Institution Press.

World Bank. 2011. "On the Edge of Uncertainty: Poverty Reduction in Latin America and the Caribbean during the Great Recession and Beyond." Poverty and labor brief, World Bank, Washington, DC.

World Bank. n.d. *World Development Indicators*. Online database. Washington, DC: World Bank. http://data.worldbank.org/data-catalog/world-development-indicators.

Economic Mobility and the Middle Class: Concepts and Measurement | 2

Social and economic mobility are integral components of economic development. At its most basic, income growth is itself a form of economic mobility (as we shall discuss further below). But the nature and extent of mobility arguably affect societies in ways that are both more subtle and more dramatic than income growth.

Economic mobility, in the sense of changes in relative rank and position, has often been said to mitigate static inequality and contribute to long-term fairness, as eloquently suggested by Milton Friedman (1962, p. 171): "Consider two societies that have the same distribution of annual income. In one there is great mobility and change so that the position of particular families in the income hierarchy varies widely from year to year. In the other, there is great rigidity so that each family stays in the same position year after year. Clearly, in any meaningful sense, the second would be the more unequal society."

Mobility also affects politics. Tocqueville ([1856] 1986) argued that greater opportunity for upward movement among the poor might make long-standing oppression and inequality less, rather than more, tolerable and that this may explain why revolution took place in France earlier than in other European countries, where oppression and exploitation were even greater. In a famous paper, Hirschman and Rothschild (1973) suggested that the relationship between mobility and political reaction might be more complicated: the upward movement of others, when unaccompanied by one's own, might be welcome at first but subsequently resented (much as the faster movement of cars in the lane next to one's own in a tunnel). The relationship between economic mobility, individual preferences for redistribution, and economic outcomes remains of crucial interest to economists today (see, for example, Piketty 1995).

Mobility is also often seen as the ex post realization of evenly spread economic opportunity ex ante, and some countries hold up that manifestation as an integral part of their very national identity. A recent U.S. article on "What Happened to Upward Mobility?" (*Time* 2011) opened thus: "America's story, our national mythology, is built on the idea of being an opportunity society. From the tales of Horatio Alger to the real lives of Henry Ford and Mark Zuckerberg, we have defined our country as a place where everyone, if he or she works hard enough, can get ahead."

There is also a long-standing and widespread view, going back at least to the Greek philosophers, that a robust middle class can play a role beneficial for both economic and political development: "It is possible for those states to be well governed that are of the kind in which the middle-class is numerous, and preferably stronger than both the other two classes, or at all events than one of them, for by throwing in its weight it sways the balance and prevents the opposite extremes from coming into existence . . . Surely the ideal of the state is to consist as much as possible of persons that are equal and alike, and this similarity is most found in the middle classes" (Aristotle [c. 350 BC] 1932).

Scratch the surface of these grand statements, however, and it quickly becomes apparent that both concepts—economic mobility and the middle class—mean very different things to different people. Mobility has long been important in sociology and, at least since the late 1970s, it has also been the subject of formal economic analysis. At the risk of considerable oversimplification, sociologists may be said to see social mobility in terms of changes in the class and occupational makeup of populations over time, largely as a result of technological and economic change. Economists, on the other hand, tend to think of mobility in terms of the transformation of a vector of incomes (or some other measure of well-being or economic achievement) in an initial period into another income vector in a second period, and possibly onward to subsequent periods.[1] And, as we shall see, even this apparently narrow economic framework for mobility comports with a number of distinct concepts and measures—distinct enough to be frequently inconsistent with one another.

The middle class is a similarly slippery, or multifaceted, concept. Philosophers, political scientists, sociologists, and economists have meant different things by the same term. Before we can meaningfully assess the extent, nature, and possible consequences of economic mobility and the growth of the middle class in Latin America in the past decade or so, it is important to be clear about what we mean by each of these concepts. This chapter therefore offers a brief review of the main definitions used in the economic analysis of mobility and the middle class, and identifies those that will be used in the remainder of the volume. Although sociological approaches

feature occasionally in subsequent chapters, the report analyzes mobility and class dynamics primarily through an economic lens. Accordingly, this chapter also focuses on the views of mobility and the middle class prominent in the economics literature. Yet it is not intended as a comprehensive review of that literature, which is not the remit of this volume. Instead, it seeks to offer a nontechnical overview of the multiplicity of definitions currently in use and to present and justify the definitions and approaches chosen for use in the analysis that follows in subsequent chapters.

The chapter is structured as follows: The next section discusses the "Spaces, Domains, and Concepts of Economic Mobility" and highlights those featured in chapters 3 and 4. "Defining the Middle Class" turns to alternative definitions of the middle class and describes how we chose one particular definition for application to Latin America in the early 21st century, particularly in chapters 5 and 6. The final section, "Linking Mobility and Middle-Class Dynamics," illustrates how one of our chosen measures of economic mobility is straightforwardly decomposed into movements in and out of poverty, vulnerability, and the middle class.

Spaces, domains, and concepts of economic mobility

To impart meaning to the view of mobility as the transformation of a vector into another over a period of time, economists must be able to answer three questions quite precisely:

The first question is: mobility of what? It concerns the *space* of economic mobility and refers to the choice of variable in the vector (or distribution) under consideration: Is it a vector of current incomes or permanent incomes? Or is it a vector of just labor earnings, or perhaps of consumption expenditure, or wealth? Is it a vector of educational attainment (measured, for instance, by completed years of schooling), or of educational achievement (measured, say, by performance on standardized tests)? In attempting to patch together a comprehensive picture of economic mobility in Latin America on the basis of the highly imperfect data that are available, the chapters that follow will draw on information from all of the above variables, except for physical and financial wealth. In each instance, the mobility space being considered will be clearly indicated to avoid misleading the reader into comparing apples with oranges.[2] In the remainder of this chapter, however, the term "income vector" is shorthand for the vector of interest in any well-defined economic space.

The second question concerns how far apart in time the two (or more) income vectors are from one another. In particular, one must distinguish between two very different *domains* of economic mobility: the *intragenerational*—when the identities of the elements of the income vectors correspond to the same individuals over time—and the *intergenerational*—when those identities refer to the same lineage across generations (that is, fathers and sons, mothers and daughters, and so on). The domain distinction is fundamental because it interacts powerfully with the different concepts of mobility described below. It is far from obvious that the most relevant concepts, or the set of key properties one would like a measure of mobility to have, are the same for mobility across generations and for mobility over a person's lifetime. It is also possible for a given society, at a particular point in time, to exhibit a great deal of mobility within generations while remaining rather immobile across them, or vice versa. For this reason, evidence on recent intergenerational and intragenerational mobility in Latin America is presented in two separate chapters, respectively chapters 3 and 4.

The third question economists must be able to answer to arrive at a meaningful measure of economic mobility refers to the *concept* of mobility one seeks to capture. The applied literature contains at least 20 different empirical measures of mobility (Fields 2010), and the differences are not merely trivial issues of functional form or relative weights. Information on (identity-preserving) changes between two vectors can be aggregated in very different ways, and these often correspond to deep distinctions in the fundamental conception of mobility one has in mind. Drawing on (and slightly adapting) the influential taxonomy of Fields (2000), one can identify three basic concepts of mobility, as follows:

- *Mobility as movement.* Informally, this concept associates mobility with movement: the more movement we observe between two distributions, the more mobile the society. Even this apparently simple concept can give rise to very different indices, however, because an element in an income vector can be characterized by three different attributes: its income level (y); its income share, $s(y)$ (that is, relative to total or mean income); and its position or rank in the distribution ($p = F(y)$). In addition, when we consider movement in levels, it matters whether we are interested in "gross" movements or flux (so that income falls are added to income gains) or in "net" or directional movement (so that, for instance, income falls are subtracted from income gains). So the "mobility as movement" concept really consists of four subconcepts:
  - *Directional income movement (IMD)* seeks to quantify the extent of *net* upward (or downward) movement in individual incomes.
  - *Nondirectional income movement (IMND)* seeks to measure the extent of *gross* movement in incomes, or flux.
  - *Share movement (SM)* seeks to assess the extent of movement in *relative* incomes (that is, changes in individual shares of the overall income pie).
  - *Positional movement (PM)* seeks to quantify the extent of reranking from one distribution to another.
- *Mobility as origin independence (MOI).* The basic property underpinning these measures is that a more mobile society is one where one's (or one's parents') initial position is a less important determinant of one's future position. In a two-period setting, mobility as origin (or time) independence can be seen as the converse of the correlation between the initial and final vectors.

- *Mobility as equalizer of long-term incomes (ELTI).* In this view, a more mobile society is one in which inequality in permanent incomes (where permanent income is defined, say, as an individual's average income across all periods) is less than the inequality at any particular point in time (or, in an alternative specification, at the initial period).

These different concepts of mobility correspond to inherently distinct notions of what mobility *is*. In general, although many indices may be consistent with each concept, a good measure of one particular concept will be a poor measure of any other. Which is to say, to choose a particular index to measure mobility, one must first decide which concept of mobility one is trying to capture. To see this, consider a simple example, illustrated in table 2.1. Imagine a three-person economy, where the initial income vector (in pesos per day, say) is (1, 10, 100). Now consider three alternative "mobility scenarios." In Scenario A, the final income vector is (2, 20, 200). In Scenario B, it is (100, 10, 1); and in Scenario C, it is (36, 37, 38). Which of these scenarios has the highest mobility? And which has the least?

The answer clearly depends on the mobility concept. In Scenario A, all incomes have doubled, so there is a good deal of income movement, both directional (IMD) and nondirectional (IMND). But each person's share of total income remains unchanged: person 1 has 1/111; person 2 has 10/111, and person 3 has 100/111 of the total pie in both initial and final vectors. So there is no SM at all! Similarly, the ranking of individuals is unchanged between the initial and final vectors, so there is no PM either. Incomes in the initial and final vectors are also perfectly correlated, so there is zero MOI. And for any measure of relative inequality—including all those that are Lorenz consistent—inequality in average incomes (1.5, 15, 150) is identical to inequality in the initial and final vectors. So there is no mobility as an ELTI.

Scenario A illustrates the point that the concepts of income movement are essentially different from the other mobility concepts. Naturally, measures of mobility designed to capture share or positional movement, or indeed MOI or ELTI, cannot be expected to accurately gauge the extent of IMD or IMND in a particular vector transformation.

As Scenario B illustrates, IMD and IMND need not always be aligned, either. In this case, a measure of the extent of *churning* or nondirectional movement in the distribution (that is, an index where income falls and income gains enter with the same sign) would record a high value, whereas a measure of growth (or directional movement) would indicate no mobility. In this particular "rank-reversal" example, there is also a large degree of PM and SM. And inequality in average incomes (50.5, 10.0, 50.5) is also lower than in either initial or final points, so some ELTI takes place.

Scenario C is an example of transformations where SM and PM yield different degrees of mobility. In this case, there is positive IMND and SM, and there is also ELTI, but there is no aggregate IMD (at least by some measures) or PM.

The broader point that table 2.1 seeks to convey is that the distinctions between the three main concepts of mobility (movement, origin independence, and the long-term equalization of incomes)—or indeed between the four subconcepts of mobility as

TABLE 2.1   How different mobility concepts rank the same vector transformation

Initial income vector	Final income vector	Mobility	No mobility
Scenario A: (1, 10, 100)	(2, 20, 200)	IMD, IMND	SM, PM, MOI, ELTI
Scenario B: (1, 10, 100)	(100, 10, 1)	IMND, PM, SM, ELTI	IMD, MOI
Scenario C: (1, 10, 100)	(36, 37, 38)	IMND, SM, ELTI	IMD, PM

Note: ELTI = mobility as equalizer of long-term incomes. IMD = directional income movement. IMND = nondirectional income movement. MOI = mobility as origin independence. PM = positional movement. SM = share movement.

movement—are not small quibbles of limited practical interest. They go to the very heart of what mobility *is*. If we are trying to determine whether mobility is higher in Peru or in Mexico at a certain point in time, or to ascertain whether it has grown or been reduced between the 1990s and the 2000s in Argentina, we might well get different answers, depending on which concept we are interested in and on what particular measure of mobility we choose to adopt. For to each of the six concepts discussed above (IMD, IMND, SM, PM, MOI, and ELTI), there corresponds a number of different specific mobility indices.

For mobility as movement and as origin independence, the problem of measuring overall mobility in a society can be decomposed into two intuitively simple steps: First, one defines an *individual mobility function.* Second, one aggregates across all individuals (or lineages) in the economy to obtain a *social mobility index.*[3] Focus note 2.1 (at the end of this chapter) provides examples of some of the most commonly used individual mobility functions corresponding to each concept of mobility and the aggregate indices they give rise to. It also illustrates each function graphically for transformations in the vector of household per capita incomes in Peru in 2004–06.

Given the broad scope of this report—covering mobility across a good number of countries, over a relatively long period, and in different spaces (such as income, consumption, and education)—attempting to systematically provide results for all mobility subconcepts in every instance seems unwise: a wide variety of measures for every example would probably lead to a bewildering array of numbers, more likely to obscure the big picture than to provide meaningful detail. We have therefore chosen to focus on a single mobility concept for each of our two domains of interest: across and within generations.

As suggested above, however, it is not obvious that the same concept serves equally well to capture the fundamental properties of mobility in these two domains. Across generations, mobility is often associated with the

notion of equality of opportunity. A mobile society is one in which the children of lawyers or doctors and those of farmers or construction workers have similar (income or educational) prospects—one where a parent's income, occupation, education, or status does not fully or substantially predetermine the son's (or daughter's).

The mobility concept most closely associated with this notion is that of origin independence.[4] The origin-independence axiom (see Shorrocks 1978) requires a measure of mobility to rise when the association between initial and final vectors falls. In practice, a social mobility index commonly used to measure MOI is the complement of the correlation coefficient between initial and final vectors:

$$d(y_0, y_1) = 1 - \rho_{01}.^5 \qquad (2.1)$$

This measure of mobility as the converse of correlation has a long tradition in statistics and economics, going back to English statistician Sir Francis Galton (1886). Another frequent measure of intergenerational mobility is the complement of the gradient in the regression of the final vector on the initial one. Classic applications in economics include Zimmerman (1992) and Solon (2002). This measure may be preferable to the correlation coefficient when one is interested not only in how much parental background explains the outcomes in the children's generation but also in how unequal those outcomes are. This is the primary measure of mobility that will be reported in the next chapter, which focuses on intergenerational mobility in Latin America.

Within a given generation, on the other hand, it is not clear that one would prefer a society where people's incomes today had no correlation at all with their incomes, say, 10 years ago. The degree of churning and economic upheaval necessary to engender such a (lack of) serial correlation would likely lead to a great deal of intertemporal variation in consumption and well-being (unless credit markets were perfect). In addition, there are both ethical and incentive-related reasons for welcoming a certain degree of temporal persistence in the rewards to effort: a society where the economic benefits from completing a demanding college education dissipated over a few years would be unlikely to be either efficient or fair.

Provided there is equality of opportunity (and intergenerational mobility in an origin-independence sense), one might reasonably choose to focus on income growth as the key desideratum of mobility within generations. And, as we have seen, the mobility concept that most closely corresponds to the idea of growth (at the individual level) is directional income movement.

Among various possible measures of directional income movement, we chose the index denoted M^3 in Fields and Ok (1999), which is simply the average of the growth rates in individual incomes between the initial and final vectors. This index is appealing for a number of reasons:

- Intuitively, it captures the microfoundations of economic growth—at the level of the individual household.
- Formally, it is the integral of the non-anonymous growth incidence curve (GIC), which plots income growth rates for each percentile of the initial income distribution.[6]
- It can be naturally interpreted as a "democratic" measure of economic growth, which differs from the conventional measure by weighting households by their population shares rather than income shares.[7]
- It can also be decomposed in a number of informative ways, including one that generates a "transition matrix-like" portrait of transitions into and out of poverty, the middle class, and other social groups one cares to define. We return to this matrix decomposition in the concluding section, "Linking Mobility and Middle-Class Dynamics," where we use it to link this measure of intragenerational mobility to the definition of the middle class proposed below.

For these various reasons, this proportional measure of directional income movement is our preferred index of mobility within generations, and it features prominently in chapter 4.

These choices give rise to a simple 2×2 matrix of concepts by domains, whereof the report will focus on a main diagonal: when assessing the extent of mobility of individuals *within* a generation, we will be primarily concerned with measures of directional income movement, while when measuring mobility *across* generations we will focus on mobility as origin independence.

Table 2.2 illustrates this conceptual matrix. As it suggests, the focus on the main diagonal does not imply absolute silence about the off-diagonal cells. It will sometimes make sense to investigate how much growth or progress took place between generations in absolute terms, just as it may occasionally be interesting to assess measures of independence between circumstances at childhood and achievements at adulthood. In the main, however, mobility between generations will be taken to mean mobility as origin independence, whereas individual mobility over the course of a number of years will be seen through the prism of directional income movement.

As noted above, and in the bottom-right cell in table 2.2, one attraction of the directional income movement concept in the intragenerational domain is that it immediately lends itself to the analysis of social group dynamics. By means of GICs, or of decompositions of our mobility measure, it allows us to identify individuals leaving or entering poverty as well as those arriving at or falling from the middle class. The demographic, educational, and occupational characteristics of these individuals; their access to or use of services; and the different policy regimes under which they live and work can be informative of the nature of upward mobility and the rise of the middle class—the virtues of which have appealed to so many since Aristotle. As the following chapters suggest, they may even allow us to

TABLE 2.2   Key mobility concepts and domains under consideration: The main diagonal

Concept and Domain	Intergenerational	Intragenerational
Origin independence	*Key desideratum* is equality of opportunity. *Main index* is the gradient of regression across generations. *Objects of analysis* include the extent to which parental characteristics affect educational achievement today and how policies might interact with that relationship.	When looking at long-term life-cycle movements (for example, from childhood to adulthood), concepts of origin independence and equality of opportunity become relevant again.
Directional income movement	Absolute progress across generations, in income or education, will also be reported.	*Key desideratum* is individual growth. *Main index* is the average of the growth rates in individual incomes (M^3). *Objects of analysis* include movements in and out of poverty and in and out of the middle class.

formulate and investigate certain hypotheses about the causes and policy effects of these changes.

But to do this, we need a definition of the social classes we are interested in, particularly the middle class. Beyond that, given the available data and the concepts of mobility we have chosen, it will help enormously if the "middle class" definition we adopt, wherever it may come from, can ultimately be expressed in income terms.

Defining the middle class

In Western civilization, the notion of social class, like much else, goes back to Greco-Roman antiquity. Aristotle's *Politics*, as we have already hinted, noted that people with different levels of wealth tended to have different political preferences and interests and suggested that there might often be conflict between the interests of the poor and those of the rich. Such conflict might be alleviated by the existence of a large group of people "in the middle," particularly if such people were "equal and alike" (Aristotle [c. 350 BC] 1932).

The Romans, often seen as more practical-minded than the Greeks, are credited with a first operational classification of people into groups formally defined as "classes." King Servius Tullius of Rome, in a visionary plan to enlarge his kingdom, extended the franchise to people outside the traditional limits of Rome and launched the first census of the Western world (McGeough 2004; Cornell 1995). During the 6th century BC, the king gathered demographic and socioeconomic information about his subjects. The purpose of the census was to classify citizens into income groups for tax purposes, called *classis*, and to establish the contributions of each family to the empire, according to their declared means. Those in the poorest class, who were unable to contribute with financial resources, were nevertheless capable of contributing by having children, who potentially would serve as soldiers. That lowest *classis* would only contribute with *prole*, the Latin word for children, and was named the *proletarius*. The notion would evolve into the modern concept of *proletariat*, a class whose only means of production is their own labor and which is then subject to exploitation by those who own capital, according to Marxian analysis.

The notion of class is, of course, central in Karl Marx's writings. Marx viewed class as being essentially defined by the ownership of the same factors of production (chiefly labor or capital). The factors one sold into the production process in turn engendered for each group a common position in a stratified social structure, characterized primarily by the exploitation of workers by capitalists. But he did allow for the existence of a small, independent group of businessmen and professionals who acquired skills, knowledge, and education to rely only on themselves and their resources to achieve a better economic position. This embryonic middle class was seen as a relatively narrow group known as the *petty bourgeoisie*, composed largely of small entrepreneurs and bureaucrats (as opposed to the *haute bourgeoisie*, the capitalists).

But as the market economy in industrial Europe during the late 19th and early 20th centuries evolved, and more complex processes in manufacturing and services also demanded education and skills, a new class of educated people emerged who did not necessarily own capital and who sold their labor in the market. This class did not fit easily within the classic Marxist framework: it did not belong to the *lumpenproletariat* or to the proletariat (the working class) in terms of their role in the dynamics of class conflict, but neither did it own capital, as capitalists did.[8]

The more modern, nuanced, and complex concept of the middle class that was needed has evolved, in large part, from the writings of Max Weber (for example, Weber [1922] 1978). In the Weberian tradition, the concept of social stratification contains three intertwined notions: *class*, *status*, and *party* (or *power*, more broadly):

- *Class* refers to the strictly economic aspect of stratification. In Weber's own words, "the factor that creates 'class' is unambiguously economic interest, and indeed, only those interests involved in the existence of the 'market'" (Weber 1946).
- *Status*, on the other hand, relates to the "lifestyle" of a group of people, the identity and prestige associated with membership, and the expression of such conditions through cultural consumption (Torche 2010). It relates to the expected

behavior of those who belong to the group, as in Akerlof and Kranton (2002). Status is not limited by the market. According to Weber, both propertied and propertyless people can belong to status groups—although there is a clear overlap between status and class. The main difference between both concepts is that while classes relate to the *production* of goods, "status groups" are stratified according to the *consumption* of goods as represented by particular "styles of life" and associated principles, values, and ideas.[9]

- *Party*, the third dimension of Weber's social structure, is related to the notion of power in social relations. An individual holds more power to the degree that he or she controls resources that are important to others, inasmuch as this individual can induce others to act in his or her own interest. As expressed in Weber's words, power is "the probability that one actor within a social relationship will be in a position to carry out his own will despite resistance, regardless of the basis on which this probability rests" (Weber [1922] 1978).

Together, and in their very different ways, Marx and Weber can be seen as the founders of the modern sociological approach(es) to class and, hence, more specifically to the middle class. Although, as we have seen, both Marx and Weber regarded economic interests, and participation in economic processes, as fundamental to the definition of social classes, they also acknowledged the importance of other aspects. Weber and his followers, in particular, noted the importance of political organization and collective action, patterns of consumption and lifestyle, and finally beliefs and a system of ideas.

When Marx and Weber were writing, however, household-level data capable of identifying individuals into social classes were extremely scarce, and the technology for manipulating and analyzing them was rudimentary. As household data have become more plentiful, and information technology revolutionized their analysis, it has become possible to take definitions of the middle class to the data. Economists, who have recently taken the lead in this process, have seldom sought to identify the middle class in terms of its educational makeup, occupational composition, or system of beliefs. Predictably, perhaps, most studies have opted for an income-based definition.

Income is a tempting variable on which to base criteria for defining the middle class: it provides a natural metric on a single dimension, facilitating the location of a "middle group." Choose two income thresholds, and you could call those below the lower threshold the "lower class," those above the higher one the "upper class," and in between them you have the middle class, much as in Aristotle's quote at the beginning of this chapter. Albeit stylized, this has been essentially how the economics literature on the middle class has evolved.

Studies differ from one another largely in terms of which two thresholds are chosen. A first group of studies select thresholds in relation to the median income of the distribution. For example, Blackburn and Bloom (1985) identify the middle class as households with per capita income between 0.60 and 2.25 times the median income in the United States. Davis and Huston (1992) use a narrower range: between 0.50 and 1.50 times the median, also for the United States. And Birdsall, Graham, and Pettinato (2000) use a range between 0.75 and 1.25 times the median for 30 countries, including high-income, transition, and Latin American economies. Some authors also call these groups "social strata" precisely to emphasize the narrowly economic nature of the concept, avoiding the sociological discussion.

Another set of studies sets the thresholds not on the income space itself but on the space of ranks or positions in their distribution: $p = F(y)$.

For example, Alesina and Perotti (1996) use the income share of the third and fourth quintiles of the distribution; Partridge (1997) uses the middle quintile; Barro (2000) and Easterly (2001) use the middle three quintiles; and Solimano (2008), the third to ninth deciles. Under this latter approach, the size

of the middle class (in terms of population) is naturally fixed by the very definition. These measures seek, instead, to quantify the share of total income appropriated by this group.

We refer to both of these groups of studies—those that define the middle-class thresholds as multiples of median income and those that define thresholds based on certain income quintiles or deciles—as using *relative, income-based definitions* of the middle class. Table 2.3 summarizes the specific cutoff points used in some of the key studies in this group.

In comparing middle classes across countries, the *relative, income-based definitions*—or at least those among them that rely on the median—face the problem of a different median income in each country, and therefore different middle classes from place to place. Imagine two countries, A and B, with median per capita incomes of US$3 and US$8 a day, respectively. If the middle class is defined as those households with per capita income ranging between 0.60 and 1.40 times the median income, a household living on US$1.8 to US$4.2 a day in country A would undoubtedly be part of the middle class in that country; however, this household would be part of the lower class in country B, where the income thresholds range between US$4.8 and US$11.2 a day.

An alternative is using an *absolute, income-based* definition, which avoids the previous shortcoming because it identifies the middle class as those households with income or consumption in a specific range of standardized international dollars (that is, at purchasing power parity [PPP] exchange rates). The fundamental question is how to define such an absolute level. So far, most absolute thresholds appear to have been picked somewhat arbitrarily. In an influential study, Milanovic and Yitzhaki (2002) divided the world population into three groups and used household surveys to identify the middle class as those households with per capita incomes between the average per capita *incomes* of Brazil and Italy (US$12–US$50 a day). Banerjee and Duflo (2008) define the middle class as those households living with a

TABLE 2.3   Income-based definitions of the middle class

Relative definitions of the middle class

Percentiles of the income distribution		
Birdsall, Graham, and Pettinato (2000)	$i \in$ middle class	$0.75\, y\,(p_{50}) \leq y_i \leq 1.25\, y\,(p_{50})$
Blackburn and Bloom (1985)		$0.60\, y\,(p_{50}) \leq y_i \leq 2.25\, y\,(p_{50})$
Davis and Huston (1992)		$0.50\, y\,(p_{50}) \leq y_i \leq 1.50\, y\,(p_{50})$
Alesina and Perotti (1996)		$p_{40} \leq p(y_i) \leq p_{80}$
Barro (1999) and Easterly (2001)		$P_{20} \leq p(y_i) \leq p_{80}$
Partridge (1997)		$p_{40} \leq p(y_i) \leq p_{60}$
Solimano (2008)		$P_{20} \leq p(y_i) \leq p_{90}$

Absolute definitions of the middle class

Banerjee and Duflo (2008)		$\$2 \leq y_i \leq \$10$ a day
Kharas (2010)		$\$10 \leq y_i \leq \$100$ a day
López-Calva and Ortiz-Juarez (2011)		$\$10 \leq y_i \leq \$50$ a day
Milanovic and Yitzhaki (2002)	$i \in$ middle class	$\$12 \leq y_i \leq \$50$ a day
Ravallion (2010)		$\$2 \leq y_i \leq \$13$ a day

Note: All values expressed in US$ at purchasing power parity exchange rates.

per capita *expenditure* of US$2–US$10 a day and analyze the consumption and employment patterns of this group in 11 developing countries.

Similarly, Ravallion (2010) recently proposed the concept of a "developing world's middle class," defined as a range between the developing countries' median poverty line and the U.S. poverty line—in other words, the range between (a) those households with per capita consumption at or above the median poverty line for 70 developing countries (US$2 a day per person), and (b) households at or below the U.S. poverty line (US$13 a day per person). Using household surveys for almost 100 developing countries, Ravallion showed that the developing world's middle class increased from 32.8 percent of the population in 1990 to 48.5 percent of the population in 2005. These figures suggest that more than 1.2 billion people joined the middle class over 1990–2005, with China accounting for a startling half of this amount.

In an even more recent study, López-Calva and Ortiz-Juarez (2011) also proposed absolute income-based thresholds to define the middle class. Like Banerjee and Duflo (2008) and Ravallion (2010), there are elements of an analogy with poverty measurement in how they go about this. But instead of choosing a particular poverty line (the upper bound on the set of the poor) as the lower bound on

the middle class, these authors looked for an income value that corresponds to a minimum requirement for the *functionings* that define the middle-class.[10] One might see the inability to attain adequate nourishment or to participate meaningfully in a minimum set of social activities as the (absence of) functionings that define poverty, and a poverty line as some demarcation in income space of what is required to attain those minimum functionings and escape poverty, in a particular society and at a particular time.

Analogously, one might search for the set of functionings that are associated with belonging to a middle class and then attempt to quantify an income level that permits their attainment in a given society at a given time. One advantage of this approach is that it moves us a little closer, however slightly, to the concept of a common "lifestyle"—including certain consumption patterns and cultural habits—that sociologists in the Weberian tradition associate with class. Sensibly, López-Calva and Ortiz-Juarez (2011) do not attempt to fully identify a vector of consumption goods associated with middle-class status. Instead, they choose one particular "functioning," namely economic security, as the defining characteristic of the middle class. And economic security is measured, in turn, as the converse of vulnerability to falling into poverty.[11]

Specifically, these authors estimate the probability of falling into poverty in three Latin American countries for which longitudinal household data are available from the early 2000s: namely Chile, Mexico, and Peru, conditional on a set of observed covariates (including demographic indicators, labor market resources, and household-level shocks).[12] Using these panels, poverty transition matrices are constructed on the basis of national poverty lines in each country, all of which are in the PPP US$4–US$5 per day range.[13] The results are shown in figure 2.1.

Figure 2.1 depicts the inverse relationship between initial incomes (on the horizontal axis) and the probability that households with those levels of (predicted) income would find themselves in poverty at the end of the five-year interval in each country. Full economic security may well be thought to correspond to a zero, or near-zero, poverty probability. However, the existence of (some unknown amount of) measurement error in any panel survey implies that mobility in any such transition matrix is likely to be overestimated and that taking a lower bound for the middle class at the 0–5 percent probability range may well be excessively conservative. López-Calva and Ortiz-Juarez (2011) suggest taking a 10 percent probability of falling into poverty as an "operational" dividing line between economic security and vulnerability. As discussed in chapter 4, that probability is slightly lower than the average upper-bound estimate for downward mobility into poverty in the region as a whole and very close to the country estimates for Argentina, Colombia, and Costa Rica. The choice of a 10 percent probability of falling into poverty in a five-year interval yields income thresholds of PPP US$8.5 per capita per day in Chile, PPP US$9.7 in Mexico, and PPP US$9.6 in Peru. The authors furthermore present some evidence that these thresholds are relatively robust to changes in the specification of their conditioning models.

The anchoring of a middle-class definition to economic security is conceptually appealing, as is the fact that these authors have applied their proposal to three Latin

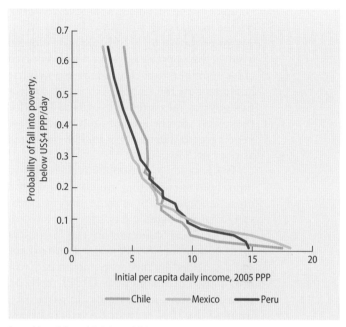

FIGURE 2.1 Income-based vulnerability to poverty in Chile, Mexico, and Peru in the 2000s

Initial per capita daily income, 2005 PPP

Chile — Mexico — Peru

Source: López-Calva and Ortiz-Juarez 2011.
Note: PPP = purchasing power parity.

American countries specifically. Like poverty, the notion of the middle class might be absolute in some capability space but not in income space. National poverty lines, which are used to inform national policy decisions, vary with aggregate incomes and are not the same in Argentina, China, and India (see Chen and Ravallion 2001). Similarly, a lower threshold of US$2 per day, as proposed by Banerjee and Duflo (2008) and Ravallion (2010), might (or might not) make sense in the poorest countries, but it is unsuitable in a Latin American context. It is well below most national poverty lines in the region, for example. Both the conceptual basis and the regional specificity of the López-Calva and Ortiz-Juarez (2011) lower threshold are therefore appealing for the purposes of this report.

One concern may remain, however, regarding the possibly arbitrary choice of a 10 percent probability of falling into poverty in a five-year interval as the dividing line between security and vulnerability, from which the monetary threshold follows.[14] We therefore asked whether an alternative, and completely independent, approach to defining the middle class would yield a very different lower threshold. Specifically, we adopted a subjective approach based on self-reported class membership. The idea—somewhat analogous to the Leyden school of subjective poverty measurement—was to look for the lowest income level around which more people regard themselves as middle class than as poor or "lower class."[15]

The best set of nationally representative household surveys that contain a question on social class as well as some objective measure of socioeconomic status for a number of Latin American countries are the *Encuestas de Cohesión Social en América Latina* (Ecosocial), fielded by the Corporación de Estudios para Latinoamérica (CIEPLAN), an influential Chilean think tank. In particular, we used the 2007 wave for seven countries, namely Argentina, Brazil, Chile, Colombia, Guatemala, Mexico, and Peru. The Ecosocial surveys do not ask individuals about actual household income, but reasonably detailed information is available on a set of assets, durable goods, and dwelling characteristics. This permits the application of a survey-to-survey income imputation method based on the poverty mapping work of Elbers, Lanjouw, and Lanjouw (2003).

Once incomes are thus imputed from the mainstream household surveys into the Ecosocial, we can observe, for each household, both a measure of "predicted income" and a class self-report. The latter records the answer to the following question: "In our society, people tend to place themselves within different social classes. Would you classify yourself as belonging to one of these?"[16] The question is asked identically in all seven countries. Answers fall into five categories: lower class, lower middle class, middle class, upper middle class, and upper class. Perhaps unsurprisingly, relatively few respondents self-describe in the extreme categories, particularly the upper class: the average density in the lower- and upper-class categories across the seven

countries was 18.5 percent and 0.8 percent, respectively. One implication of this is that a grouping of the three "middle-class" categories dominates over the two extremes at all income ranges, providing no meaningful insight.

One obvious alternative is to consider the lower and lower-middle categories jointly as a group below the middle class, and the three upper categories as a joint "middle class and the elite" amalgamation. This approach will not help us to shed light on the upper threshold of the middle class, to which we return below, but it may help us understand where Latin Americans themselves perceive the lower bound of the middle class. In five of the seven Ecosocial countries for which the analysis was possible, we therefore plotted the density functions of the income distribution of all those who considered themselves as lower or lower-middle class, and separately the densities of those who considered themselves as "middle or upper class." Figure 2.2 illustrates the results for Mexico. Our proposed "subjective approach" would treat the income at which the two functions cross—that is, the lowest income at which more people see themselves as middle class than otherwise—as the lower threshold for the middle class.

For Mexico, this income level is PPP US$9.6 per capita per day—remarkably close to the US$9.7 line obtained by the vulnerability approach of López-Calva and Ortiz-Juarez (2011), which was reported above. In Peru, it is PPP US$10.5, also not far from the US$9.6 line yielded by the vulnerability approach. Of course, as is to be expected from the application of two completely different approaches such as these to a question as tenuous as the membership of the middle class, the two answers do not always coincide.[17] Table 2.4 presents the lower middle-class thresholds obtained from the subjective approach for all five countries where the exercise was possible, namely Brazil, Chile, Colombia, Mexico, and Peru. The lines are presented both in household per capita income terms and in terms of income per earner; and, in each case,

FIGURE 2.2 **Distribution of self-reported class status in Mexico, 2007**

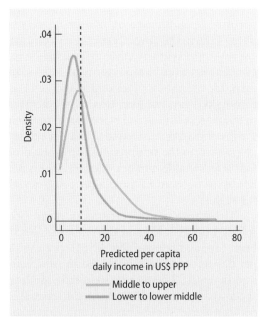

Sources: *Encuestas de Cohesión Social en América Latina* (Ecosocial) by the Corporación de Estudios para Latinoamérica (CIEPLAN) 2007; *Encuesta Nacional de Ingreso y Gastos de los Hogares* 2008 by the Mexican Instituto Nacional de Estadística y Geografía (INEGI).
Note: Densities are weighted by class size. PPP = purchasing power parity.

TABLE 2.4 **Middle-class thresholds from self-reported class status, selected Latin American countries, 2007**

	Lower threshold (per capita income)		Lower threshold (income per earner)	
	US$ PPP	Percentile	US$ PPP	Percentile
Brazil	16.3	84	26.2	82
Chile	20.3	83	33.2	77
Colombia	9.3	69	17.1	57
Mexico	9.6	68	19.9	66
Peru	10.5	76	18.1	74

Sources: Ecosocial 2007 and SEDLAC harmonized data.
Note: PPP = purchasing power parity. SEDLAC = Socioeconomic Database for Latin America and the Caribbean, jointly managed and maintained by the Centro de Estudios Distributivos, Laborales y Sociales (CEDLAS) of the Universidad de la Plata in Argentina, and the World Bank.

the rank of that income in the corresponding distribution is given. The latter are rather similar across the two distributions (except in the case of Colombia), suggesting robustness across income normalizations.

In our preferred income concept, namely household per capita income, these subjective thresholds range from US$9.3 (in Colombia) to US$20.3 (in Chile) at PPP exchange rates. Though the number for Chile, in particular, indicates that the subjective approach can generate lower bounds that are considerably higher than those obtained from the vulnerability approach, the exercise also suggests that the lower envelope of subjective lower thresholds in our sample (of around PPP US$9–US$10 per day) is remarkably close to the lines yielded by the vulnerability approach.

Given the scope for measurement error and imprecision of various kinds that are inevitably associated with the two procedures, and the various imputations and estimations that are carried out in each, we take these numbers as indicators of a broad order of magnitude rather than as precise point estimates. We do draw comfort from the fact that two conceptually appealing approaches—one based on the attainment of an objective functioning (economic security) and another based on self-perceptions of class—yield very similar lower bounds for the middle class in Latin America. But we do not read a great deal into decimal points and are happy to follow the recommendation in López-Calva and Ortiz-Juarez (2011) of adopting PPP US$10 per capita per day as our operational lower bound for the Latin American middle class in the chapters that follow.

Determining the upper income threshold

In principle, of course, the upper bound of the middle class should matter as much as the lower bound. Yet inspection of table 2.4 suggests that self-reported middle-class status is already associated with people fairly high up in the continent's income distribution. As we will see in much more detail in chapter 5 (which describes the nature, profile, and trends of the regional middle class), our US$10 line falls approximately on the seventh decile of the continent's overall distribution, as obtained from the household surveys in

SEDLAC.[18] If one were to apply, for example, Kharas's (2010) suggested upper threshold for the middle class of US$100 per capita per day to that household-survey-based mixture of distributions, only 0.5 percent of the continent's population would be counted as being the elite, or "above the middle class."[19] Naturally, this 0.5 percent figure reflects the well-known—and severe—shortcomings of household survey representativeness at the top of the income distribution. Income underreporting by richer households in surveys of this kind has long been known to be a common problem. More important still are the effects of survey noncompliance at the top end of the distribution.[20]

Although the existence of these survey problems is widely acknowledged, estimates of their extent in each country or methods to correct for them are much scarcer. In richer countries, a lot of work on the distribution of top incomes has recently relied on anonymized tax record data (see, for example, Piketty and Saez 2003; Atkinson, Piketty, and Saez 2011). A great deal has been learned from this approach, and it is encouraging that similar methods are now being applied to Latin America (Alvaredo 2010). Nevertheless, it is not clear that this work has evolved sufficiently to help us define a realistic upper threshold for the middle class in Latin America at this time. This is for two reasons: First, the tax record data that are needed for analyzing top incomes have only recently been made available to researchers.[21] Second, most of the top-income analysis so far has focused exclusively on the analysis of tax record data, which, in the Latin American case, would clearly be inferior to household survey data for the lower (and possible middle) income ranges, given the narrow coverage of the income tax in most of the region as well as problems of tax avoidance and evasion. Combining tax record data and household survey data—although a promising avenue of research for truly understanding the income distribution of middle-income countries—remains a frontier issue on which, to our knowledge, little progress has been made.

The practical implication is that the analysis of the nature and evolution of the Latin American middle class in this volume will perforce remain based on household survey data. Given the uncertainty surrounding survey representativeness at the very top, two implications would seem to follow, in turn, for the choice of an upper middle-class threshold: First, less attention should be paid to it, and less confidence placed on it, than on the lower threshold. Second, it may be preferable to err on the side of a lower threshold so that a reasonable number of observations are left above it, even in the poorer countries of the region.

With those considerations in mind, we follow López-Calva and Ortiz-Juarez (2011) here, too, and adopt a PPP US$50 per capita per day upper bound for the Latin American middle class. This is precisely half the line suggested by Kharas (2010), and it leaves 2.2 percent of the (survey-based) Latin American population in the "elite," rather than 0.5 percent. But the analysis that follows will place much less emphasis on the class divide at the top than it will on the bottom threshold. That analysis will be concentrated in chapters 5 and 6, which focus, respectively, on a description of the size, nature, and evolution of the middle class and on the implications for economic policy.

Distribution of four economic classes in Latin America

Our middle-class thresholds—PPP US$10 and PPP US$50 per capita per day—are shown in figure 2.3, which depicts the density function for the Latin America-wide income distribution. This continental distribution was constructed from the Socioeconomic Database for Latin America and the Caribbean (SEDLAC) data set mentioned above and represents 500 million individuals from 15 countries, or 86 percent of the region's population. We will return to the continental distribution in chapter 5, but it is included here so that the income thresholds derived in this section can be pictured in context. In

FIGURE 2.3 **Four economic classes, by income distribution, in selected Latin American countries**

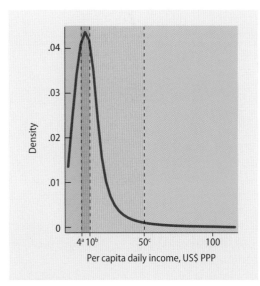

Source: SEDLAC (Socioeconomic Database for Latin America and the Caribbean) data.
Note: PPP = purchasing power parity. Countries include Argentina, Bolivia (2008), Brazil, Chile, Colombia, Costa Rica, Dominican Republic, Ecuador, El Salvador, Honduras, Mexico (2010), Panama, Paraguay, Peru, and Uruguay.
a. US$4 PPP = moderate Latin American and Caribbean poverty line.
b. US$10 PPP = lower bound of Latin American middle class.
c. US$50 PPP = upper bound of Latin American middle class.

addition to the lower and upper bounds of the middle class, figure 2.3 also indicates the Latin American moderate poverty line of PPP US$4 per capita per day.

One consequence of having sought to define a lower threshold for the middle class, which is endogenously derived from the vulnerability approach (and validated by the subjective approach) is that there is no reason why that threshold should then coincide with the poverty line. Indeed, in our case, the lower bound of the middle class is considerably higher than the moderate poverty line of US$4 a day commonly used by the World Bank for the Latin American and Caribbean region. This implies, of course, that there are four—not three—economic classes in our analysis. We refer to the people with incomes between US$4 and US$10 per person per day, who are too well-off to be considered poor but too vulnerable to be regarded as middle-class, as the *vulnerable class*.[22] This

is by no means a small group: it includes 37.6 percent of the continent's population, including its modal resident!

The existence and characteristics of this group provide a number of useful insights. At the most basic level, perhaps, it suggests that escaping poverty—as most countries and international agencies define it—is not enough to join the ranks of the comfortable-sounding, economically secure middle class. There is a narrow but populous purgatory between those two states, characterized by considerable vulnerability and a high risk of falling back into poverty. As a group, they are likely to be central to the continent's social policy design, political dynamics, and broad social contract, and we will return to them often in subsequent chapters. Before we get there, however, the next section describes the analytical framework used to link the two (multifaceted) concepts discussed so far in this chapter: economic mobility and the middle class.

Linking mobility and middle-class dynamics: A matrix decomposition

As noted in chapter 1, this volume aims to shed light on three aspects of the microeconomic dynamics underpinning the recent growth process in Latin America and the Caribbean:

First, as economies grow (and, in many cases, become less unequal), are greater opportunities being seized by all Latin Americans or only by those whose families have long hoarded the keys to prosperity? This is largely a question of mobility across generations, and it is addressed in chapter 3, which investigates the extent to which success in our societies today—in school or at work—is determined by who our parents were.

Second, how does growth manifest itself at the level of the individual worker or student? How do the aggregate GDP growth figures translate into growing incomes for individuals and their families? These questions about income growth, or income movement within a person's lifetime, are addressed in chapter 4.

Third, as incomes grow at the lower end of the income distribution, raising millions of Latin Americans out of poverty, is it true that the middle class is growing across the continent? How are these middle classes defined? Who was already part of them, and who are the new entrants? Do the "old" and "new" middle classes look alike? Do they have similar backgrounds? Do they think and act in similar ways? What will a larger (and possibly different) middle class mean for savings, growth, and the shaping of economic policy in Latin America?

The link between the last two questions—between mobility as income movement and the growth of the middle class—is probably self-evident. If middle classes grow, it is because more people have incomes that are large enough to earn them membership. Conveniently, this obvious link can be intuitively formalized in terms of a matrix decomposition of M^3: the measure of mobility as directional income movement described early in this chapter (and more formally in focus note 2.1 at the end of the chapter). This decomposition is used for much of the analysis in chapter 4.

As noted earlier, that measure of social mobility M^3 is simply an average of household per capita income growth rates. It can thus be decomposed as the sum of all proportional income gains and all proportional income losses. For any given income vector transformation, this "horizontal" decomposition separates overall mobility into that attributable to the "gainers" and that associated with the "losers." Exploiting the fact (discussed in more detail in focus note 2.1) that the measure corresponds graphically to the area under the non-anonymous growth incidence curve (na-GIC), figure 2.4 illustrates this decomposition for the 2004–06 interval in Peru. In this figure, the area in green corresponds to a measure of gross upward mobility in Peru during the period, while the area in orange measures gross downward mobility.[23] The difference between two—that is, the integral of the

FIGURE 2.4   Horizontal decomposition of mobility in Peru, 2004–06

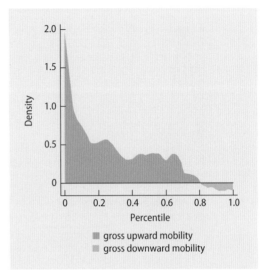

Source: Encuesta Nacional de Hogares (ENAHO) 2004 and 2006 by the Instituto Nacional de Estadística e Informática (INEI) de Perú.

na-GIC—measures total mobility as directional income movement.

The same measure of social mobility can also be decomposed "vertically," by social class at origin. One could simply partition the initial income vector by deciles, or in any other way, and measure aggregate mobility (both upward and downward) within each subgroup of the initial population. Because a partition ensures that each household belongs to one and only one subgroup, the sum of all such measures of subgroup mobility would yield total mobility once again.

For our purposes, and given the income-based definition of the middle class described previously, it makes sense to partition the initial income vector into four groups. Using the PPP US$4 per capita per day poverty line commonly applied to Latin American and Caribbean countries in World Bank studies, as well as the US$10–US$50 per day middle-class thresholds, one could decompose economic mobility by group at origin in the manner depicted in figure 2.5, once again for Peru (2004–06). The area under the na-GIC up until the percentile corresponding to an income of US$4 a day yields

FIGURE 2.5 Vertical decomposition of mobility in Peru, 2004–06

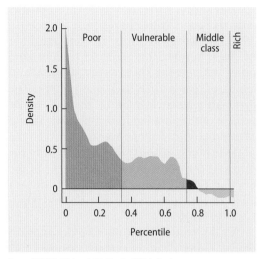

Source: ENAHO 2004 and 2006 by the INEI de Perú.

overall mobility among the originally poor. The area under the GIC and between the percentiles corresponding to US$4 and US$10 in figure 2.5 measures mobility among those originally vulnerable in Peru. Similarly, the area between the percentiles corresponding to US$10 and US$50 per day shows mobility among the middle class (at origin), and that above US$50 measures mobility among the rich elite.

To shed light on poverty dynamics, or on the dynamics of the middle class, one can combine the horizontal and vertical decompositions just described. Because M^3 is perfectly additively separable, the decomposition into "winners and losers" and the decomposition by social group at origin can be combined into what Ferreira and Lugo (2012) call a matrix decomposition of mobility as directional income movement. As those authors show, this decomposition is simply the sum of population-weighted average net income gains (or losses) for each cell in a transition matrix. Indeed, the sum can be stacked so that all those who were initially poor are in one row, while all those in the next group are immediately below, and so on. In such a matrix, the rows correspond to the social

group at origin, and the columns to the social group at destination. Entries in each cell give the average income gain for that subgroup, weighted by its population share.

Table 2.5 provides a schematic illustration of how the elements in the decomposition can be presented in a matrix or table format. To keep the picture as simple as possible, the middle class and the elite have been grouped together, so that each panel has 9, rather than 16 cells. This is merely a presentational simplification, although, in light of our earlier discussion of the nature of household survey data for the rich in Latin America, it might be a sensible option in the actual analysis as well.

Table 2.5 shows that the overall amount of mobility in a particular society, over a given period, can be separated out into the net income gains or losses among nine groups, or cells. These cells can be grouped according to different criteria, depending on the object of interest. We highlight three such possibilities: In a first cut, the nine cells can be divided with respect to whether income movement was sufficient for individuals to "change class." Three cells (A, E, and I) represent "stayer groups": people whose incomes have not changed enough to move them across classes. They stay poor (A), stay vulnerable (E), or stay middle or upper-class (I). Another three groups (B, C, and F) are the upwardly mobile "climbers": their income gains were enough for them to leave poverty or near-poverty behind and to join the ranks

TABLE 2.5 Matrix decomposition of M^3: A schematic representation

Origin (rows) or destination (columns)	Poor	Vulnerable	Middle class and above
Poor	A	B	C
Vulnerable	D	E	F
Middle class and above	G	H	I

Source: Ferreira and Lugo 2012.
Note: M^3 = the measure of economic mobility as directional income movement. The rows correspond to the social group at origin, and the columns to the social group at destination. Entries in each cell represent the average income gain for that subgroup, weighted by its population share.

of the near-poor or the middle class, respectively. The final three groups (D, G, and H) are the downwardly mobile "sliders": they live in households where income losses led to falling back into vulnerability or, worse, into poverty.

A second cut focuses on transitions in and out of poverty, and hence on a subset of five cells in the matrix. This decomposition suggests a natural definition of chronic poverty: those who started out and remain poor (A). It also identifies those who left poverty (B and C) or who fell back into it (D and G).

A third possible cut narrows in on the five cells of greatest relevance for those interested in middle-class dynamics: Cell I contains those who were and remain middle-class (or elite), while cells C and F include those who have recently joined the ranks of the middle class (from vulnerability or directly from poverty). Cells G and H consist of people whose falling income suggests that they have been displaced from the middle class.

Naturally, the information presented in each of these cells may be the actual elements of the decomposition of M^3, or it may be other information of interest about these population subgroups. Table 2.6 illustrates three possible alternatives.

Panel A presents the actual decomposition for Peru in 2004–06, which we have been using as an example. M^3, which gives the average rate of growth in household per capita incomes across the Peruvian income distribution over this period, was 0.4 (or 40 percent). As the marginal distributions in table 2.6 (panel A) show, all of this growth took place among those who were originally poor or vulnerable (with 26 percentage points coming from the poor). But this growth moved enough people across social classes that, if we look by destination, 24 of the 40 percentage points of growth were for households that ended up in the middle class in 2006!

But how many people moved across social groups? And what were their average income gains and losses? This information is conflated in the entries into the decomposition matrix in panel A but can easily be separated out. Panel B of table 2.6 presents only the population shares for each cell. In 2004, 34 percent of the population was poor in 2004, but by 2006, only 29 percent were poor: 22 percent simply stayed poor, and another 7 percent fell back into poverty. The Peruvian middle class (and elite) made up 26 percent of the population in 2004, but almost 12 percent joined them over the period—the overwhelming majority *not* directly from the ranks of the poor. Because 8 percent of the population fell from the middle class, that class grew to almost 30 percent of the population in 2006.

While panel B shows the population shares, panel C shows average income gains (or losses) for each group.[24] One can see that those few people who made it straight from poverty to the middle class (2 percent of the population, from panel B) experienced a remarkable 420 percent growth over the period. Conversely, the unfortunate 1 percent who fell two classes did so by losing almost 80 percent of their incomes. And so on.

Our preferred measure of intragenerational mobility, M^3, can therefore be used for much more than simply comparing the extent of directional income movement across countries or over time, important though that may be. By means of the matrix decomposition above, it can also shed light on how growth was distributed across the population and what that means in terms of class dynamics. Using a standard poverty line, as well as the more original definition proposed in the "Defining the Middle Class" section, the decomposition allows us to investigate the extent of chronic poverty and contrast it with the magnitude of movements both out of and into poverty. It permits us to investigate the stable middle class as well as those who have recently ascended to or fallen from its ranks. The analysis in chapters 4 and 5 draws on these and other tools to gain a better understanding of the nature of intragenerational mobility and the growth

TABLE 2.6   Matrix decomposition of *M³* in Peru, 2004–06

a. Decomposition of *M³*				
	2006 (destination)			
	Poor	**Vulnerable**	**Middle class +**	**Total 2004**
2004 (origin) Poor	0.06	0.14	0.06	0.26
Vulnerable	−0.02	0.02	0.14	0.14
Middle class +	−0.01	−0.03	0.04	0.00
Total 2006	0.03	0.13	0.24	0.40

b. Population shares in the transition matrix				
	2006 (destination)			
	Poor	**Vulnerable**	**Middle class +**	**Total 2004**
2004 (origin) Poor	0.22	0.10	0.02	0.34
Vulnerable	0.06	0.23	0.10	0.40
Middle class +	0.01	0.07	0.18	0.26
Total 2006	0.29	0.41	0.30	1.00

c. Average income growth in the transition matrix				
	2006 (destination)			
	Poor	**Vulnerable**	**Middle class +**	**Total 2004**
2004 (origin) Poor	0.28	1.34	4.21	0.77
Vulnerable	−0.44	0.13	1.37	0.36
Middle class +	−0.79	−0.47	0.21	−0.02
Total 2006	0.10	0.32	0.80	0.40

Source: ENAHO 2004 and 2006 by the INEI de Perú.
Note: M^3 = the measure of economic mobility as directional income movement.

of the middle class in Latin America over the past one or two decades. By identifying individuals belonging to each of the cells in table 2.5 and analyzing their characteristics, we hope not only to paint an accurate portrait of social dynamics in Latin America but also to begin investigating their determinants and, in particular, how public policy in various realms may have promoted or impeded upward mobility.

| Focus Note 2.1 | *Mobility concepts and measures* |

Most measures of mobility as movement or origin independence can be constructed in two steps:

1. First, define an individual mobility function as some measure of the distance between an individual's income in the initial and final vectors, respectively, y_0, y_1. If we denote each "individual" by the position he or she occupies in the initial vector or distribution, $p_0 = F_0(y)$, then the individual mobility function can be written in general terms as

$$m(p_0) = d(y_0(p_0), y_1(p_0)).[25]$$ (F2.1.1)

2. The second step is aggregation, wherein information across all individual mobility functions in the population is combined into a single summary index. One simple and appealing aggregator is arithmetic averaging:

$$M(Y_0, Y_1) = \int_0^1 d(y_0(p_0), y_1(p_0)) dp_0.$$ (F2.1.2)

Table F2.1 provides a simple example of individual mobility functions for each of the subconcepts 1 (a–d) and 2, as well as a graphical depiction of what the function or profile looks like in an actual recent vector transformation in Latin America, namely that in Peru, between 2004 and 2006.

TABLE F2.1   Sample mobility functions and graphical representation of Peru, 2004–06

Concept	Individual mobility function: an example	Graphical representation of the profile: Peru, 2004–06
Directional income movement	$d(y_0, y_1) = y_1 - y_0$	Differences in income
Nondirectional income movement	$d(y_0, y_1) = \lvert y_1 - y_0 \rvert$	Absolute differences in income

Focus Note 2.1 *(continued)*

Concept	Individual mobility function: an example	Graphical representation of the profile: Peru, 2004–06
Share movement	$$d(y_0, y_1) = \frac{y_1}{m_1} - \frac{y_0}{m_0}$$ μ_t: mean income in time t	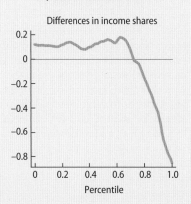 Differences in income shares
Positional movement	$$d(y_0, y_1) = \text{rank}_1 - \text{rank}_0$$	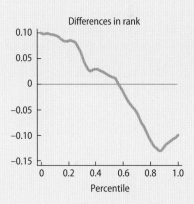 Differences in rank
Mobility as origin independence	$$d(y_0, y_1) = \frac{1}{2}\left(\frac{y_0 - m_0}{s_0} - \frac{y_1 - m_1}{s_1} \right)$$ μ_t: mean income in time t s_t: standard deviation of income in time t	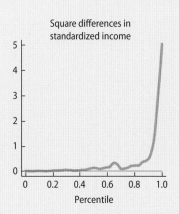 Square differences in standardized income

(focus note continued next page)

Focus Note 2.1	*Mobility concepts and measures* *(continued)*

Visual inspection of the income mobility function diagrams (in the third column of table F2.1) clearly reveals how each particular measure is sensitive to different ranges of the distribution and maps the same underlying distributional change differently into its own metric. Although each concept (and index) summarizes a complex distributional change in a different way, and thus contributes to one's overall understanding of the process, it is infeasible to present all such indices for all mobility episodes examined in this volume. Choices had to be made and, as argued in the text, we have chosen to focus on mobility as directional income movement for the intragenerational domain and on mobility as origin independence for the intergenerational.

The specific index we use for mobility as directional income movement is a simple, yet interesting, transformation of the individual mobility function in the first row of table F2.1. If one takes the individual income distance function as a proportion of the initial income, rather than as the absolute difference, we have

$$d(y_0, y_1) = \frac{y_1(p_0) - y_0(p_0)}{y_0(p_0)}. \qquad \text{(F2.1.3)}$$

If expressed as a function of the original percentile p_0, this is simply a non-anonymous growth incidence curve, $g(p_0) = \frac{y_1(p_0) - y_0(p_0)}{y_0(p_0)}$, described by Grimm (2007) and Bourguignon (2011): it gives the growth rate of individual incomes (between periods 0 and 1) for those people initially in position p_0 of the original distribution. This is an identity-preserving (that is, non-anonymous) version of the well-known growth incidence curve introduced by Ravallion and Chen (2003): $g(p) = \frac{y_1(p) - y_0(p)}{y_0(p)}$, which considers the proportional income differences between those in percentile p in the final distribution and those in the same percentile in the initial distribution.

Aggregating equation (F2.1.3) across individuals to obtain a measure of social mobility yields

$$M(Y_0, Y_{11}) = \int_0^1 \frac{y_1(p_0) - y_0(p_0)}{y_0(p_0)} dp_0 \int_0^1 g(p_0) dp_0 \qquad \text{(F2.1.4)}$$

Equation (F2.1.4) is a well-known mobility index. Its log-approximation is the M^3 measure in Fields and Ok (1999). It has the appealing feature that it corresponds to the area under the non-anonymous growth incidence curve.

Notes

1. To assess mobility, economists must keep track of the individual identity of income recipients as the income vector (or distribution) evolves though time.

2. However, given differences in the way questions are asked and surveys collected across countries and over time, comparing different varieties of apples will often be inevitable.

3. When the individual mobility function is written as a function of the individual's position in the initial income vector, it corresponds to what van Kerm (2009) calls an *income mobility profile*.

4. Ferreira and Gignoux (2011) show that this family of intergenerational mobility measures is isomorphic to a widely used measure of ex ante inequality of opportunity.

5. As shown by D'Agostino and Dardanoni (2006), this social mobility function can be obtained as an aggregation of the individual mobility function shown in the last row of focus note 2.1 (at the end of the chapter):

$$d(y_0, y_1) = \frac{1}{2} \frac{1}{n} \sum \left(\frac{y_0 - \mu_0}{s_0} - \frac{y_1 - \mu_1}{s_1} \right)^2 = 1 - \rho_{01}.$$

6. Both the anonymous and non-anonymous growth incidence curves (GICs) are briefly introduced in focus note 2.1, at the end of the chapter.

7. Omitting subscripts for simplicity:

$$M^3 = \int \frac{\Delta y}{y} f(y_0) dy_0 \text{ , whereas growth in mean}$$

incomes is $\frac{\Delta \mu}{\mu} = \int \frac{\mu y}{y} \frac{y}{\mu} f(y_0) dy_0$. See Klasen (1994) for a related discussion.

8. The origin of these concepts is in Marx's classic writings, such as Marx and Engels' *The German Ideology* ([1845] [1932] 1998), where they propose the concept of the *lumpenproletariat* as the lowest class among the working class or *proletariat*.

9. The importance of "thoughts, perceptions, expressions, and actions" to the "symbolic aspect of class structure" has been famously emphasized more recently by Bourdieu (1980; 1987) and others.

10. The term "functionings" is commonly used in development economics to denote the set of activities and achievements ("beings and doings") that a person is capable of, following Sen (1985). The set of feasible functionings, from which a person chooses those that he or she actually enjoys or exercises, is often called one's "capabilities."

11. In another link with the sociological literature, López-Calva and Ortiz-Juarez (2011) refer to the view that class positions are inherently intertwined with vulnerability and risk, as discussed, for instance, in Goldthorpe and McKnight (2004).

12. The data sets used are the *Socioeconomic Characterization Survey* (CASEN Panel) for 2001 and 2006 for Chile; the Mexican Family Life Survey (MxFLS) for 2002 and 2005 for Mexico; and the *National Household Survey* (ENAHO Panel) for 2002 and 2006 for Peru.

13. The same vector of covariates is also used as independent variables in a household income regression. The results allow the authors to map predicted conditional probabilities of falling into poverty (in an interval of roughly five years early in the last decade) to (predicted) average initial household incomes. See López-Calva and Ortiz-Juarez (2011) for details.

14. As noted, however, the threshold is anchored by being close to the average upper-bound estimate of actual vulnerability to poverty in the region (see chapter 4).

15. In the so-called Leyden approach to subjective poverty identification, households with certain demographic characteristics were asked what income they felt a household like theirs needed to "make ends meet." The answers were typically found to increase with household (objective) incomes, and the level at which the two (actual and answered) incomes crossed was taken as the poverty line (see, for example, Hagenaars and van Praag [1985]).

16. The question in Spanish is: "*En nuestra sociedad la gente tiende a ubicarse en distintas clases sociales. ¿Se siente Ud. perteneciente a alguna de estas clases?*"

17. In particular, they are very different for Chile, where the vulnerability approach yields a threshold of PPP US$8.50 per day compared with PPP US$20.30 per day for the subjective approach.

18. SEDLAC, (Socioeconomic Database for Latin America and the Caribbean), is jointly managed and maintained by the Centro de Estudios Distributivos, Laborales y Sociales (CEDLAS) of the Universidad de la Plata in Argentina, and the World Bank. See http://cedlas.econo.unlp.edu.ar.

19. Kharas's (2010) proposal was motivated by the fact that average daily per capita income in the United States in 2009 was $98.77.
20. See, for example, Korinek, Mistiaen, and Ravallion (2006).
21. So far, the only analysis of tax record data in Latin America and the Caribbean is for Argentina (Alvaredo 2010). Other countries in the region for which there is ongoing work include Belize, Brazil, Chile, Colombia, Guyana, Jamaica, St. Vincent, and Trinidad and Tobago. For more details, see the World Top Incomes Database, http://g-mond .parisschoolofeconomics.eu/topincomes/.
22. One might also call them the "near-poor" or the "lower middle class." The latter terminology is more consistent with the domestic classification chosen, for example, by Brazil.
23. The figure has been constructed from the percentile distribution in the initial period. Hence, each point in the line formally represents the average income growth within each percentile.
24. As the attentive reader will have guessed, the products of the cells in panels B and C of table 2.6 yield the corresponding entries in panel A, up to an error of approximation.
25. Just as "income" is used here as shorthand for whichever variable is appropriate to capture the mobility space of interest, so "individual" is used as shorthand for the identity of the elements in the income vector. In the intragenerational domain, these would generally correspond to actual individuals, whereas in the intergenerational domain they would usually denote lineages: parents and their children.

References

Akerlof, George A., and Rachel E. Kranton. 2002. "Identity and Schooling: Some Lessons for the Economics of Education." *Journal of Economic Literature* 40 (4): 1167–201.

Alesina, Alberto, and Roberto Perotti. 1996. "Income Distribution, Political Instability, and Investment." *European Economic Review* 40 (6): 1203–28.

Alvaredo, Facundo. 2010. "The Rich in Argentina over the Twentieth Century 1932–2004." In *Top Incomes over the Twentieth Century vol. II: A Global Perspective*, ed. A. Atkinson and T. Piketty, 253–98. Oxford: Oxford University Press.

Aristotle. (c. 350 BC) 1932. *Politics*. Translated by H. Rackham. Cambridge, MA: Harvard University Press.

Atkinson, Anthony B., Thomas Piketty, and Emmanuel Saez. 2011. "Top Incomes in the Long Run of History." *Journal of Economic Literature* 49 (1): 3–71.

Banerjee, Abhijit V., and Esther Duflo. 2008. "What Is Middle Class about the Middle Classes around the World?" *Journal of Economic Perspectives* 22 (2): 3–28.

Barro, Robert J. 1999. "Determinants of Democracy." *Journal of Political Economy* 107 (6): 158–83.

———. 2000. "Inequality and Growth in a Panel of Countries." *Journal of Economic Growth* 5 (1): 5–32.

Birdsall, Nancy, Carol Graham, and Stefano Pettinato. 2000. "Stuck in the Tunnel: Is Globalization Muddling the Middle Class?" Working Paper 14, Center on Social and Economic Dynamics, Brookings Institution, Washington, DC.

Blackburn, McKinley L., and David E. Bloom. 1985. "What Is Happening to the Middle Class?" *American Demographics* 7 (1): 18–25.

Bourdieu, Pierre. 1980. *The Logic of Practice*. Translated by Richard Nice. Stanford, CA: Stanford University Press.

———. 1987. "What Makes a Social Class? On the Theoretical and Practical Existence of Groups." *Berkeley Journal of Sociology* 32: 1–27.

Bourguignon, François. 2011. "Non-anonymous Growth Incidence Curves, Income Mobility, and Social Welfare Dominance." *Journal of Economic Inequality* 9 (4): 605–27.

Chen, Shaohua, and Martin Ravallion. 2001. "How Did the World's Poor Fare in the 1990s?"*Review of Income and Wealth* 47 (3): 283–300.

Cornell, Tim J. 1995. *The Beginnings of Rome*. New York: Routledge.

D'Agostino, Marcello, and Valentino Dardanoni. 2006. "The Measurement of Mobility: A Class of Distance Measures." Unpublished manuscript, University of Palermo, Italy.

Davis, Joe C., and John H. Huston. 1992. "The Shrinking Middle-Income Class: A Multivariate Analysis." *Eastern Economic Journal* 18 (3): 277–85.

Easterly, William. 2001. "The Middle Class Consensus and Economic Development." *Journal of Economic Growth* 6 (4): 317–35.

Elbers, Chris, Jean O. Lanjouw, and Peter Lanjouw. 2003. "Micro-Level Estimation of Welfare." *Econometrica* 71(1): 355–64.

Ferreira, Francisco H. G., and Jérémie Gignoux. 2011. "The Measurement of Educational Inequality: Achievement and Opportunity." Policy Research Working Paper 5873, World Bank, Washington, DC.

Ferreira, Francisco H. G., and Maria A. Lugo. 2012. "Decomposition of Measures of Income Movement." Unpublished manuscript, World Bank, Washington, DC.

Fields, Gary S. 2000. "Income Mobility: Concepts and Measures." In *New Markets, New Opportunities? Economic and Social Mobility in a Changing World*, ed. Nancy Birdsall and Carol Graham, 101–33. Washington, DC: Brookings Institution and Carnegie Endowment Press.

———. 2010. "Does Income Mobility Equalize Longer-Term Incomes? New Measures of an Old Concept." *Journal of Economic Inequality* 8 (4): 409–27.

Fields, Gary S., and Efe A. Ok. 1999. "Measuring Movement of Incomes." *Economica* 66 (264): 455–71.

Friedman, Milton. 1962. *Capitalism and Freedom.* Chicago: University of Chicago Press.

Galton, Francis. 1886. "Regression toward Mediocrity in Hereditary Stature." *Journal of the Anthropological Institute of Great Britain and Ireland* 15: 246–63.

Goldthorpe, John H., and Abigail McKnight. 2004. "The Economic Basis of Social Class." CASE paper 80, Centre for Analysis of Social Exclusion, London School of Economics and Political Science, London.

Grimm, Michael. 2007. "Removing the Anonymity Axiom in Assessing Pro-Poor Growth." *Journal of Economic Inequality* 5 (2): 179–97.

Hagenaars, Aldi J. M., and Bernard van Praag. 1985. "A Synthesis of Poverty Line Definitions." *Review of Income and Wealth* 31 (2): 139–54.

Hirschman, Albert, and Michael Rothschild. 1973. "The Changing Tolerance for Income Inequality in the Course of Economic Development." *Quarterly Journal of Economics* 87 (4): 544–66.

Kharas, Homi. 2010. "The Emerging Middle Class in Developing Countries." Working Paper 285, Development Centre, Organisation for Economic Co-operation and Development, Paris.

Klasen, Stephan. 1994. "Growth and Well-Being: Introducing Distribution-Weighted Growth Rates to Reevaluate U.S. Postwar Economic Performance." *Review of Income and Wealth* 40 (3): 251–72.

Korinek, Anton, Johan A. Mistiaen, and Martin Ravallion. 2006. "Survey Non-Response and the Distribution of Income." Policy Research Working Paper 3543, World Bank, Washington, DC.

López-Calva, Luis F., and Eduardo Ortiz-Juarez. 2011. "A Vulnerability Approach to the Definition of the Middle Class." Policy Research Working Paper 5902, World Bank, Washington, DC.

Marx, Karl, and Friedrich Engels. (1845) (1932) 1998. *The German Ideology.* Amherst, NY: Prometheus.

McGeough, Kevin M. 2004. *The Romans: An Introduction.* Oxford: Oxford University Press.

Milanovic, Branko, and Shlomo Yitzhaki. 2002. "Decomposing World Income Distribution: Does the World Have a Middle Class?" *Review of Income and Wealth* 48 (2): 155–78.

Partridge, Mark D. 1997. "Is Inequality Harmful For Growth? Comment." *American Economic Review* 87 (5): 1019–32.

Piketty, Thomas. 1995. "Social Mobility and Redistributive Politics." *Quarterly Journal of Economics* 110 (3): 551–84.

Piketty, Thomas, and Emmanuel Saez. 2003. "Income Inequality in the United States, 1913–1998." *Quarterly Journal of Economics* 118 (1): 1–39.

Ravallion, Martin. 2010. "The Developing World's Bulging (but Vulnerable) Middle Class." *World Development* 38 (4): 445–54.

Ravallion, Martin, and Shaohua Chen. 2003. "Measuring Pro-Poor Growth." *Economics Letters* 78 (1): 93–99.

Sen, Amartya K. 1985. *Commodities and Capabilities.* Oxford: Oxford University Press.

Shorrocks, Anthony F. 1978. "Income Inequality and Income Mobility." *Journal of Economic Theory* 19 (2): 376–93.

Solimano, Andres. 2008. "The Middle Class and the Development Process." Serie Macroeconomía del Desarrollo 65, United Nations and Economic Commission for Latin America and the Caribbean, Santiago, Chile.

Solon, Gary. 2002. "Cross-Country Differences in Intergenerational Earnings Mobility." *Journal of Economic Perspectives* 16 (3): 59–66.

Time. 2011. "What Happened to Upward Mobility?" November 14.

Tocqueville, Alexis de. (1856) 1986. *L'Ancien Régime et la Révolution.* Paris: Robert Lafont.

Torche, Florencia. 2010. "Social Status and Public Cultural Consumption: Chile in Comparative Perspective." In *Social Status and Cultural Consumption*, ed. T. W. Chan and J. H. Goldthorpe, 109–38. Cambridge, U.K.: Cambridge University Press.

Van Kerm, Philippe. 2009. "Income Mobility Profiles." *Economics Letters* 102 (2): 93–95.

Weber, Max. 1946. "Class, Status, Party." In *From Max Weber: Essays in Sociology*, ed. Hans H. Gerth and C. Wright Mills. New York: Oxford University Press.

———. (1922) 1978. *Economy and Society.* Ed. Guenther Roth and Claus Wittich. Berkeley: University of California Press.

Zimmerman, David. 1992. "Regression toward Mediocrity in Economic Stature." *American Economic Review* 82 (3): 409–29.

Mobility across Generations | 3

If income mobility were very high, the degree of inequality in any given year would be unimportant, because the distribution of lifetime income would be very even. . . . An increase in income mobility tends to make the distribution of lifetime income more equal.

—Paul Krugman (1992), "The Rich, the Right, and the Facts."

In spite of the remarkable achievements obtained during the past decade, income inequality in Latin America remains high by international standards and certainly a major concern for policy makers. Arguably, however, high inequality might be socially acceptable if coupled with strong social mobility. This is especially true in the case of mobility across generations. To the extent that equal opportunities are provided to children from different parental backgrounds, some inequality of outcomes might be socially acceptable, or even desirable, because it may provide the right incentives for exerting effort and, through this channel, foster economic efficiency and future growth. Indeed, it has been argued that individuals living in a society characterized by a great degree of generational mobility are more likely to accept existing inequalities than individuals living in a world where their fortunes are highly dependent on the socioeconomic statuses of their parents (Bénabou and Ok 2001).

Parental background influences children's outcomes through a variety of channels. Even before children are born, maternal nutrition and health during gestation have an impact on children endowments at birth (Currie 2009). In turn, there is increasing empirical evidence suggesting that these birth endowments have an influence on adult outcomes, including educational attainment and incomes (Currie 2011). A schematic simplification of the complex relationship between parental background and their children's income is presented in figure 3.1, which draws from Haveman and Wolfe (1995).

Parents affect children through heredity of genetic endowments, which in turn affects children's schooling and income, an aspect first formalized by the seminal work of Becker and Tomes (1979). In addition, parental ability influences their own educational attainment and thus their income. Together, these determine the level of "home investments" in offspring (including time spent

FIGURE 3.1   **The intergenerational association between parental background and children's income**

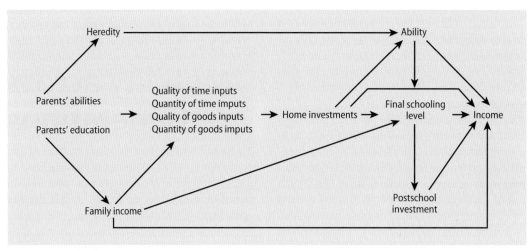

Source: Haveman and Wolfe 1995.

with the children and the quality and quantity of goods and services delivered to them), which, in turn, will affect the final schooling level. Furthermore, parental income exerts a direct influence on final schooling (through the choice of school) and on the children's eventual income (through networks and connections in the labor market). Finally, the schooling level attained by the children will affect their income later in life and further experience through the labor market (postschool investments). All of these factors, in turn, affect their own children's earnings and income.

Haveman and Wolfe's (1995) diagram (figure 3.1) focuses on the direct and indirect links between parental background and children's income. In doing so, it pays little attention to the external factors that shape parental influences on children's outcomes. Three key actors mediate the process of intergenerational mobility: the schooling system, the government, and the labor market.

It is generally understood that better-managed, better-endowed schools are more likely to succeed in bringing up children's human capital. However, the role of schools in promoting intergenerational mobility is far from being settled for at least two reasons: First, there is great heterogeneity

among schools in how they treat differences in children's endowments. Some schools have more inclusive policies and try to bring the worst-performing kids closer to the average. Others put more emphasis on the better-endowed kids, trying to enhance and develop their full potential. Second, the importance of the school in promoting equal opportunity is confounded with the role of parental background. Most naturally, parents do not choose schools for their children randomly. There is instead substantial positive sorting: that is, parents with more resources send their children to better-endowed schools.

The government is the second fundamental actor that shapes the complex relationship between parental background and children's outcomes. Governments indeed have the capacity to alter this relationship through a number of different channels. A primary intervention is through the provision of public schools. Access to high-quality universal education can certainly help to level the playing field. Additionally, the government can influence the sorting process that characterizes schooling choice—for instance, through fellowships and voucher programs. As emphasized by Solon (2004), the progressivity of public investment in human capital is a key government intervention to enhance intergenerational income mobility.

The final mediator between parental background and children's well-being is the labor market. An inefficient labor market that favors connections and nepotism instead of rewarding talent will hinder intergenerational income mobility. On the other hand, higher returns to schooling are expected to be associated with a higher investment effort of parents in the human capital of their children, increasing the association between parents and children's incomes (Solon 2004).

Chapter focus and objectives

In this chapter, we discuss the impact of parental background on a variety of outcomes for their children, including educational attainment; educational achievement; and, in the few cases where data for Latin America are available, income. An important limitation of the analysis is that data sets featuring the same measure of socioeconomic status across generations (for example, pertaining to education, occupation, or income) are generally not available for Latin America. For this reason, we use different approximations of the complex concept of parental background, including proxies for the permanent income of the parents, their ethnicity, their schooling, and their occupational status. In a few cases we also try to evaluate the role of policies and institutions in shaping differences over time and across countries in the observed patterns of intergenerational mobility.

As discussed in chapter 2, the particular concept of mobility adopted throughout the chapter is that of *origin independence*. (See box 3.1 for a discussion of the chosen measure of origin independence.) This is the concept of choice of most intergenerational studies (Solon 2002; Zimmerman 1992).

To illustrate this concept, we will focus on two polar cases, following Solon (1999): Imagine two societies with the same level and distribution of income and thus the same proportion of rich and poor. In the first society, children's income and level of education

are completely determined by the socioeconomic status of their parents. Poor children are born from poor families, and rich children are born from rich families. This society is thought to display no intergenerational mobility. At the other extreme, in the second society, the relative socioeconomic position of parents is completely uninformative of the income or education of their offspring. The probability that children born from poor families will go to college and end up rich is equal to that of children born from rich families. In this case, there is perfect intergenerational mobility. The main goal of this chapter is to understand where Latin America stands in the continuum of possibilities delimited by these two extremes. How do Latin American countries compare with middle-income and rich countries in other regions? Can we provide some tentative evidence on the determinants of the relative position of these countries?

This chapter pays special attention to the influence of parental background on the educational outcomes of Latin American children. This emphasis contrasts with most of the literature on intergenerational mobility, in which income or earnings are central to the analyses. The rationale for putting education center stage is twofold: First, for Latin American countries, there is greater data availability on education across generations than on income or earnings. These microdata sets are also available for a large number of countries, allowing benchmarking of Latin America with respect to other developed and developing countries. The second rationale is of substance. Among observable and measurable human characteristics, education is the most important determinant of income, as emphasized by the enormous literature on the returns from education.[1] In addition, the increasing availability of data sets measuring cognitive test scores in a large number of countries has shown a strong positive effect of educational achievement on labor-market performance (Neal and Johnson 1996; McIntosh and Vignoles 2001; Currie and Thomas 2000). Moreover, the education of a person affects not only his or her wages but also his

---

BOX 3.1   Assessing the association of socioeconomic status across generations

There are different ways to measure the association in outcomes across generations. Perhaps the simplest and most common application relates an outcome variable of the parent generation, denoted by the subscript 0, with the same outcome for their children, denoted with subscript 1, in the following linear fashion:

$$y_1 = \alpha + \beta y_0 + \varepsilon, \qquad \text{(B3.1a)}$$

where β is a measure of the persistence in incomes across generations; and

$1 - \beta$ is a measure of intergenerational mobility.

The outcomes differ across studies, but the most common applications consider the log of incomes in each generation (see Black and Devereux 2011 and Björklund and Salvanes 2011 for recent overviews) so that β represents the intergenerational elasticity of income. An alternative measure is the correlation coefficient (ρ) between the vectors y_1 and y_2, which standardizes the intergenerational gradient by the ratio of the standard deviations in the two generations:

$$\rho = \beta \, \frac{\sigma(y_0)}{\sigma(y_1)}. \qquad \text{(B3.1b)}$$

The gradient and the correlation might provide different pictures in specific instances and countries. For instance, the gradient in one country might be reduced over time simply because there has been a reduction in the inequality of outcomes in the children's generation, while the correlation would remain unaffected. Both metrics have advantages and disadvantages, and there is no clear ranking between the two. One advantage of the gradient is

that it is less prone to classical measurement error in the outcomes of the children. Perhaps more important, the gradient is to be preferred if the researcher is interested not only in how much parental background explains the outcomes in the children's generation but also in how unequal those outcomes are.

To provide an idea of what a "typical" degree of inequality in the parental generation represents for their children's outcomes, our preferred measure discussed in the chapter will be $\beta \times \sigma(y_0)$. The reading of this measure is simple. It states by how much children's outcomes change (in the units in which y_1 is measured) when parental background increases by one standard deviation.

We will consider a variety of outcomes for the children's generation throughout the chapter, and in most cases we will not be able to measure the same outcomes for their parents, as suggested in equation (B3.1a), but instead we can measure some indicators that are likely to be correlated with such outcomes. In the case of educational quality, for instance, we can measure cognitive tests only for the kids, while parental background is approximated by different indicators of socioeconomic status, including indices of physical asset holdings, education, and occupation. We view these outcomes of the parents as proxies for a latent variable, the test score, which is not observed in the data, as in Ferreira and Gignoux (2011).

To facilitate the interpretation of the results, in some cases we will discuss the differences in children's outcomes between two representative families at the extremes in the distribution of socioeconomic status. Thus, we often will discuss differences in outcomes of the children among parents who have tertiary education against parents who did not finish primary. Sometimes, the index of socioeconomic status is multidimensional. In these cases, we label "poor" and "rich" families as those that are at the bottom and top quintile of the distribution of the outcome variable (or set of variables), respectively.

---

or her probability of employment. Hence, a society that is not displaying substantial mobility in education across generations is unlikely to have a great deal of intergenerational income mobility, unless markets work in a very inefficient manner (for example, by not rewarding education).

An important caveat should be highlighted at the outset: correlations do not necessarily imply causality. The patterns discussed here may not reflect a direct causal effect of parental socioeconomic status on the education or socioeconomic status of the children. Instead, they will include both direct and indirect effects of growing up in a more advantageous background. Both educational and socioeconomic outcomes may be determined, at least in part, by other unobserved individual or family characteristics such as hard-wired genetic traits and environmental factors related to where individuals live (their neighborhoods, housing, schools, and so on). Children from rich and better-educated families tend to live in richer neighborhoods where unemployment, crime, and violence are lower and the overall quality of services is higher. In addition, rich children are more likely to attend better schools, with better teachers and more inputs, and to interact with other kids from better-educated parents. All these factors are most likely to affect the performance of children in school as well as later in life. Many of these factors are unobserved in most of the data sets used in this chapter and will thus be partially captured by parental background.

This chapter aims to uncover some empirical regularities in Latin America, but in most cases does not attempt to assess causality. Hence, drawing specific policy conclusions from the analysis will often be difficult, precisely because we cannot isolate the specific channel through which the intergenerational association emerges. In an attempt to overcome this limitation, we discuss in boxes throughout the chapter specific examples where either natural experiments or specific characteristics of programs in one country have allowed researchers to identify the causal impact of policies on the extent of intergenerational mobility. We complement the analysis with cross-county regressions, which exploit the variability of policies across countries to provide an indication of what seems to work or not at the aggregate level.

Our analysis starts with the evolution of educational attainment in Latin America and differences among rich and poor children in years of schooling. We next study the influences of parental background on educational achievement, measured by test scores in international assessments. We then briefly discuss the link between educational mobility and income mobility. Having established the

facts, the last part of this chapter discusses the policies and institutions that appear to be related to the different degrees of intergenerational mobility found both across and within countries.

Educational attainment: How important is parental background?

The reduction of poverty and inequality during the 2000s, alluded to in chapter 2, was anticipated by a rapid expansion of educational attainment. Has this expansion at the same time become more egalitarian? Has the schooling gap between rich and poor narrowed? Are the sons and daughters of less-favored households today more likely to finish primary and secondary schooling on time than they were 20 years ago? How does Latin America compare with other regions regarding the intergenerational association of education?

Parental influence on years of schooling

We start by examining the last question, and the message obtained is quite clear: the Latin American region is characterized by substantial educational persistence across generations. Recent estimates of the correlation in schooling across generations in different countries of the world suggest that Latin America presents the highest persistence of education across generations. Hertz et al. (2007) provides an excellent overview of these differences across countries. The study produced an impressive data set of associations in *years of schooling* between parents and children in 42 countries, for different birth cohorts spanning the last 50 years.

Figure 3.2 is based on their estimates, showing the average effect of one standard deviation of parental years of schooling on children's schooling (see box 3.1 for details on measurement issues). According to this metric, Latin American countries are undoubtedly among the less educationally mobile regions in the sample. In the extreme, in Peru, one standard deviation in parental

FIGURE 3.2 **Impact of parental education on children's years of education, selected countries**

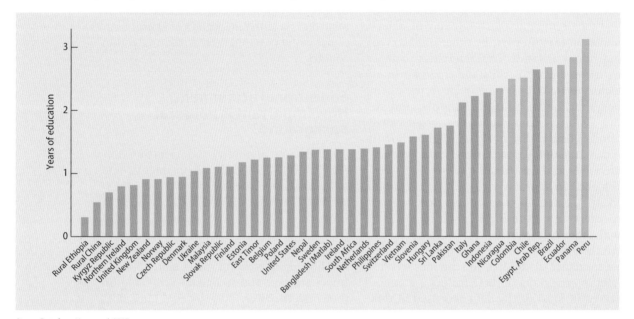

Source: Data from Hertz et al. 2007.
Note: Bars represent the impact of one standard deviation of parental years of schooling on the years of schooling of children. The impact is averaged across birth cohorts born between 1930 and 1980.

education (about 3.5 additional years of education) is associated with more than 3.0 additional years of schooling in the next generation. Peru is closely followed by Panama, Ecuador, Brazil, Chile, Colombia, and Nicaragua. The only non-Latin American country in the study group that displays a similar level of educational persistence across generations is the Arab Republic of Egypt.

The fact that Latin American countries cluster at the top of the persistence of education across generations is especially remarkable, considering that the sample includes both developing and developed economies. As expected, Scandinavian countries tend to display low educational persistence. Perhaps more surprising is the low association between the years of schooling of parents and their children in Northern Ireland and the United Kingdom, which contrasts with the result found later in the chapter, where Anglo-Saxon countries display substantial persistence when the outcome considered is student achievement (test scores) rather than attainment (schooling). It should be noted

that, in some low-income countries such as rural Ethiopia, persistence in attainment is low not because of low grade persistence (the regression coefficient) but because of the low parental schooling level even among the country's most highly educated. The standard deviation of years of schooling among parents in this case is extremely low, at an average of 0.5.

However, educational mobility in Latin America has improved in the past two decades. Across cohorts born during different periods, we observe a mild increase in intergenerational mobility of education in Latin America, especially during the past couple of decades. Figure 3.3 shows the evolution of the association between education of the parents and children in the seven Latin American countries, included in Hertz et al. (2007). In all Latin American countries, with the exception of Nicaragua, intergenerational mobility increased between those born in the 1920s and 1930s and those born in the 1970s. In some cases such as Chile, the reduction in the relationship between parental and children's

FIGURE 3.3 **Evolution of intergenerational persistence in education across birth cohorts in seven Latin American countries, 1930s–80s**

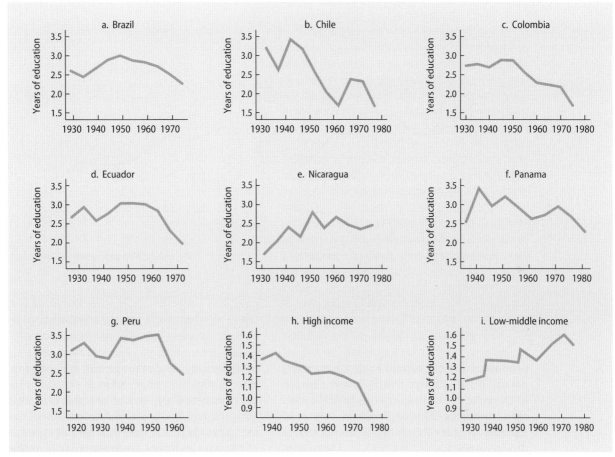

Source: Data from Hertz et al. 2007.
Note: Lines represent the estimated effect of one standard deviation of parental years of schooling on the years of schooling of children, across cohorts.

education is quite impressive: the impact of one standard deviation of parental schooling level on children's years of education more than halves during the period. It should be noted, however, that regardless of the moderate improvements in mobility, the levels of educational intergenerational persistence in Latin America remain substantially higher even among the youngest cohorts, compared with either developed countries or developing countries.

Naturally, changes in our estimates of the association between parental and children's education, as shown in figure 3.3, are driven by two factors: changes in the β coefficients

of a regression of children's education on parental education and changes in the standard deviation of parental education (see box 3.1). When we unbundle the two effects, we find that, in most countries, the β's have declined, driving the increase in mobility we are documenting.

Figure 3.4 shows this pattern in two countries: Colombia and Peru. In Colombia, we observe a sharp decline in the β coefficient (leaving the standard deviation fixed), which drives the overall increase in mobility we document in spite of the hump-shaped evolution in the inequality of education in the parents' generation. In Peru, the hump is even more

FIGURE 3.4 **Evolution of intergenerational persistence in education across birth cohorts in Peru and Colombia, 1920s–80s: Decomposition between parental inequality and β**

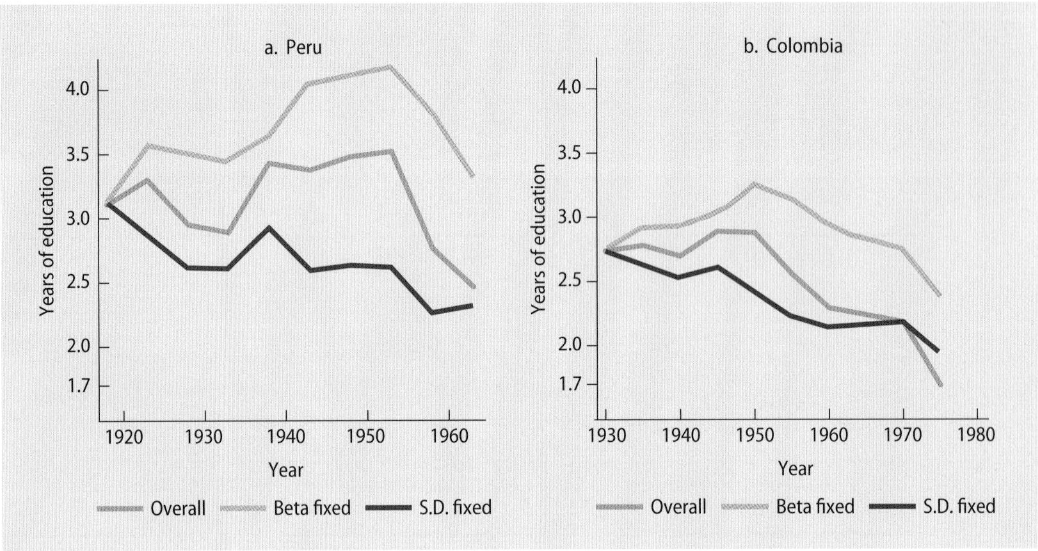

Source: Data from Hertz et al. 2007.
Note: S.D. = standard deviation. The overall effect represents the estimated effect of one standard deviation of parental years of schooling on the years of schooling of children, across cohorts. "Beta fixed" is the effect of a changing standard deviation in the education of the parents, keeping the beta fixed at the level obtained in the first available cohort in each country. "Standard deviation fixed" does the opposite exercise: it keeps the standard deviation of parental education fixed at the level of the first birth cohort available and allows the betas to change over time.

pronounced. Educational inequality among parents (leaving β fixed) increases steadily up to the cohort of children born in 1955, and then it reverses. This explains the very mild increase in overall mobility despite a steady decline in the β.

Parental influence on the educational gap

The next few figures show the evolution of an alternative measure of educational attainment: the *educational gap*.[2] This indicator is defined as the difference between *potential* years of education and the years of *completed* education. For instance, if the starting age of primary education is 6, a 10-year-old child should have, by the end of the school year, four years of schooling (the exact number depends also on the month of birth and of the interview). This is the maximum potential years completed. If this is the case for a given child, his or her educational gap would be equal to 0. If, instead, the child just finished third grade, his or her educational gap would be equal to 1. Similarly, if the child started

school at the required age but dropped out after completing only the first grade, his or her educational gap would be equal to 3. The advantage of using this indicator relative to the previous one is that it allows us to look at the gap at different schooling ages in the 1990s and 2000s and thus obtain a more recent picture of intergenerational mobility.

The educational gap of children at schooling ages in Latin America is large, but it has unambiguously declined during the past two decades. Figure 3.5 shows the educational gap at ages 10, 15, and 18 for the Latin American average.[3] On average, the schooling gap in the mid-1990s was 1.3 years for kids aged 10, and the gap was 5.0 years for kids aged 18. By 2009, the gap more than halved for both ages.

What is the impact of parental background on the children's schooling gap? Because we rely on household surveys, we now have two possible proxies for parental background: education and income. The broad messages with the two measures are fairly consistent, so we concentrate on education to avoid repetition. Across all ages,

FIGURE 3.5   **Average children's educational gap in Latin America, 1995–2009**

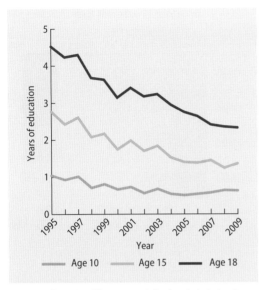

Source: Data from SEDLAC (Socioeconomic Database for Latin America and the Caribbean).
Note: Lines represent the (population weighted) average schooling gap across Latin American countries, for children aged 10, 15, and 18, respectively. The sample includes a maximum of 15 countries in the region. In some years, however, some countries have no survey so they are excluded from the calculation. The minimum number of countries is 10, for the first three years of the period considered. Similar trends are found if the additional countries are excluded.

FIGURE 3.6   **Differences in the educational gap between the top and bottom income quintiles in Latin America, 1995–2009**

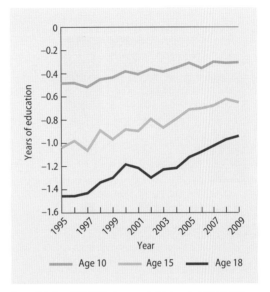

Source: Data from SEDLAC (Socioeconomic Database for Latin America and the Caribbean).
Note: Lines represent the expected reduction in the schooling gap associated with one standard deviation of parental education. Other covariates in the regression are children's gender, living in an urban area, and country fixed effects. The estimated effect of parental education on the educational gap is always statistically different from zero (confidence bands are omitted for clarity).

the children of more-educated parents present a lower schooling gap than the children of less-educated parents, but the differences associated with parental background in the children's schooling gap narrowed during the past 15 years (as shown in figure 3.6). In 1995, one standard deviation of parental education was associated with an additional 0.5-year gap at age 10; with a 1.0-year gap at age 15; and with a 1.5-year gap at age 18. By 2009, the gap had declined to 0.3, 0.6, and 1.0 year for each of the age categories, respectively.

Mobility at the top and mobility at the bottom

The discussion so far has focused on a single average parameter for the whole population in each point in time, but there is no reason to think that the extent of mobility in a society is equal at different points of the distribution of parental background. Indeed, numerous

studies show that a constant-elasticity relationship between the child's and parent's socioeconomic status is not supported by the data (for example, Behrman and Taubman 1990; Zimmerman 1992; Dearden, Machin, and Reed 1997). Most of these studies find that there is more upward mobility at the bottom than downward mobility at the top of the distribution. However, the importance of poverty traps in Latin America can turn around these results.

Table 3.1 presents cross-tabulations of schooling gaps (in columns) as a function of the level of completed education of the parents (in rows) for the first (circa 1995) and last (circa 2009) years in our sample in the region. For simplicity, we focus our discussion on children aged 15.

Several aspects are worth noting:

- First, there has been great mobility at the bottom. The share of children whose parents had less than primary education

TABLE 3.1   Relationship between parental education and children's average educational gap at age 15 in Latin America, 1995 versus 2009

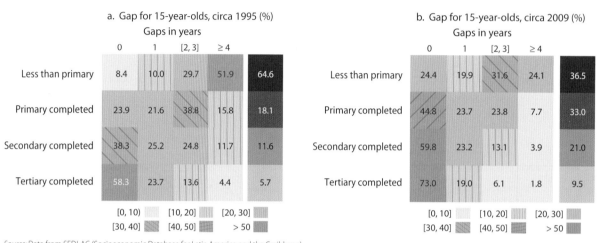

Source: Data from SEDLAC (Socioeconomic Database for Latin America and the Caribbean).
Note: Each row (of green-shaded squares) adds up to approximately 100 horizontally. The red column on the right represents the distribution of parental education and thus adds up to 100 vertically. "Educational gap" is defined as the difference between potential years of education at a given age and the years of completed education at that age.

almost halved between 1995 and 2009, from 65 percent to 36 percent.

- Although 50 percent of the children in the bottom group of parental background presented more than four years of educational gap in 1995, by 2009 this share dropped to less than 25 percent.
- The latter percentage remains far from the share of children with a similar gap among parents with tertiary education (a mere 1.8 percent in 2009), but the absolute distance between children with highly educated parents and children with low-educated parents fell dramatically during the period.

We should note that the closing of the schooling gap between the rich and the poor observed in Latin America is not driven solely by the general educational improvement in the population but also by the fact that the educational gap today is less dependent on parental background than it was a decade ago. It is naturally the case that, as poorer children are able to attend and finish school, the schooling gap between rich and poor children is bound to drop because richer children cannot go beyond their grade. However, using different metrics, we have found

that an important factor in the reduction of this gap is a genuine reduction in the dependence of children's outcomes on parental background.[4]

Cross-country heterogeneity

The evolution across countries of the association between parental education and children's educational gap at age 15 is presented in figure 3.7. The common denominator is that, in all countries and periods, the schooling gap is larger for those children raised in households with a low parental background than for those children raised in households with a high parental background. This is true whether we measure parental background through the parents' education or their income. That is, no country shows complete independence of children's educational outcomes with respect to parental background.

Encouragingly, for most of the countries and children's ages we considered, the differences in the schooling gap associated with parental education in 2009 are lower than in 1995. We also observe some convergence across countries. Ecuador, Brazil, and Bolivia (in that order) are the countries that made the greatest progress in reducing the children's

FIGURE 3.7 **Impact of parental background on children's educational gap at age 15 in Latin America, 1995–2009**

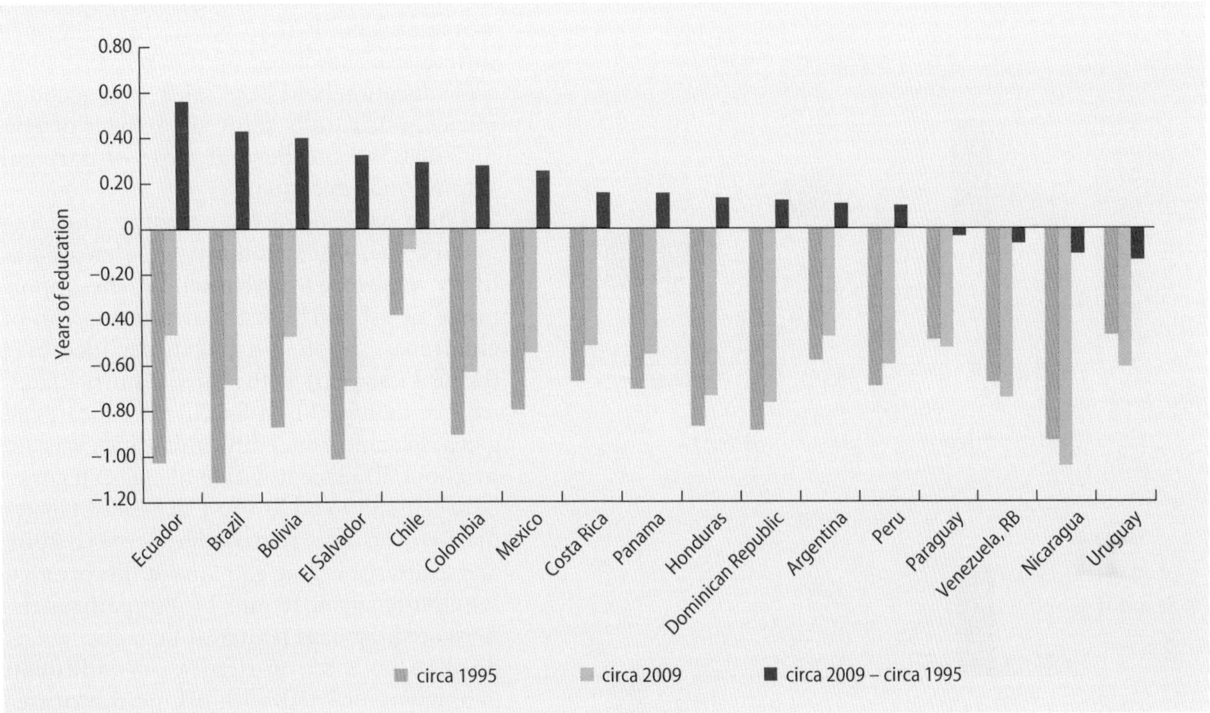

Source: Data from SEDLAC (Socioeconomic Database for Latin America and the Caribbean).
Note: "Educational gap" is defined as the difference between potential years of education at a given age and the years of completed education at that age. The green and orange bars represent the expected reduction in the schooling gap associated with one standard deviation of parental education in 1995 and 2009, respectively. The red bar is the difference between the two. Other covariates in the regression are children's gender, living in an urban area, and country fixed effects. The estimated effect of parental education on the educational gap is always statistically different from zero and so are the differences between 1995 and 2009.

educational gap associated with parental education, but their starting levels of inequality of opportunity in this particular dimension were among the highest in 1995. Uruguay is the country that made the least progress during the period, but it had started from a fairly low level of inequality associated with parental background. Most saliently, throughout this period, Chile managed to reduce the differences in schooling gaps across socioeconomic groups almost completely: by 2009, one standard deviation in parental education is associated with less than 0.1 years of additional schooling gap.

The role of ethnicity

The role of parental background in the determination of their children's educational attainment probably goes well beyond that

captured by the income or education of the parents. Ethnicity has been and remains a significant source of disparity in Latin American countries (Justino and Acharya 2003; Busso, Cicowiez, and Gasparini 2005; Chong and Ñopo 2008) and hence is likely to be an important determinant of the children's educational attainment (Cruces et al. 2011).

Our next exercise concentrates on three countries where existing microdata sets allow for a similar definition of ethnicity: Brazil, Ecuador, and Guatemala. In the three cases, we identify ethnic minorities as those who define themselves as nonwhite.[5] Ethnic minority households tend to be concentrated at the bottom of the income and education distribution. Therefore, taking into consideration the previous analysis, we would expect ethnic minority children to present lower educational attainment levels. Our interest

FIGURE 3.8 **Impact of ethnic minority status on children's educational gap in Brazil, Ecuador, and Guatemala**

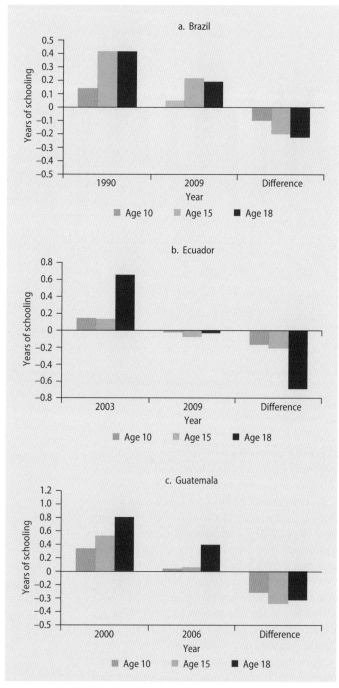

Source: Data from SEDLAC (Socioeconomic Database for Latin America and the Caribbean).
Note: "Educational gap" is defined as the difference between potential years of education at a given age and the years of completed education at that age. The first two sets of bars represent the coefficient associated with ethnicity in a schooling gap regression for each country, children's age, and year. The last set of bars is the difference between the two years. The regressions include as control variables the maximum education of the parents (and its square), household income (and its square), sex, urban/rural dummy, and regions dummies.

lies, however, in determining whether children of ethnic minority groups are doing worse in schools than white children, once differences associated with parental income and education have been taken into account. Hence, our results show the impact of ethnicity above and beyond those of parental income and education.

Once we control for parental schooling and income, ethnic minority children are less likely to succeed in school. Yet the importance of ethnicity in the determination of children's schooling gaps has declined over the past few years in the three countries studied (see figure 3.8). In Brazil, the educational gap associated with ethnic minorities was cut by about 50 percent within all age categories between 1990 and 2009. The case of Guatemala is even more remarkable: between 2000 and 2006 the ethnic gap almost disappeared for children aged 10 and 15. But perhaps the most striking case is that of Ecuador, which displays in 2009 no significant additional penalty associated with ethnic minorities within the three age categories considered.

The importance of educational achievement

Closing the schooling gap between children living in poor households and those from rich households is an important step towards achieving more equal opportunities. However, substantial differences may remain in the quality of schooling received by children with different parental backgrounds. To understand the influence of parents on student achievement, we use two similar cross-country harmonized data sets that include detailed information about parental background and student test scores. The most comprehensive is the 2009 Program for International Student Assessment (PISA), which tests student at age 15 in 65 countries, including Organisation for Economic Co-operation and Development (OECD) countries, nine Latin American countries, and other rich and poor countries outside Latin America and the OECD (OECD 2011). The second data set used is the Second Regional

Student Achievement Test (SERCE), an assessment sponsored by the United Nations Educational, Scientific, and Cultural Organization (UNESCO) and carried out in 2006 in 17 Latin American countries (UNESCO 2009). The harmonized questionnaires tested children attending the sixth grade of primary school.

Both the PISA and SERCE data sets share various characteristics and enable the assessment of the relationship between children's test scores and their parents' socioeconomic backgrounds. Test scores in both data sets are standardized to have an average across countries of 500 points and a standard deviation of 100. Parental background is measured through an index of economic, social, and cultural status (ESCS). In the case of PISA, the index includes information on household asset holdings, occupation, and educational attainment of the parents (see OECD 2011). In SERCE, we follow a similar procedure for

constructing the index and include 11 household asset holdings and dwelling characteristics as well as parental schooling.[6]

Intergenerational persistence in achievement in Latin America is fairly high.[7] With the exception of Mexico, the region's countries do not fare well in terms of independence of achievements in secondary education from parental background, either compared with more-developed countries or with countries at a similar level of development from other regions.

Figure 3.9 presents estimates of the effect of parental background on children's test scores in all 65 countries and economies included in the PISA sample. In Argentina, Peru, and Uruguay, an improvement of one standard deviation of the ESCS of the parents is associated with an increase of around 45 points in the test scores, which is about half a standard deviation of test scores included in the sample. Brazil, Chile, Colombia, and

FIGURE 3.9 **Influence of parental background on secondary students' PISA test scores across countries and economies, 2009**

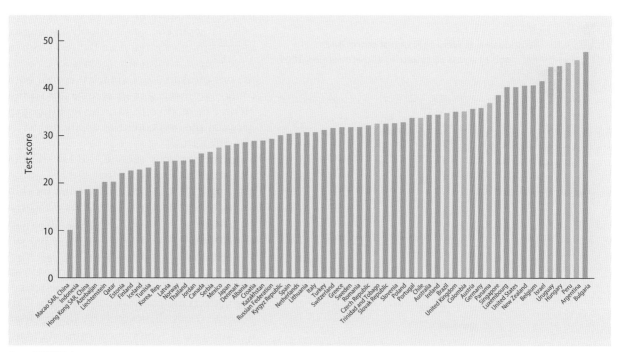

Source: PISA 2009 data.
Note: ESCS = PISA index of economic, social, and cultural status; PISA = Program for International Student Assessment. The bars represent the effect on reading test scores of one standard deviation of change in the ESCS index. Other variables included in the regression as controls include gender of the pupil, urban/rural dummy, and immigration status (first- or second-generation). Standard errors are clustered at the school level, and in all cases, the estimated effects are significant at the 5% level.

Panama show slightly more intergenerational mobility but are well below the cross-country PISA average. This result is consistent with findings in Ferreira and Gignoux (2011), which uses the *R*-squared of a similar regression to gauge the extent of (in)equality of opportunities in Latin America with respect to other regions.

The message regarding achievements is particularly worrying for two reasons: First, not only is equity low in Latin America but average performance is also quite poor by international standards. Second, the estimates of parental background in the student test scores from developing countries in data sets like PISA or SERCE are likely to be downward-biased. We elaborate on both of these points in turn.

The high influence of parental background on student achievements in Latin America is coupled with low levels of efficiency. This combination amplifies the troubling nature of intergenerational mobility in the region. Figure 3.10 shows the bivariate association between average scores and the impact of

parental ESCS on children's reading tests across countries and economies.

There is no clear association between the two measures. In other words, there does not seem to be a clear trade-off between efficiency, as measured through average test score, and equity. The vertical and horizontal lines show the cross-country averages for both axes. With the exception of Mexico, Latin American countries are clustered in the southeast quadrant of the graph, characterized by lower-than-average performance and lower-than-average intergenerational mobility (in other words, higher-than-average impact of parental ESCS on the children's test scores).

The importance of looking at these two dimensions together can be illustrated with a couple of examples. In absolute terms, the impact of one standard deviation of parental background on the test scores of the children in Panama and Germany is similar. However, the average test score in Panama is around 360, while in Germany it is almost 500. Hence, in relative terms, the impact of parental background on the test scores is much larger in Panama. Similarly, the impact of parental background on the test score in Argentina is almost three times as large as the one measured in Indonesia, even if both countries present similar average test scores. Hence, in relative terms, the mobility gap between the two countries is larger than in absolute terms.

In the previous section, we saw that in all Latin American countries there is a positive impact of parental background on children's educational attainment, as measured by schooling gaps. This positive impact has two components: children from better-off backgrounds are less likely to drop out from school and, among those who remain in school, they are also less likely to fall behind. Both effects are confirmed by the data. This poses a serious challenge to the investigation of educational achievement using standard surveys such as PISA and SERCE because these data are representative of the population of children attending school at a given age (in PISA) or in a given grade (in SERCE)

FIGURE 3.10   Relationship of average PISA test scores and intergenerational mobility across 65 countries and economies, 2009

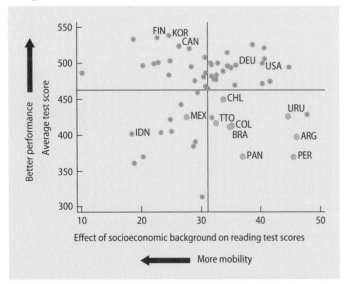

Source: PISA 2009 data.
Note: PISA = Program for International Student Assessment. The effect of socioeconomic background on reading test scores is calculated as described in figure 3.9. The horizontal line represents the average test score in the sample. The vertical line represents the average effect of parental background on test scores in the sample.

but not of the entire child population of that age.[8] When working solely with OECD countries in the PISA sample, this is not a great limitation because enrollment rates at age 15 are high (Hanushek and Woessman 2011). However, in developing countries, the enrollment rates are much lower, especially in secondary education.

The implication is that estimates of the association between parental background and test scores for developing countries are likely to be downward-biased due to selection. As a result, the gap in equity between high-income and low-income countries is most likely larger than observed. Indeed, this will be the case if the following three conditions are satisfied:

1. Enrollment rates in developing countries are lower than in developed countries.
2. The probability of attending school increases with parental background.
3. Children who do not attend school perform no better than those with similar backgrounds who do attend school.

Conditions 1 and 2 are indeed confirmed by the data. We have no direct evidence of condition 3, but it is reasonable to believe it is also met.

Lugo and Messina (2012) discuss the problem of selection into schools and propose a correction based on building bounds around the estimated effects of parental background on children's test scores in the case of Latin American countries.[9] The authors combined information (from national household surveys, PISA, and SERCE) on enrollment rates and test score data for children from different socioeconomic backgrounds to construct reasonable lower and upper bounds of test scores for the nonobserved population. (For a detailed explanation and results for PISA, see focus note 3.1 at the end of this chapter.) We present here results for SERCE, which measures cognitive development in children attending sixth grade of primary school, and focus on the gap in test scores between children with high-educated parents (tertiary) and low-educated parents (no education).

In countries where almost all children attend school, the lower and upper bounds of the differences in sixth-grade test scores are close to each other. In Chile, for instance, children whose parents completed tertiary education score around 120 points more (that is, more than one standard deviation) than those whose parents have no education (figure 3.11, panel b). Although this test score difference is large, the bounds around it are quite tight.

In contrast, in countries where a significant proportion of children do not attend school, the distances between the lower bound of the gap and the upper bound can be quite large. The extreme example is Guatemala, where a 12-year-old child born from tertiary-educated parents will most certainly attend school at age 12, as is the case in Chile for any kid. However, if the child had parents with no education, he or she would have only a 60 percent chance of being at school (figure 3.11, panel a). As a consequence, the difference in performance between children from parents with no education and those with tertiary education lies somewhere between 80 and 180 test-score points (that is, between one and two standard deviations). Importantly, although the estimate from the distribution of those children attending school indicates that the gap in Guatemala is among the smallest in the region, the bounds clearly suggest that it is possible that, instead, the gap between the highest and lowest parental background is indeed the largest of all (figure 3.11, panel b).

For PISA estimates, bounds are much wider than in SERCE. However, in most of the cases, the estimated effects without taking into account the sample selection are very close to the lower bound. Considering that enrollment rates are lower in Latin American countries than in most OECD countries, this implies that the distance in intergenerational mobility between the two groups of countries is even larger than what we have discussed so far.

Do we observe similar improvements in intergenerational educational mobility when we consider achievements rather than educational attainment? Unfortunately, the

FIGURE 3.11   **Enrollment and inequalities in reading test scores, selected countries, 2006**

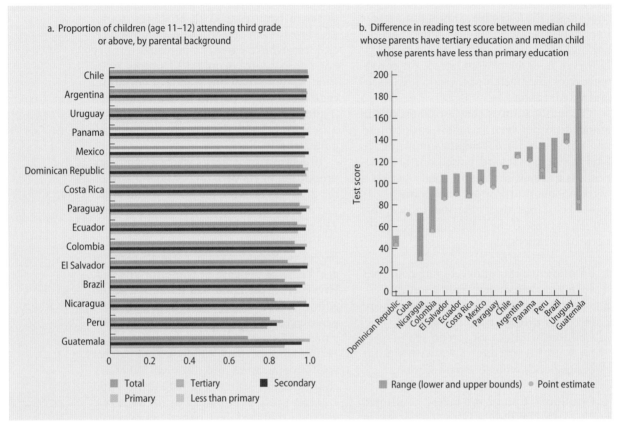

a. Proportion of children (age 11–12) attending third grade
or above, by parental background

b. Difference in reading test score between median child
whose parents have tertiary education and median child
whose parents have less than primary education

Legend (panel a): Total, Tertiary, Secondary, Primary, Less than primary

Legend (panel b): Range (lower and upper bounds) • Point estimate

Source: Lugo and Messina (2012); SEDLAC (Socioeconomic Database for Latin America and the Caribbean) data.

Source: Lugo and Messina (2012), based on SERCE 2006 and SEDLAC (Socioeconomic Database for Latin America and the Caribbean) data.
Note: Range represents upper and lower bounds. The dots are the point estimates.

evidence is much scarcer. The PISA study started collecting information in 2000, so we could in principle discuss evidence of the evolution of the socioeconomic gradient in test scores in the past decade. However, several data limitations make this comparison quite problematic:

• We have observed an important improvement in educational attainment during the past decade in Latin America. Hence, raw estimates of the changes in the socioeconomic gradient of student achievements are likely to be affected by changes in selection over time.

• The index of socioeconomic status was constructed differently in the 2000 and 2009 waves of PISA.

• There is some indication that the scores from the worst-performing children in PISA 2000 were left censored, diminishing the variance in the test scores.

The first and last concerns are likely to bias the comparison of 2000 and 2009 scores against finding improvements because they suggest that the impact of parental background on test scores in PISA 2000 is likely to be downward-biased with respect to 2009. Keeping all these caveats in mind, there is no evidence of an improvement in the socioeconomic gradient of student achievements in the past decade in Latin America. Estimates relying on the same methods used to construct figure 3.9 for the few countries where data is available show very limited changes over time, and sometimes even negative ones.[10]

From educational to income mobility

In the previous sections we have seen that intergenerational mobility in educational attainment and achievement in the Latin American region is generally low compared with other regions—although, at least in the case of attainment, it has improved in the past decades. To the extent that the level of education attained is related to incomes and wealth later in life, one would wonder whether similar improvements in income mobility are observed. The present section tries to shed some light on this question.

To study intergenerational persistence of income, one would ideally need income data for parents and their children (once they are adults). Indeed, these types of data have been used to study mobility in high-income countries, as described in box 3.2. Unfortunately, no Latin American country has the similar long-term panel surveys needed to perform similar analyses. One possibility to overcome this limitation is to use retrospective information on parental background such as education and occupation to build estimates of parental income, which can be related in a second stage to the income of the children. In a recent paper, Corak (forthcoming) compiled methodologically comparable estimates of fathers' and sons' earnings mobility across a large host of countries, using data from 19 studies. In most cases, estimates of parental income are obtained using retrospective information on parental education and occupation. Earnings mobility is computed as the elasticity of earnings between the two generations when both are of similar age.

How does Latin American generational income mobility compare with that of other countries? Figure 3.12 presents country estimates from Corak (forthcoming) in panel a, together with its relationship to the current level of earnings inequality (panel b). Two striking features emerge from these figures. First, Latin American countries are

FIGURE 3.12 **Intergenerational earnings elasticity between fathers and sons and its relationship to earnings inequality**

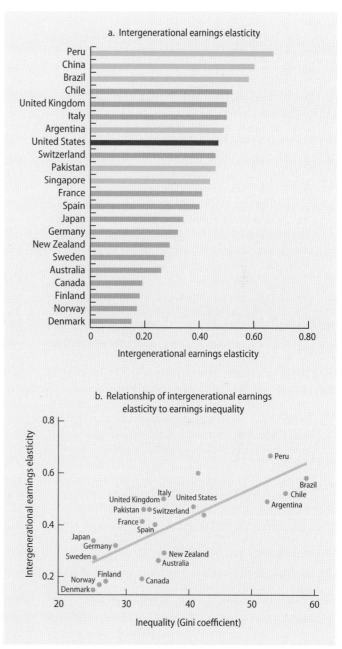

Source: Corak, forthcoming.
Note: Bars shaded in orange are not OECD member countries in panel a.

among the economies with the highest levels of intergenerational dependence. In Peru, for instance, if one father earns 100 percent more than another, then the son of the

---

BOX 3.2   Income mobility in high-income countries

The importance of family background for children's economic status in developed countries has been studied intensively in Nordic countries and in the United States, relying mostly on three different approaches: intergenerational associations of income, sibling similarities, and the relationship between inequality of income and unequal opportunities. The results of these studies, summarized by Jäntti (2012), show a similar pattern across methodologies, revealing evidence against the traditional notion of "American exceptionalism"—which consists of, among other aspects, a belief in a greater rate of upward social mobility in the United States than in other countries. The discomfort with the "end of the American dream," made explicit by the Occupy Movement, is probably not all that surprising.

Analyzing the joint distribution of fathers' and sons' income (intergenerational associations) through quintile group mobility matrices, Jäntti (2012) shows that, for the Nordic countries, approximately 25 percent of sons born into the poorest quintile remain in that position, while around 10 to 15 percent reach the very top quintile. In contrast, the author finds that more than 40 percent of U.S. males born in the poorest quintile remain there, reflecting a much lower upward mobility. Similarly, the probability that the son of a lowest-quintile parent makes it into the top-quintile group is lower in the United States than in all of the Nordic countries, and the top-to-bottom mobility is also lower in the United Kingdom and the United States than in Nordic countries, as shown by Atkinson (1981) and more recently by Jäntti (2012). Fewer than 10 percent of U.S. males born into the richest quintile fall all the way down to the bottom quintile, while this is typically the case for around 15 percent of Nordic males. In more central parts of the income distribution, all countries are remarkably similar.

A fuller account of the impact of family background on economic status can be found by studying the extent to which siblings' economic characteristics resemble each other. Siblings share part of the attributes that parents transfer to their children, which are partially related to income, such as values and aspirations. The correlation in income between

siblings can thus be considered as a lower bound on the impact of family background on economic status. When analyzing international sibling correlations of earnings in Nordic countries and the United States, Björklund and Jäntti (2009) show that Norway stands out as having much smaller correlations than Denmark, Finland, and Sweden: 0.14 for Norway compared with around 0.25 for the other countries. At the opposite extreme, the correlation in the U.S. is approximately 0.50, that is, more than double the Nordic countries' average.

An alternative approach to examining the importance of family background on people's income is present in the literature of equality of opportunities. This research has been inspired by developments in political and social philosophy (see Arneson 1989; Cohen 1989; and Roemer 1993, 1998). In different ways, these authors argue that not all inequality need be ethically unacceptable (see Almås et al. 2011). Individuals should be held accountable for outcomes for which they *can* be held responsible, such as level of effort exerted at work, but not for those outcomes for which they are not responsible, such as the color of their skin or the place of birth. Consequently, inequalities due to effort are viewed as ethically acceptable, whereas inequalities related to circumstances beyond individuals' control are, in turn, ethically unacceptable.

Often, groups are defined by a few observable parental traits—typically parental income, occupation, and education (see Roemer et al. 2003)—to compute the extent to which tax-and-transfer regimes in 11 rich countries equalize opportunities among citizens for income acquisition. In this context, equality of opportunity in incomes is achieved when the distributions of postfiscal income are the same for different "types" of citizen ("types" being defined according to parental socioeconomic status). The authors find that high-income countries tax income at close to, and sometimes possibly in excess of, equality-of-opportunity norms. These results are particularly present among northern European economies—such as Sweden and Denmark—which tended to do well in achieving equality of opportunity.

high-income father will make, as an adult, 67 percent more than the son of the relatively lower-income father. This is in sharp contrast with the elasticity found, say, in Norway (0.17) but also in Spain (0.40) or the United States (0.47).

The second interesting result from Corak is that low generational mobility goes hand in hand with high inequality. Countries with low mobility (high intergenerational earnings elasticity) tend to have high levels of inequality. (See, in particular, that all four of the Latin American countries in the sample appear in the far right side of panel b.) In contrast, highly mobile societies are also the ones presenting the lowest levels of cross-sectional inequality (not only lower lifetime inequality). In the next section, we will describe some of the potential underlying causes of this observed relationship. We examine whether specific market structures and policies that are correlated with children's unequal access to education interact with the level of education or wealth of their parents.

Examining changes over time in the intergenerational association of income is an even harder task. In an attempt to shed some light on this issue, Azevedo et al. (2012) use retrospective information from household surveys in Colombia and Mexico. These surveys ask all household heads and their spouses about the households' possession of a number of assets generally associated with household wealth at two points in time: when they were 10 years old and at the time the survey is administered. Combined with the educational attainment of adults in the household and their parents, one can construct two indices of socioeconomic status, one for each generation, using a methodology similar to the one described in previous sections (see Azevedo et al. 2012 for details). This method allows the researchers to assess the extent to which the position of children in the overall wealth distribution is associated with the position their parents held. Such an association is examined employing a similar methodology to the one previously outlined in box 3.1 to estimate the β coefficient as a measure of intergenerational persistence.[11]

Confirming previous evidence, the authors find that the association between socioeconomic status of parents and children in both countries is fairly high, with an intergenerational elasticity of 0.56 in Colombia and 0.48 in Mexico. Both associations are highly significant. However, the two countries have followed different trends. In the case of Colombia, we observe an increase in intergenerational mobility across cohorts. The elasticity of the index of socioeconomic status is 0.66 for the oldest cohort (ages 56–64), while the elasticity for those age 41–55 is 10.0 percentage points lower, at 0.56, and in the case of the youngest cohort it declines to 0.47. In the case of Mexico, however, the association in the asset index is larger for the younger cohort, at 0.56, against 0.43 for the older one.

Policies and intergenerational educational mobility

What are the determinants of cross-country differences in intergenerational mobility? Are there institutional factors, policies, and macroeconomic environments that favor mobility across generations? These are extremely difficult questions, but they remain at the core of the policy analysis of intergenerational mobility. As we discussed in the introduction to this chapter, the transmission of socioeconomic status from one generation to the next is a combination of exogenous biological factors, endogenous optimizing behavior of parents, macroeconomic or environmental conditions, and collective policies (Solon 2004). However, none of these factors operates in isolation. The optimizing behavior of parents and policies, for instance, interact with each other, complicating the interpretation of estimates of intergenerational mobility in a cross-country context.

The literature on the determinants of intergenerational mobility is rather thin, which is not surprising considering the extreme complexity of simply measuring this social phenomenon. There is a limited literature that looks at correlations of policies and institutional variables and different proxies of intergenerational mobility across countries, including Woessmann et al. (2009) and Causa and Chapuis (2009), both focused on OECD countries, and Ferreira and Gignoux (2011) for both OECD and non-OECD countries. In this section, we extend this literature to consider a larger set of countries and indicators of intergenerational mobility. Box 3.3 briefly outlines the methodology.

We complement the general overview of the role of policies (provided with the cross-country analysis) with selected examples where sharp policy changes have helped

to identify the causal impact of a particular policy intervention on intergenerational mobility. It should be noted that even this analysis is not exempt from the typical limitations of quasi-experimental settings. The fact that some policy worked in a particular context does not guarantee that it would have the same impact in a different macro or institutional environment. For all of these reasons, rather than providing definitive answers, the aim of this section is to highlight particular aspects of the institutional and policy environments that appear to be important for the determination of mobility across generations.

BOX 3.3   Cross-country analysis of policies and institutions and intergenerational mobility

Cross-country comparisons can shed light on the importance of policies and institutions in the determination of intergenerational mobility, but they present clear limitations. Countries are very different in many respects. Moreover, institutional aspects are highly correlated within countries. Both aspects make it almost impossible to isolate the impact of a particular policy on the outcome of interest. Moreover, in many instances, institutional indicators are imperfect measures of the complex real-life phenomena they are meant to summarize. The increasing availability of panel data can help us start to compare apples to apples. Relying on changes in policies and institutions within countries brings us closer to identifying their actual impact, even if they are not the definitive answer since comovement in other confounding factors limits the power of identification.

Here, we estimate cross-country regressions of the following format:

$$y_{ic} = \alpha + \beta X_{ic} + \gamma_1 ESCS_{ic} + \gamma_2 (ESCS_{ic} \times P_c) + \mu_c + \varepsilon_{ic}, \quad \text{(B3.3a)}$$

where subscript ic represents individual i living in country c, X_{ic} is a set of control variables, and μ_c is a country fixed effect.

$ESCS_{ic}$ is an index of socioeconomic status that captures a wide array of parental background characteristics, including education, occupation, and some tangible asset holdings (the exact variables changing with the data set). We will consider two outcome variables (y_{ic}): test scores from PISA and the schooling gap. Importantly, data on schooling gaps are available for repeated cross-sections in each country. In this case, we add to equation (B3.3a) time dummies that capture common factors that shock countries. For schooling gap regressions, standard errors are robust to country-year. In PISA, instead, standard errors are robust to correlation within schools.

Our interest lies in the impacts of policies (P_c) on the socioeconomic gradient of the test score or educational gap. Thus, we are interested in

$$\frac{\partial y_{ic}}{\partial ESCS_{ic}} = \gamma_1 + \gamma_2 P_c. \quad \text{(B3.3b)}$$

This equation indicates that socioeconomic background is associated with the educational outcome directly and through the level of the policy variable or institution we are considering. A positive (negative) γ_2 implies that in countries with higher provision of the policy, the educational outcomes of children are more (less) strongly associated with parental background.

Expenditures on education and educational outcomes

We start the analysis by focusing on expenditures. There is an important debate in the literature on the impact of public education expenditures on educational outcomes. Harbison and Hanushek (1992) review 12 case studies in developing countries, and only half of them reported a positive association. Rajkumar and Swaroop (2008) argue that differences across countries may be related to differences in governance. In countries where corruption is high and the quality of bureaucracy is low, higher spending in education or health may not need to be translated into better outcomes. They also offer cross-country evidence that is in line with the proposed hypothesis.

The debate about the efficacy of public spending in education is important for the Latin American region because even if public expenditures in education are still low today relative to other developed and developing countries, it is undeniable that an important effort was devoted to "catch up" during the past decade. According to UNESCO data, between 1999 and 2009, expenditures per student in primary and secondary education as a percentage of gross domestic product (GDP) per capita in the region grew by almost 50 percent—from 10.5 percent to 15.1 percent in the case of primary education, and from 11.9 percent to 16.9 percent in secondary education. Has this increase in resources helped close the gap in attainment and achievements between the poor and the rich?

We pool individual data from different countries and years (1990–2009) with public expenditure data on education expenditures in primary and secondary education, measured at the country level to estimate the association between public expenditures and individual schooling gaps, following the methodology explained in box 3.3. We find that public expenditures per student in primary and secondary school have indeed helped to reduce the schooling gap between rich and poor children (figure 3.13).

FIGURE 3.13   Impact of public education expenditures on the schooling gap between rich and poor

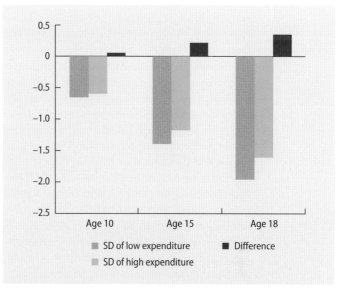

Source: Data from SEDLAC (Socioeconomic Database for Latin America and the Caribbean).
Note: SD = standard deviation.
The green and orange bars represent the effect of a one-SD increase in parental education on schooling gaps in countries with low and high levels of public expenditure on education per pupil as a percentage of GDP, respectively. The estimated effects are obtained from three independent regressions (one per age), including Latin American household surveys from the period 1995–2009. The dependent variable is the student gap, and the coefficients of interest are the highest level of parental education and its interaction with public education expenditures (see box 3.3 for details). Regressions include as control variables gender of the student, urban status, country, and time fixed effects. Standard errors are clustered by country. All estimates are statistically different from zero at standard levels of testing.

The differences in the gap between a high-spending country (see the orange bar, corresponding to Costa Rica) and a low-spending one (the green bar, corresponding to Peru) is 0.08 years of schooling at age 10. At age 15, differences in the gap between low-spending (Dominican Republic) and high-spending (Brazil) country-years are 0.18, and at age 18 the gap differs by 0.28 years of education. Although these differences are sizable (and statistically significant at 1 percent), it is clear that they explain only a small part of the reduction of the gap observed in the region throughout the period.

The effects of parental background are evaluated at different levels of public expenditures. In the case of children aged 10, expenditure levels in primary education in 2006 are considered. Low expenditures correspond to Peru, and high expenditures correspond to Costa Rica. For children aged 15 and 18, expenditures in secondary education in 2006 are considered. High and low expenditures correspond to Brazil and the Dominican Republic, respectively

Higher public educational expenditure might be associated with a lower schooling gap for several reasons. Schools receiving more funding can devote more resources to the poor and those students lagging behind, either in the form of physical inputs (such as books and stationery) or by providing special tuition and extra-support lessons. Higher investments also can result in better school infrastructure in remote areas, where poor families are likely to be concentrated. This is probably particularly important for enrollment and attainment in secondary schools, where the opportunity cost of studying is higher, especially in families where credit constraints are important.

Gauging evidence of the particular channels through which additional public spending influences educational attainment is hard at the macro level, but some lessons can be learned. Regarding the importance of resources, we have included in our cross-country regressions pupil-teacher ratios and found that assigning fewer students per teacher helped to reduce the gap between the rich and the poor in primary schools, although not in secondary schools. Box 3.4, drawn from Solis (2011), presents evidence from a quasi-natural experiment in Chile on the importance of credit constraints for enrollment in tertiary education. The impact of having access to student loans for the poor is hard to dispute: among those eligible for a student loan, having access to credit after completion of high school completely eliminates the enrollment gap in college between the rich and the poor.

As we argued before, we expect credit constraints to be a more important factor limiting access to education as we move up the educational ladder. Higher education is more expensive than secondary education, and the opportunity cost of studying at age 18 is higher than at age 14. This implies that

as Latin America gradually closes the educational gap in primary and secondary schooling, the importance of credit constraints in limiting intergenerational educational mobility is likely to increase. Moreover, the recent success in Latin America in closing the gap in secondary education, and the resulting increase of workers with high school credentials in the labor market, is reducing the returns to secondary education (see Aedo and Walker 2011). Hence, limited access to credit, by limiting access to tertiary education, is likely to be hindering those human capital investments that present the highest marginal returns in Latin America.

The impact of public educational expenditures on educational achievement—as opposed to educational attainment—is ambiguous. In this case, we work with cross-sectional data only (PISA) and the full sample, which includes the 50 countries for which we have expenditure data. On average, we find that *higher* public expenditures per pupil are associated with a *larger gap* in test scores between the rich and the poor, but this result is not uniform across countries. In developing countries, public expenditures appear to be mildly progressive,[12] whereas in developed countries, larger gaps are associated with more spending.

The importance of school quality and children's sorting in intergenerational mobility

Affluent parents interested in providing the best possible education for their children are likely to send them to better schools even when this implies paying an additional fee, an option that may not be available for parents with fewer resources and limited access to credits. The implication for analyses using assessment data such as PISA or SERCE is that it will be difficult to disentangle the impact of school and parental inputs because children are not randomly allocated across schools. Instead, in all educational systems where parents have some freedom of choice, there is sorting across schools according to parents' and children's preferences. Indirect

BOX 3.4   Tuition loans in Chile: Is the alleviation of credit constraints a good policy to close the gap in educational attainment between rich and poor?

Tertiary education is costly for the students. Costs include not only student fees, which vary greatly across countries, but also the forgone income associated with the loss of hours worked. Naturally, families in need may not be able to afford this income loss, and difficult access to credit can make the option of a college education simply unaffordable for the most vulnerable households. However, assessing the importance of credit constraints for tertiary education is not straightforward, and the evidence until recently has been highly inconclusive. Keane and Wolpin (2001); Card (2001); Carneiro and Heckman (2002); and Brown, Scholz, and Seshadri (2009), among others, rely on different identification techniques to obtain little agreement on the importance of credit constraints for the intergenerational mobility of education. Still, none of these papers has been able to observe credit constraints directly.

The difficulty in assessing the importance of credit constraints lies in the fact that the intention of accessing credit is generally not observable. Credit-constrained families might not apply for a loan if they think the likelihood of obtaining it to be very low. In parallel, children from poor families might also be less likely to enroll in college because they lack the necessary qualifications or hold different values transmitted by their parents, among other reasons. A recent paper by Solís (2011) takes advantage of a natural experiment to isolate the impact of credit constraints on the probability of attending college and to study differences in such probabilities across poor and more affluent families.

The experiment is simple. A financing program in Chile offers tuition loans to students who fulfill three criteria: (a) apply for the loan, (b) belong to the lowest four income quintiles of the income distribution, and (c) obtain a score above 475 points on the College Admission Test (*Prueba de Selección Universitaria*, PSU). The structure of the loan is such that it creates a sharp discontinuity. Similar students who apply for the loan might be successful by just one-point difference in the PSU score. Students obtaining a very high score (say, 550) and students obtaining a very low score (say, 400) are likely to be very different in many observed and unobserved characteristics and would have also different incentives to go to college. Instead, one may argue that

students scoring in the vicinity of the threshold, say, one or two points above or below, are likely on average to be very similar. If students immediately above the threshold present a higher probability of enrollment in college than those immediately below, this can be interpreted as a strong sign of credit constraints.

In figure B3.4.1, panel a, the author shows that the program was properly implemented; only those students who obtained a PSU above 475 were eligible for the loan. Importantly, the loan take-up among those who were eligible was fairly high (panel b), at 30 percent, and increasing with the PSU score. Panel c shows that college enrollment increases sharply, on average, for those who obtain a PSU score above 475. The probability of enrollment is around 17 percent for the students who are immediately below the 475 threshold. In contrast, the probability of enrollment jumps to 35 percent for those immediately above the threshold. Hence, having access to the loan doubles the probability of enrollment. Solís (2011) interprets this as strong evidence of binding credit constraints.

Most crucially, the loan appears to help reduce the gap between the rich and the poor. Panel d shows the probability of enrollment by income quintile for two groups of students: those who score 475 or 476 on the PSU and thus are eligible for the loan (the treated group) and those who obtained a PSU score of 474 or 473 and hence are ineligible (the control group). Several aspects are worth noting: Enrollment rates among the control group increase monotonically with income. In contrast, enrollment rates among those with access to the loan seem to be independent of their income level. Hence, for those students who are around the cutoff—that is, those who obtain a PSU score of around 475—the inclusion into this program completely eliminates the gap of college enrollment by family income. This, of course, does not mean that the program wipes out all influences of family background into children's access to higher education in the population because children from affluent families are more likely to obtain a higher PSU score than are children from poorer backgrounds. Indeed, the mean test score of children in the top quintile was 527, whereas it was 468 for those in the bottom quintile.

(Box continues next page)

BOX 3.4   Tuition loans in Chile: is the alleviation of credit constraints a good policy to close the gap in educational attainment between rich and poor?   *(continued)*

FIGURE B3.4.1   Tuition loans and school enrollment in Chile

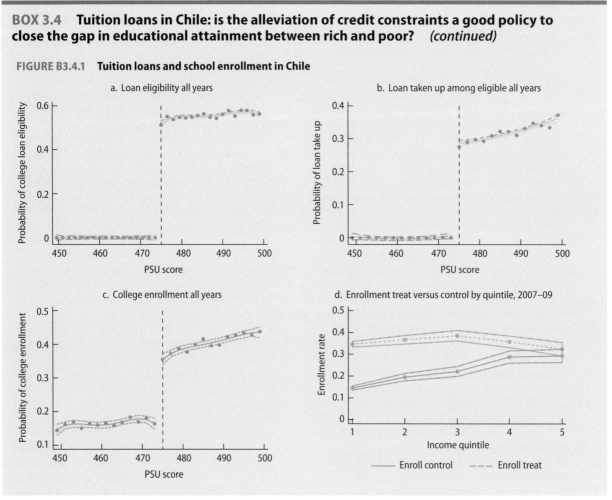

Source: Solís 2011.
Note: PSU = *Prueba de Selección Universitaria* (College Admission Test).

evidence about the extent of parental influence that is channeled through the schooling system can be obtained by comparing the amount of sorting in different regions.

Is there more sorting among schools in Latin America than in other economic areas? A first take at this question compares the impact of the socioeconomic status (ESCS) on children's test scores as estimated in figure 3.9 with the impact resulting from adding to the regression school fixed effects. This latter estimation will be labeled as the "direct" impact of ESCS, as opposed to the first result, labeled "overall" impact, which includes not only (a) the direct association from, among other factors, genetic traits

that are inheritable, effort, and time spent with the children, but also (b) indirect effects through parental choices and investments, including the type of schools the children are attending. It should be noted that although the direct impact estimates the effect of parents on children's test scores that is not confounded with the school, this estimate cannot be interpreted as the "true" impact, precisely because the allocation of kids to schools is not random. For convenience, we group countries in seven groups:[13]

• Latin America and the Caribbean
• Anglo-Saxon (excluding United Kingdom and United States)

- Nordic
- Continental Europe
- United Kingdom and United States
- Remaining low- and middle-income countries
- Remaining high-income countries.

The green bars in figure 3.14 show the overall impact of ESCS on children's test scores. As we discussed earlier, Latin American countries show a high degree of intergenerational persistence: the impact of one standard deviation in ESCS is higher only in the combined group of the United Kingdom and the United States. At the other extreme of the graph, Nordic countries present the highest levels of mobility. The orange bars show the direct impact of parents, once school effects have been controlled for. Note that Latin American countries now fall to the opposite extreme of the distribution, showing the lowest influence of parental ESCS on the children's test scores.

Interestingly, once we control for school effects, the Nordic countries appear to have the highest level of persistence across generations in the six groups of countries considered. Similarly, the overall and direct effects in the United Kingdom and United States are not very different. These findings have two possible interpretations: (a) The first is that, in Latin American countries, there is much more sorting of children across schools than in Nordic countries. In this candidate explanation, schooling inputs might even be the same across schools. The differences between the green and orange bars simply reflect sorting and not differences in schooling quality. (b) Alternatively, the distance between the green and orange bars may be a sign not only of sorting but also of differences in school quality between the schools attended by rich and poor children. In this alternative explanation, the fact that there is a much larger gap between the overall and direct effect in Latin America than in the Nordic countries would be a sign not only of higher sorting but also of the importance of the schooling system in the determination of mobility across generations. In this case, rather than

FIGURE 3.14 **Direct and overall impact of parental background on children's test scores**

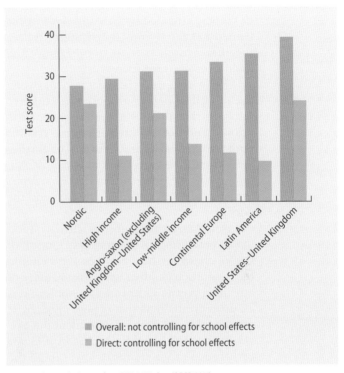

Source: Authors' calculations from PISA 2009 data (OECD 2011).
Note: ESCS = PISA index of economic, social, and cultural status; PISA = Program for International Student Assessment. The bars represent the effect of one standard deviation in ESCS on children's test scores, for each group of countries. Group-specific regressions include as control variables gender of the pupil, urban dummy, immigration status, and country dummies. The orange bar regressions include school fixed effects, whereas the green bars do not.

mitigating the existing socioeconomic disparities, the schooling system in Latin America would exacerbate them.

To shed further light on the importance of sorting versus school inequality, our next exercise assesses the differences in the inputs of the typical schools attended by the rich and the poor. Our conclusion is that differences between schools attended by the rich and those attended by the poor are larger in Latin America than in any other group of countries, suggesting that inequality in schooling inputs in Latin America is likely to play a more important role than in other regions in widening the achievement gap between children from different backgrounds. Figure 3.15 shows differences in the characteristics of the schools frequented by the rich (top quintile of the ESCS distribution) and the poor (bottom quintile) in Latin American countries compared with those of schools attended by rich and poor in the United Kingdom and United States (taken together) as well as those in other low- and middle-income countries.

The metric used is the ratio between the quintiles; hence, an outcome equal to 1 means that there is an equal proportion of poor and rich children attending schools with a particular characteristic. The further away from 1 the outcome is in any direction, the greater the difference in that characteristic in schools attended by the rich and the poor.

Latin American countries clearly stand out as presenting an unequal distribution of school characteristics between the rich and the poor. Rich children have a probability of attending private-independent schools that is 22 times greater than that of poor children. If the school is government-dependent but privately operated, the difference is by a factor of 10. Such ratios are much lower in all the other regions. The only exception that comes close is in the United Kingdom and United States. There is an important difference between Latin America and these two countries, however. In Latin American countries, the differences between public and private provision translate into important inequalities in a wide range of observable school characteristics:

- Schools attended by the rich have much more autonomy in hiring and firing teachers as well as in selecting teachers' pay.
- Schools attended by the rich also have more autonomy in selecting the course contents and in administering their budgets.
- The percentage of fully certified teachers, a measure of teaching quality, in the schools attended by the rich is 50 percent larger than in the schools the poor attend.

In contrast, the observable inputs in U.K. and U.S. schools are much more similar across income groups, with no particular aspect standing out as a major difference.

This similarity might be related to the fact that the publicly owned and operated schools in these two countries operate under rules and manners similar to those of private schools—a likeness that suggests a role for governments in homogenizing standards that appears to be missing in Latin America. Some differences are detected in the case of other low- and middle-income countries, but these tend to be smaller than those observed in Latin America. Nordic countries (not shown in figure 3.15) constitute an interesting example of equality of inputs: although rich children outnumber the poor in attendance at privately operated schools, there are no significant differences between private and public schools in any of the dimensions of educational inputs.

School systems and the influence of parental background on schooling outcomes

Are these schooling characteristics associated with more intergenerational mobility or with less? We have established that school characteristics are not uniformly distributed among children with different socioeconomic backgrounds, at least in Latin America. In a different dimension, the importance of each of these characteristics varies greatly across countries. Some countries such as the Netherlands allow for great autonomy of schools in hiring and firing teachers. Others, such as Colombia, are much more restrictive in the role they assign to schools in personnel policies. Keeping the caveat that the same incidence of a given policy in two countries might hide different patterns (for example, depending on the level of sorting), it is of interest to understand the association, on average, of each of the schooling dimensions on intergenerational mobility.

To that end, we have built country-level indicators from PISA using a wide range of the school dimensions from the data set. Naturally, these variables tend to be highly correlated across countries. To limit the dimensionality problem in the data, we conducted a factor analysis of all the institutional

FIGURE 3.15 **Differences in school characteristics between the top and bottom quintile of the ESCS**

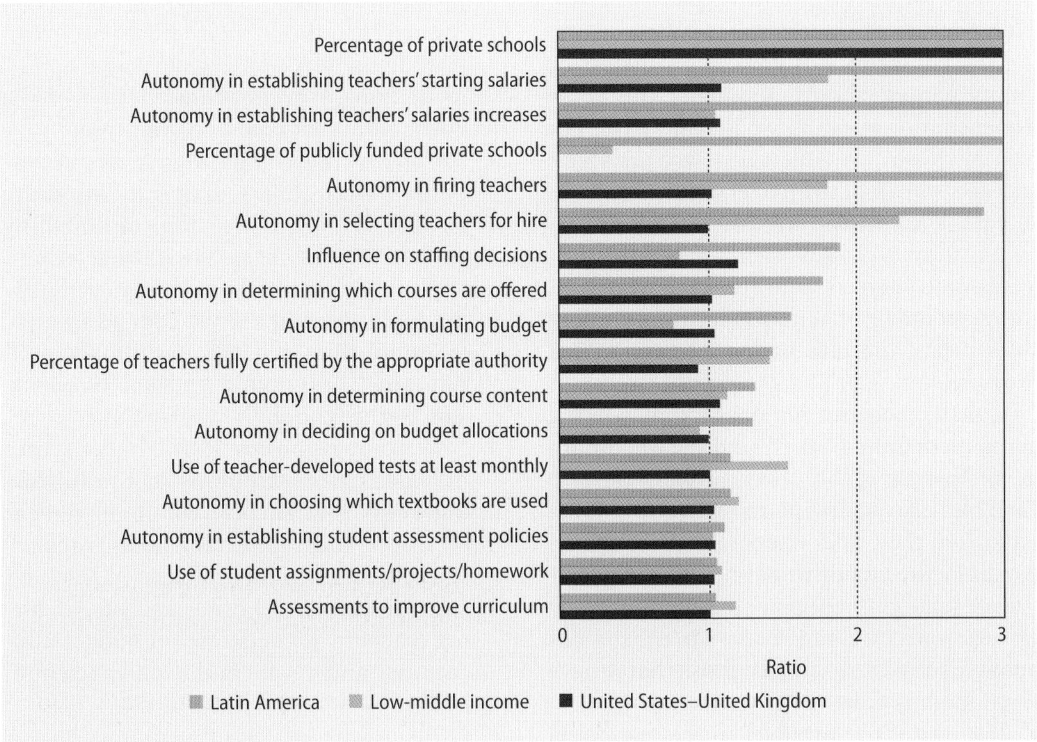

Source: Data from PISA 2009 (OECD 2011).
Note: ESCS = PISA index of economic, social, and cultural status; PISA = Program for International Student Assessment. Each bar shows the ratio in the characteristics of the schools frequented by the rich (top quintile of the ESCS distribution) and the poor (bottom quintile) in Latin American countries as opposed to the United Kingdom and United States (considered jointly).

variables in PISA except for three variables that appeared to be crucial, hence warranting separate appearances in the regressions: (a) the share of students attending private independent schools, (b) the share of students attending private but partially government-subsidized private schools, and (c) the amount of tracking in the system.

School tracking has been found to be an important obstacle to intergenerational mobility. Using international data sets similar to ours from primary and secondary schools, Hanushek and Woessmann (2006) find that early tracking systems lead to more educational inequality because tracking accentuates the role of family background on student performance. Ammermüller (2005) studies the importance of the number of school types available in the system, obtaining similar conclusions. Brunello and Checchi (2007)

examine the impact of parental background across countries and time as a function of the age when tracking takes place and the length of tracking systems in a variety of student outcomes, including educational attainment, enrollment in college, employment, training, and wages. They find that tracking has a detrimental impact on educational attainment among students from lower parental background because it limits the possibility of attending tertiary education. However, the specialization induced by tracking systems appears to reduce the impact of parental background on learning outcomes among adults.

Most previous studies have looked at a particular form of tracking, namely, the early separation of children among well-defined segments in the educational process, typically specializing in general and vocational education. This form of tracking is not particularly prevalent in Latin America. However, educational systems also differ regarding the importance of grouping students by ability within schools, and hence this is the dimension of tracking we discuss here. For this purpose, we construct two variables: (a) *class tracking*, the percentage of students in each system who are divided by ability into different classes within schools for at least some subjects and (b) *grade tracking*, the percentage of schools that use student assessments to decide students' retention and promotion.

Considering the importance of sorting across economic background between public and private schools, we also keep the two variables characterizing the share of private schools in the country separate in the analysis. As before, we distinguish between purely private schools (those that are fully funded by private sources) and privately managed but publicly subsidized schools (those that receive some funding from the government).

The rest of the variables in the regression analysis are constructed using factor analysis, which reduces the dimensions of the institutional variables. The factor analysis of the remaining 22 variables suggests the existence of four well-identified groups of indicators. In what follows, we describe them and list the variables with the larger loadings in each of the categories:

- *High frequency of assessment practices.* A high score indicates that student assessments are done frequently in the schools. In particular, three variables are summarized by this factor: (a) the incidence of at least monthly teacher-developed tests, (b) incidence of at least monthly teacher's judgment ratings, and (c) incidence of at least monthly student assignments or projects or homework.
- *Accountability.* A high score indicates higher importance of student assessments in the system. Six variables are behind this factor: (a) assessments to compare the school with district or national performance, (b) monitoring of the school's progress from year to year, (c) comparing the school with others schools, (d) informing parents about their child's progress, (e) judging teachers' effectiveness, and (f) identifying aspects of instruction or the curriculum that could be improved.
- *Autonomy regarding students and course contents.* Higher scores indicate more autonomy of schools in (a) establishing student assessment policies, (b) determining course content, (c) choosing textbooks used, (d) determining the courses offered, (e) establishing student disciplinary policies, and (f) approving students for admission to the school.
- *Autonomy regarding staff.* Higher scores indicate more autonomy in the following areas that involve the management of school staff: (a) establishing teachers' starting salaries, (b) establishing teacher's salaries increase, (c) firing teachers, (d) hiring teachers, (e) deciding on budget allocations, and (f) formulating the school budget.

As comprehensive as this list of variables may seem at first sight, our study of the association of policies and the socioeconomic gradient of educational achievement cover only a subset of the policies that may be related to cross-country differences. In particular, because of data availability, all the policies analyzed pertain to interventions at the school level. Even within this domain, some potentially important variables such as those related to key infrastructure and equipment are not considered. In rural areas in poor countries, school availability of basic infrastructure (such as well-kept roofs and heating) and inputs (such as textbooks) may be an important constraint on children's learning.

Moreover, our analysis leaves out important influences that governments may have on the socioeconomic gradient of education by acting directly at the family level. These include not only taxes and transfers but also targeted programs to directly increase parents' competencies in an attempt to indirectly improve children's behavior and development. Little is known regarding the impact of such programs on the educational outcomes of the children.[14] On the side of subsidies, the prominent importance of conditional cash transfers (CCTs) in Latin America during the past decade is undeniable. Although there is a consensus that CCTs have been an effective tool in increasing educational attainment of poor children, their impact on educational achievement is still subject to debate (see box 3.5).

We proceed to analyze the association between each of these variables and the socioeconomic gradient of student achievement, following the methodology described in box 3.3. In table 3.2, we show regression results, highlighting the interaction term between the

---

BOX 3.5   Conditional cash transfers and children's educational outcomes

Conditional cash transfers (CCTs) are programs that transfer cash, generally to poor households, on the condition that those households make specified investments in the human capital of their children. Health and nutrition conditions generally require periodic checkups, growth monitoring, and vaccinations for children less than five years of age, prenatal care for mothers, and attendance by mothers at periodic health information talks. Education conditions usually include school enrollment, attendance on 80–85 percent of school days, and occasionally some measure of performance. Most CCT programs transfer the money to the mother of the household or to the student in some circumstances. Interest in CCTs has grown enormously in the past 10 years (Fiszbein et al. 2009).

In terms of educational outcomes, adults with more exposure to CCT programs have completed more years of schooling than have those with less exposure. There is also some evidence that CCT programs promote cognitive development in early childhood. Rigorous impact evaluations of the Mexican CCT program *Oportunidades* (originally known as *Progresa*) indicate that it has significantly increased the enrollment of children, particularly girls and especially at the secondary school level. The results imply that children will have an average of 0.7 years of extra schooling because of *Oportunidades*, although this effect may increase if children are more likely to go on to upper secondary school as a result of the program. Using panel data for Mexico for 1997–99 (Behrman, Gaviria, and Székely 2001; Skoufias and Parker 2001; Schultz 2004), it is shown that *Oportunidades* resulted in higher school attainment among indigenous children and a significant reduction in the gap between indigenous and nonindigenous children in other outcomes (Bando, López-Calva, and Patrinos 2005). Longer-run impacts include positive effects on schooling, reductions in work for younger youth (consistent with postponing labor force entry), increases in work for older girls, and shifts from agricultural to nonagricultural employment (Behrman, Parker, and Todd 2010).

In terms of the program's effect on occupational mobility, *Oportunidades* has a positive effect on job insertion because it increases beneficiaries' educational attainment. In addition, those who received the transfer for more than six years through primary and secondary education received salaries that were 12 percent and 14 percent higher, respectively, than the nonbeneficiaries (Rodríguez-Oreggia and Freije 2008). An updated version of this study shows that if migrants are included in the analysis, the effect on earning could be as high as 44 percent (Rodriguez-Oreggia 2011).

In Colombia, an interesting randomized trial compared three designs:

- A standard design
- A design that postponed part of the monthly transfers until children reenroll in school
- A design that lowered the reward for attendance but rewarded graduation and tertiary enrollment.

The two nonstandard designs significantly increased enrollment rates at both the secondary and tertiary levels while delivering the same attendance gains as the standard design. Postponing some of the attendance transfers until the time of reenrollment appeared particularly effective for the most at-risk children (Barrera-Osorio et al. 2011).

A number of evaluations have concluded that the higher enrollment levels have not resulted in better performance on achievement tests, even after accounting for selection into school (see, for example, Fiszbein et al. 2009; Ponce and Bedi 2010).

(Box continues next page)

BOX 3.5   Conditional cash transfers and children's educational outcomes   *(continued)*

Thus, the potential for CCTs to improve learning on their own may be limited. To be clear, CCTs are not designed to improve children's performance at school but rather to increase enrollment. Still, it is interesting to see whether CCTs have had a positive indirect effect on achievement or whether other tools should be used for that purpose.

There are various reasons why CCTs may have had only modest effects on "final" outcomes. One possibility is that CCTs, as currently designed, do not address some important constraints at the household level. These constraints could include poor parenting practices, inadequate information, or other inputs (or lack thereof) into the production of education. Another possibility is that the quality of services is so low—perhaps especially for the poor— that increased use of CCTs alone does not yield large benefits in terms of student achievement.

TABLE 3.2   Interaction of school practices and parental background on reading test scores

	Interaction of policy variable with		
	Parental education (1)	Home possessions (2)	ESCS (3)
Highest education of parents	6.987***		
	(0.489)		
Home possessions		26.37***	
		(1.388)	
Index of socioeconomic status (ESCS)			34.67***
			(1.448)
Teacher qualification	−0.00821*	−0.0731***	−0.0564***
	(0.00422)	(0.0144)	(0.0141)
Incidence of private schools	0.00895	0.0504	−0.0582
	(0.0280)	(0.104)	(0.0998)
Incidence of publicly funded private schools	−0.0591***	−0.113***	−0.214***
	(0.00573)	(0.0200)	(0.0222)
Grade tracking	0.00987*	0.0777***	0.0314**
	(0.00536)	(0.0151)	(0.0158)
Class tracking	0.0148***	0.00741	0.0707***
	(0.00489)	(0.0140)	(0.0155)
High frequency of assessments	−0.559***	0.809*	−0.157
	(0.177)	(0.446)	(0.556)
Accountability	−0.824***	−2.553***	−3.205***
	(0.175)	(0.490)	(0.613)
Autonomy in selecting courses and determining student	1.050***	2.404***	3.583***
	(0.149)	(0.446)	(0.497)
Autonomy in selecting staff and budget	0.703***	−0.698	1.723***
	(0.141)	(0.462)	(0.476)
Constant	331.4***	434.0***	436.2***
	(2.105)	(1.767)	(1.693)
Observations	422,332	428,984	428,516
R-squared	0.330	0.340	0.375

Source: Data from PISA 2009.
Note: PISA = Program for International Student Assessment. ESCS = PISA index of economic, social, and cultural status. Results correspond to a pooled regression for all countries, with country-fixed effects and as control variables gender, urban dummy, and immigration status. Standard errors (in parentheses) are clustered at the school level.
*** $p < 0.01$, ** $p < 0.05$, * $p < 0.1$

institutional variable of interest and parental background. For robustness, we run the regressions for three alternative measures of parental background: parental education, an index of home asset holdings, and the overall ESCS index. Figure 3.16 then highlights the impact of the variables that proved to be significant in the ESCS regression by depicting the effect of one standard deviation of parental background on the average test score in two scenarios: in a representative country where the level of the policy variable is high and in a representative country where such a level is low.

Countries with a larger share of publicly funded private schools tend to have a smaller socioeconomic gradient, controlling for other school factors. One standard deviation in the average ESCS in a country like Indonesia (where 34 percent of all schools are publicly funded private schools) results in test scores that are nine points lower than in a country like Uruguay, where no private school received government subsidies. A possible interpretation of this result is that government funding of private schools increases the choice of schools available to worse-off families, hence decreasing inequality of educational opportunities. This result is consistent with Woessmann et al. (2009).

On the other hand, there is no significant difference in the socioeconomic gradient for countries with either a high or low incidence of private nonsubsidized schools. Hence, it is the combination of private management but guaranteed public financing that is associated with a lower gap in achievements between the rich and the poor. This combination of publicly funded but privately operated systems has been proven to be causally related to higher performance in other contexts, for example in the Netherlands, where more than 80 percent of the students are enrolled in these types of schools, but education is free for the compulsory first 10 years of schooling (Patrinos 2012). In Latin America, prominent examples of this mixed system are the voucher programs in Chile and Colombia, which also appear to be related to less inequality in educational achievements (see box 3.6)

FIGURE 3.16   School practices and reading test scores for high and low values of selected policies

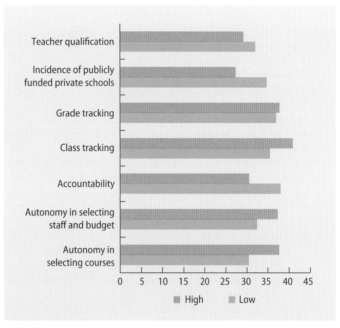

Source: Data from PISA 2009.
Note: ESCS = PISA index of economic, social, and cultural status; PISA = Program for International Student Assessment. Bars represent the effect of one standard deviation of ESCS on test scores when the policy is set at a high level (green bar) and a low one (orange bar). School variables in the graph include only those whose interaction with ESCS is significant in the regression and for which the difference between high and low are statistically significant at 5 percent level. Results correspond to a pooled regression for all countries, with country-fixed effects and as control variables gender, urban dummy, and immigration status. Standard errors are clustered at the school level.

A priori, the impact of teacher quality on the achievement gap between rich and poor kids is not clear. Better-educated teachers might be frustrated with poor-performing students and concentrate on bringing those more capable upward, increasing the gap between poor and high performers. On the other hand, better-educated teachers are more likely to be better trained to deal with classes that are more heterogeneous and hence more able to increase the pace without leaving behind the worst-performing students. Our results suggest that the latter effect appears to be dominant, inasmuch as countries with a higher proportion of teachers with an ISCED5A (International Standard Classification of Education) certification, an indicator of teacher quality, present a lower gap in test scores between rich and poor students.

BOX 3.6   Voucher systems in Chile and Colombia: Did they help the achievements of the poor?

Chile was one of the first countries to implement a school choice program for the stated purpose of improving efficiency in education. But as important as the 1981 program was, the nationwide implementation presents two important difficulties for evaluating its impact. First, participation was not randomized; therefore, it is difficult to disentangle the effects of the program from the inherent difference in populations due to self-selection. Second, it is a universal program, implying that the counterfactual of no vouchers is difficult to construct (Hoxby 2003).

In spite of these difficulties, the school choice program in Chile has been subject to a high level of scrutiny. The earlier literature presents mixed results, to say the least, but identification of causal impacts is difficult for the aforementioned reasons (see, for example, Aedo 1997; Aedo and Larrañaga 1994; Contreras 2001; Rodríguez 1988; Gallegos 2002; Mizala and Romaguera 2000). More recently, several strategies to overcome the problem of self-selection using the Heckman correction method (see, for example, Sapelli and Vial 2004) and instrumental variables (IV) approaches (see, for example, Auguste and Valenzuela 2004; Gallegos 2002; Hsieh and Urquiola 2006) have been proposed. According to an evaluation by Henríquez et al. (2012), voucher schools run by Sociedad de Instrucción Primaria (SIP) that serve low-income students obtain test scores that are up to one standard deviation higher than those obtained by public schools, and up to 70 percent of one standard deviation higher than private voucher schools in Santiago. Furthermore, the performance of SIP schools is similar to that of private nonvoucher schools, which typically serve the elite families in Chile. Long-term benefits of vouchers have been examined with IV estimates and show significant effects in the labor market (Bravo, Mukhopadhyay, and Todd 2010; Patrinos and Sakellariou 2011).

Colombia, in an effort to increase access to secondary schools, offered funding to private schools that enrolled students from poor families. This became known as the secondary school voucher program, the *Programa de Ampliación de Cobertura de la Educación Secundaria* (PACES). Launched in 1991, the program provided the poorest third of its population with access to secondary education. Running until 1997, PACES covered more than a quarter of a million students. The vouchers were renewable through to the end of high school as long as the student continued to progress. More than three-quarters of the beneficiaries renewed their vouchers. The vouchers could be used at private academic and vocational schools, and about 40 percent of private schools accepted them. The unit costs for participating private schools were 40 percent lower than for nonparticipating private schools.

Due to oversubscription in the program, available places were allocated by lottery. This created a natural, randomized experiment that enabled researchers to undertake rigorous impact evaluations of the program and test several hypotheses. The results for this targeted voucher program are encouraging. Researchers found that voucher beneficiaries had higher educational attainment: they were 10 percent more likely to finish the eighth grade three years after they won the vouchers. They were also 5–6 percent less likely to repeat a grade. They scored 0.2 standard deviations higher on achievement tests than nonvoucher students. And they were 20 percent more likely to take the college entrance exam than students who had not won a voucher in the lottery. They were also 0.6–1.0 percent less likely to be married and 2.5–3.0 percent less likely to be working (Angrist et al. 2002). In a study of longer-term effects, Angrist, Bettinger, and Kremer (2006) found that the program improved scores for both average students and those over the 90th percentile.

Yet another study tested whether vouchers increased educational productivity or were purely redistributive, benefiting recipients by giving them access to more desirable peers at others' expense. Among the voucher applicants to vocational schools, lottery winners were less likely to attend academic secondary schools and thus had peers with less-desirable observable characteristics. Despite this, lottery winners had better educational outcomes. Hence, in this population, vouchers improved educational outcomes through channels beyond redistribution of desirable peers (Bettinger, Kremer, and Saavedra 2010).

School accountability is a last factor associated with a lower socioeconomic gradient in student achievements. Countries where students' assessments are used to compare schools with others and where year-to-year performance is monitored are, on average, more equitable (once we control for other factors). In randomized evaluations that can identify the causal effects of increasing accountability in schools, the evidence suggests a positive role for accountability in promoting the performance of the system.

Consistent with the literature summarized above, in countries prone to use pupils' assessments to assign them to grades and classes, the test score gap between rich and poor kids is larger. The differences in the impact of one standard deviation in ESCS on test scores in the United States—where class tracking is prevalent (88 percent of schools use this method in one way or another)—is more than 6 percentage points larger than in other countries such as Brazil, where only 10 percent of the schools use such tracking.

Regarding school autonomy, the expected impact on the socioeconomic gradient of the children's test scores is, in principle, ambiguous. On the one hand, school autonomy may allow greater influence of parents in transforming children's potential into higher achievements (Ammermüller 2005). To the extent that sorting according to parental preferences or resources is important in a country, it may lead to larger inequalities in achievement. On the other hand, greater school autonomy may allow schools to adapt their curriculum and structure to try to mitigate possible learning difficulties or delays of less-well-off children.

The two variables capturing autonomy of schools (autonomy regarding students and course contents and autonomy regarding staff) yielded similar results in the analysis. In both cases, higher school autonomy is associated with a higher degree of intergenerational persistence, but the magnitude of the effect is larger in the case of more autonomy regarding students and course contents. In this case, the difference in the socioeconomic gradient

between high- and low-autonomy countries is about 7 points in the PISA test score.

Conclusions

This chapter has documented the extent of intergenerational mobility in Latin American countries and compared it with other developed and developing economies. The comparative analysis allowed us to draw several conclusions:

- On the positive side, the 2000s showed a notable decline in the inequality of opportunities related to educational attainment. The children born to households that are disadvantaged (whether due to the parents' lower education or lower income) are less likely to be delayed in schools today than they were in the 1990s.
- Similarly, delays in school attainment associated with ethnic minority groups are less prevalent today than they were in the recent past.
- In educational achievement, the evidence is scarcer and more complicated to evaluate, but it suggests very limited, if any, improvements during the 2000s.
- The negative note comes from the long road ahead that must be traveled to achieve an equal-opportunity environment for Latin American children. In spite of the progress made, Latin American countries display some of the lowest levels of intergenerational mobility in income or education in the world.

The chapter has also provided some tentative evidence of the correlates of cross-country differences in educational achievement, and has reviewed some of the key findings from the impact evaluation literature in this area:

- Better teachers, more accountable and transparent schools, and a mixed system of public funding with private provision are associated with more intergenerational mobility in the sense that children's educational outcomes are less affected by parental background.

- School tracking (that is, the grouping of students according to their ability or performance) and school autonomy appear instead to work to the detriment of students from poor socioeconomic backgrounds and in favor of those with better-educated or higher-income parents.
- An important factor that appears to be behind the strong intergenerational educational persistence in Latin America is the high inequality of the region's educational system. The differences in the characteristics of the schools attended by children from advantageous backgrounds and those attended by children from poor socioeconomic backgrounds are larger in Latin America than in most of the other regions covered in this chapter.

Bounding the estimates of parental background on student achievement

Test-score data sets such as SERCE and PISA, as used in this chapter, allow us to estimate the gap in school achievement according to pupils' parental background. The problem is that, most often, social scientists and policy makers are interested in the degree of interdependency for the society as a whole rather than only among those attending school. This becomes particularly relevant when comparing countries with varying rates of school enrollments. For instance, almost all children aged 15 in Chile are enrolled in seventh grade or above, whereas in Peru only 6 out of 10 are (see figure F3.1A). Similarly, almost all 12-year-old Uruguayans attend third grade or above, while 70 percent of Guatemalans do. More important, these proportions vary significantly, depending on the socioeconomic status of the child's family. Case in point: a Guatemalan child born from secondary-educated parents will most certainly attend school at

age 12, as is the case in Uruguay for any child, but if he or she had parents with no education, the child has only a 60 percent chance of being in school at age 12.

The problem in calculating the importance of parental background on children's achievements for the whole population using schooled-based data sets is that information on the test scores that the nonenrolled children would have had *were they in school* is not available. Additionally, selection into school is most likely not random, so that the observed distribution is unlikely to be a good indication of test scores for the nonenrolled children. One alternative is to construct reasonable lower and upper bounds on the distribution of test scores for the nonobserved population and combine it with the observed one. This approach to missing data has been proposed by Manski (1994) and Manski and Pepper (2000) and used by, among others, Blundell et al. (2007) to study wage

FIGURE F3.1A   School enrollment rates, selected Latin American countries
percentage

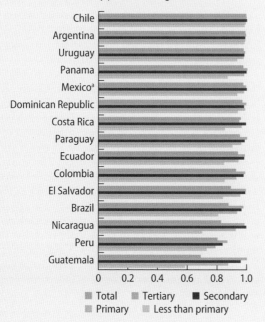

a. Proportion of children (age 11–12) attending 3rd grade or above, by parental background

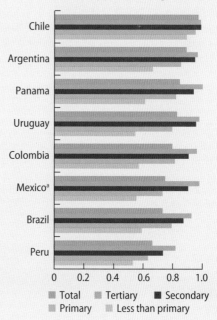

b. Proportion of children (age 15) attending 7th grade or above, by parental background

Source: Lugo and Messina 2012.
a. For Mexico, the data is from the state of Nuevo León (NLE).

(Box continues next page)

| Focus Note 3.1 | *Bounding the estimates of parental background on student achievement*   (continued) |

inequality and educational and gender differentials in the United Kingdom, to allow for the nonrandom selection into work.

Lugo and Messina (2012) apply Manski's approach to test score data from SERCE and PISA for children aged 11–12 and 15, respectively. Bounds are constructed, imposing positive selection into school in a weak sense; that is, children currently not in school are assumed to perform no better than those in school with similar backgrounds. Strictly speaking, the assumption is that, conditional on parental background, the test score distribution of nonenrolled individuals is first-order, stochastically dominated by the distribution of enrolled children. For each level of parental education, the observed distribution of test scores is combined with the two extreme distributions for the nonenrolled to compute the lower and upper bounds.

Formally, the method can be described as follows. The cumulative distribution function of interest is that of children's test scores, conditional on parental education, denoted $F(ts/pe)$, where ts is the test score and pe is the level of parental education, expressed as a categorical variable. Selection is indicated by the indicator function E. When a child attends school, $E = 1$, whereas when he or she does not, $E = 0$. While $F(ts/pe)$ is not observed, because of nonrandom selection, we can write

$$F(ts/pe) = F(ts/pe, E = 1)P(pe)$$
$$+ F(ts/pe, E = 0)[1 - P(pe)], \quad \text{(F3.1a)}$$

where $P(pe)$ is the probability of attending school, conditional on parental education. Lugo and Messina (2012) calculate these probabilities (enrollment rates) from national household surveys.

The assumption of positive selection into school implies that

$$F(ts/pe, E = 1) \leq$$
$$F(ts/pe, E = 0) \; \forall ts, \; \forall pe \quad \text{(F3.1b)}$$

Under this assumption, the bounds to the distribution of test scores is

$$F(ts/pe, E = 1) \leq F(ts/pe) \leq F(ts/pe, E = 1)$$
$$P(pe) + [1 - P(pe)]. \quad \text{(F3.1c)}$$

For each of these two distributions on either side of the inequality, one can compute the median test score for each level of parental education. The median derived from the distribution on the left will give the upper bound for that level of parental education, denoted by $ts^{(u)}(pe)$, while the median derived from the right side of the inequality will give the lower bound of test score, $ts^{(l)}(pe)$.

From here, one can compute the differences between test scores of children from different parental education (for example, tertiary versus primary) as follows:

$$ts^{(l)}(pe = tertiary) - ts^{(u)}(pe = primary)$$
$$\leq D \leq ts^{(u)}(pe = tertiary)$$
$$- ts^{(l)}(pe = primary). \quad \text{(F3.1d)}$$

These results are presented in figure F3.1b.

As explained in the chapter, in countries where the selection is small, the lower and upper bounds of the differences in sixth-grade test scores are very close to each other. In these cases, one can get a fairly accurate estimate of the true gap in performance. See, for instance, Argentina, Chile, or Uruguay, where although the difference in test scores is significantly high (above one standard deviation), the bounds are extremely tight so that the point estimate is a fairly good approximation of the true difference.

Instead, in countries where a significant proportion of children do not attend school, the distances between the lower estimates of the gap and the upper bound can be quite large. An extreme case is that of Guatemala when comparing the differences in test scores for children of tertiary-educated parents with those whose parents had no education. The bounds indicate that the true test score difference lies somewhere between 80 and 180 (that is, between one and two standard deviations). Importantly, although the estimate from the observed distribution (black dot) will indicate that the gap in Guatemala is among the smallest in the region, the bounds will indicate that it is possible that, instead, the gap between the highest and lowest parental background is indeed the largest of all. Similar results, though to a lesser extent, are found in Brazil, Colombia, and Nicaragua, where their position in the region in terms of degree of intergenerational dependence differ once we incorporate information on the nonenrolled individuals.

Focus Note 3.1   *(continued)*

FIGURE F3.1B   **Inequalities in reading test scores of sixth-grade students, selected Latin American countries, 2006**

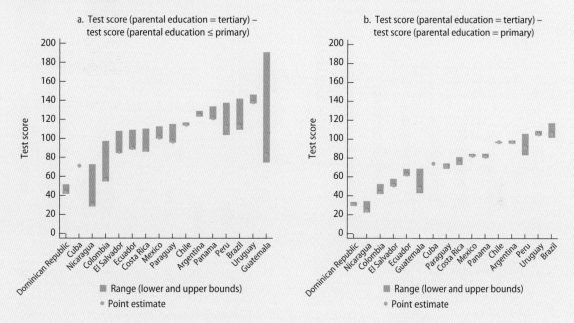

Sources: Lugo and Messina 2012; SERCE and SEDLAC (Socioeconomic Database for Latin America and the Caribbean) data.

The problem of nonenrollment is, naturally, more acute for older children. PISA surveys children aged 15 who are enrolled in school in seventh grade or above. As shown in figure F3.1c, the proportion of children of that age who are not in school or fall behind significantly is, in some countries, quite large. This leads to much larger bounds in the estimates of the performance gap, with the notable exception of Chile, where, even for children of lower socioeconomic background, the enrollment rate is 97 percent. According to these results, one can be confident that the test-score gap between children from primary and tertiary parental education is larger in Chile, Peru, and Uruguay than in Brazil, Colombia, and Panama. Similarly, irrespective of performance of nonattendant children, the differences in test scores by parental education are larger in Uruguay than in Chile.

Focus Note 3.1   *Bounding the estimates of parental background on student achievement* *(continued)*

FIGURE F3.1C   **Inequalities in reading test scores at age 15, selected Latin American countries, 2009**

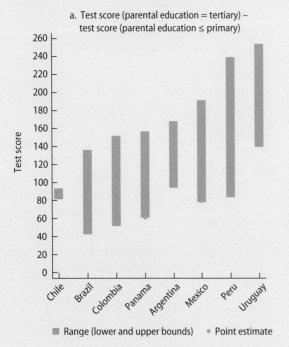

a. Test score (parental education = tertiary) –
    test score (parental education ≤ primary)

Test score

Chile, Brazil, Colombia, Panama, Argentina, Mexico, Peru, Uruguay

■ Range (lower and upper bounds)   ● Point estimate

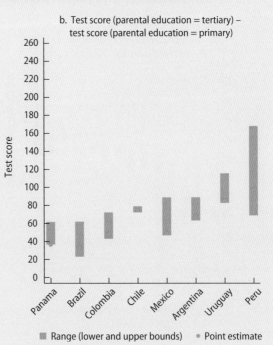

b. Test score (parental education = tertiary) –
    test score (parental education = primary)

Test score

Panama, Brazil, Colombia, Chile, Mexico, Argentina, Uruguay, Peru

■ Range (lower and upper bounds)   ● Point estimate

Sources: Lugo and Messina 2012; PISA and SEDLAC (Socioeconomic Database for Latin America and the Caribbean) data.

Notes

1. See Card (2001) and the references therein for an overview.
2. The educational gap and its relationship with parental background are studied in Andersen (2001) for a cross-section of Latin American countries and in Behrman, Gaviria, and Székely (2001) for 16 Latin American countries during the period 1980–96.
3. The schooling gap is calculated for children living with their parents because other information is not available in the household surveys. For this reason, we do not calculate the schooling gap for individuals older than 18.
4. Fields (1996) proposes a decomposition of the R-squared in a regression that allows separating the contributions of each different variable (or set of variables) in the explanation of the overall variance. Like the correlation coefficient, this measure is invariant to the variance in either parental background or children's schooling gaps. Using this proposed methodology, we find that the percentage of the variance in the schooling gap explained by parental income and education declines steadily in the Latin American region.
5. Evaluating the evolution of the educational gap associated with ethnic minorities is particularly challenging when the information comes from household surveys and hence is self-declared. The decision to declare belonging to a certain ethnic minority group (or not) depends on social norms and attitudes toward ethnic minorities, which are likely to change over time. This in turn introduces a problem of selection that we are not addressing in this chapter. For this reason, the results regarding differences in educational gaps associated with ethnicity should be interpreted with caution.
6. The index was constructed using principal component analysis in two steps: first, on asset holdings and dwelling characteristics; second, combining the resulting index with the maximum years of schooling of the parents.
7. In the chapter, we will restrict the attention to results from the reading literacy test, which was the focus of the 2009 PISA survey, but results are qualitatively similar for math.
8. An additional challenge from PISA is that it is representative only of urban areas. This introduces serious limitations in cross-country comparisons, considering that the distribution of the population across urban and rural areas varies greatly across countries, and in particular between developing and developed countries.
9. A related approach is proposed by Ferreira and Gignoux (2011).
10. Aedo and Walker (2011) study the changes in the gradient of socioeconomic status on PISA test scores in seven Latin American countries between 2000 and 2009, also finding mixed results.
11. The main difference is that we need to control for life-cycle effects because we are comparing adults of different ages with parents of different ages. This is done by including in the regressions a full set of dummy variables for fathers' and children's ages.
12. We define developing countries as those with a GDP per capita purchasing power parity below US$20,000 in 2009.
13. Each group is composed of the following countries: "Nordic countries" include Denmark, Finland, Iceland, Norway, and Sweden. "Anglo-Saxon" countries include Australia, Canada, Ireland, and New Zealand. "Continental Europe" includes Austria, Belgium, France, Germany, Greece, Italy, Liechtenstein, Luxembourg, the Netherlands, Portugal, Spain, and Switzerland. "High-Income" economies include Croatia; the Czech Republic; Estonia; Hong Kong SAR, China; Hungary; Indonesia; Israel; Japan; Kazakhstan; the Republic of Korea; Jordan; Kyrgyzstan; Latvia; Macao SAR, China; Poland; Qatar; the Slovak Republic; Slovenia; Shanghai, China; Taiwan, China; Singapore; and Dubai (United Arab Emirates). "Low-Middle Income" countries include Albania, Azerbaijan, Bulgaria, Lithuania, Montenegro, Romania, the Russian Federation, Serbia, Tunisia, Thailand, and Turkey. "Latin America" includes Argentina, Brazil, Chile, Colombia, Mexico, Panama, Peru, Trinidad and Tobago, and Uruguay. "United Kingdom-United States" includes the United Kingdom and United States.
14. The School Management Support program (*Apoyo a La Gestión Escolar*; AGE) in Mexico is a randomized trial that doubled resources and hence the school responsibilities of parent associations in highly disadvantaged rural communities in four high-poverty states with a high concentration of indigenous peoples. Gertler, Patrinos, and Rodríguez-Oreggia

(2012) found that AGE improved learning outcomes by almost a quarter of a standard deviation. A separate component designed to test the impact of training parents in organizing themselves (but with no cash grant) also proved successful compared with a group of schools receiving neither grants nor training. The effects of training alone are slightly higher than the cash grant, though the schools are not directly comparable.

References

Aedo, Cristian. 1997. "Organización Industrial de la Prestación de Servicios Sociales." Research Network Working Paper 3001, Inter-American Development Bank, Washington, DC.

Aedo, Cristian, and Osvaldo Larrañaga. 1994. "Educación Privada vs. Pública en Chile: Calidad y Sesgo de Selección." Unpublished paper, postgraduate program in economics, Latin American Institute of Doctrine and Social Studies and Georgetown University, Washington, DC.

Aedo, Christian, and Ian Walker. 2011. *Skills for the 21st Century in Latin America and the Caribbean*. Directions in Development Series. Washington DC: World Bank.

Almås, Ingvild, Alexander W. Cappelen, Thori J. Lind, Erik Sorensen, and Bertil Tungodden. 2011. "Measuring Unfair (In)Equality." *Journal of Public Economics* 95 (7–8): 488–99.

Ammermüller, Andreas. 2005. "Educational Opportunities and the Role of Institutions." Research Memoranda 004, ROA, Research Centre for Education and the Labour Market, Maastricht, Netherlands.

Andersen, Lykke. 2001. "Social Mobility in Latin America: Links with Adolescent Schooling." Research Network Working Paper 3130, Inter-American Development Bank, Washington, DC.

Angrist, Joshua, Eric Bettinger, Erik Bloom, Elizabeth King, and Michal Kremer. 2002. "Vouchers for Private Schooling in Colombia: Evidence from a Randomized Natural Experiment." *American Economic Review* 92 (5): 1535–58.

Angrist, Joshua, Eric Bettinger, and Michael Kremer. 2006. "Long-Term Educational Consequences of Secondary School Vouchers: Evidence from Administrative Records in Colombia." *American Economic Review* 96 (3): 847–62.

Arneson, Richard. 1989. "Equality and Equality of Opportunity for Welfare." *Philosophical Studies* 56 (1): 77–93.

Atkinson, Anthony B. 1981. "On Intergenerational Income Mobility in Britain." *Journal of Post Keynesian Economics* 3 (2): 194–218.

Auguste, Sebastian, and Juan P. Valenzuela. 2004. "Do Students Benefit from School Competition? Evidence from Chile." Doctoral dissertation, University of Michigan, Ann Arbor.

Azevedo, João Pedro, Alejandro Gaviria, Roberto Angulo, and Gustavo Nicolás Paez. 2012. "Social Mobility in Colombia." Unpublished paper, World Bank, Washington, DC.

Bando, Rosagenla, Luis F. López-Calva, and Harry A. Patrinos. 2005. "Child Labor, School Attendance, and Indigenous Households: Evidence from Mexico." Policy Research Working Paper 3487, World Bank, Washington, DC.

Barrera-Osorio, Felipe, Marianne Bertrand, Leight L. Linden, and Francisco Perez-Calle. 2011. "Improving the Design of Conditional Transfer Programs: Evidence from a Randomized Education Experiment in Colombia." *American Economic Journal: Applied Economics* 3 (2): 167–95.

Becker, Gary S., and Nigel Tomes. 1979. "An Equilibrium Theory of the Distribution of Income and Intergenerational Mobility." *Journal of Political Economy* 87 (6): 1153–89.

Behrman, Jere R., Alejandro Gaviria, and Miguel Székely. 2001. "Intergenerational Mobility in Latin America." *Journal of the Latin American and Caribbean Economic Association* 2 (1): 1–44.

Behrman, Jere R., Susan W. Parker, and Petra Todd. 2010. "Do Conditional Cash Transfers for Schooling Generate Lasting Benefits? A Five-Year Followup of PROGRESA/Oportunidades." *Journal of Human Resources* 46 (1): 93–122.

Behrman, Jere R., and Paul Taubman. 1990. "The Intergenerational Correlation between Children's Adult Earnings and Their Parents' Income: Results from the Michigan Panel Survey of Income Dynamics." *Review of Income and Wealth* 36 (2): 115–27.

Bénabou, Roland, and Efe A. Ok. 2001. "Social Mobility and the Demand for Redistribution: The Poum Hypothesis." *The Quarterly Journal of Economics* 116 (2): 447–87.

Bettinger, Eric, Michael Kremer, and Juan E. Saavedra. 2010 "Are Educational Vouchers Only

Redistributive?" *Economic Journal* 120 (546): F204–F228.

Björklund, Anders, and Markus Jäntti. 2009. "Intergenerational Income Mobility and the Role of Family Background." In *The Oxford Handbook of Economic Inequality*, ed. W. Salverda, B. Nolan, and T. M. Smeeding, 491–521. Oxford, U.K.: Oxford University Press.

Björklund, Anders, and Kjell G. Salvanes. 2011. "Education and Family Background: Mechanisms and Policies." In *Handbook of the Economics of Education*, *Vol. 3*, ed. E. Hanushek, S. Machin, and L. Woessmann, 201–47. San Diego: Elsevier

Black, Sandra E., and Paul J. Devereux. 2011. "Recent Developments in Intergenerational Mobility." In *Handbook of Labor Economics*, ed. O. Ashenfelter, R. Layard, and D. Card, 1487–1542. San Diego: Elsevier.

Blundell, Richard, Amanda Gosling, Hidehiko Ichimura, and Costas Meghir. 2007. "Changes in the Distribution of Male and Female Wages Accounting for Employment Composition Using Bounds." *Econometrica* 75 (2): 323–63.

Bravo, David, Sankar Mukhopadhyay, and Petra E. Todd. 2010. "Effects of School Reform on Education and Labor Market Performance: Evidence from Chile's Universal Voucher System." *Quantitative Economics* 1 (1): 47–95.

Brown, Meta, John K. Scholz, and Anath Seshadri. 2009. "A New Test of Borrowing Constraints for Education." Working Paper 14879, National Bureau of Economic Research, Cambridge, MA.

Brunello, Giorgio, and Daniele Checchi. 2007. "Does School Tracking Affect Equality of Opportunity? New International Evidence." *Economic Policy* 22 (52): 781–861.

Busso, Matias, Martin Cicowiez, and Leonardo Gasparini. 2005. "Ethnicity and the Millennium Development Goals in Latin America and the Caribbean." Joint publication of Economic Commission for Latin America and the Caribbean (of the United Nations), Inter-American Development Bank, United Nations Development Programme, and World Bank, Washington, DC.

Card, David. 2001. "Estimating the Return to Schooling: Progress on Some Persistent Econometric Problems." *Econometrica* 69 (5): 1127–60.

Carneiro, Pedro, and James J. Heckman. 2002. "The Evidence on Credit Constraints in Post-Secondary Schooling." *The Economic Journal* 112 (482): 705–34.

Causa, Orsetta, and Catherine Chapuis. 2009. "Equity in Student Achievement Across OECD Countries: An Investigation of the Role of Policies." Economics Department Working Paper 708, Organisation for Economic Co-operation and Development, Paris.

Chong, Alberto, and Hugo R. Ñopo. 2008. "The Mystery of Discrimination in Latin America." *Journal of the Latin American and Caribbean Economic Association* 8 (2): 79–115.

Cohen, Gerald A. 1989. "On the Currency of Egalitarian Justice." *Ethics* 99 (4): 906–944.

Contreras, Dante. 2001. "Evaluating a Voucher System in Chile: Individual, Family, and School Characteristics." Working Paper 175, Facultad de Ciencias Económicas y Administrativas, Universidad de Chile, Santiago.

Corak, Miles. Forthcoming. "Inequality from Generation to Generation: The United States in Comparison." In *The Economics of Inequality, Poverty and Discrimination in the 21st Century*, ed. Robert Rycroft. Santa Barbara, CA: ABC-CLIO.

Cruces, Guillermo, Marcelo Bergolo, Fedora Carbajal, Adriana Conconi, and Andres Ham. 2011. "Are There Ethnic Inequality Traps in Education? Empirical Evidence for Brazil and Chile." Joint publication of the Center for Distributive, Labor and Social Studies of the Universidad Nacional de La Plata and Consejo Nacional de Investigaciones Científicas y Técnicas, Argentina.

Currie, Janet. 2009. "Healthy, Wealthy, and Wise: Socioeconomic Status, Poor Health in Childhood, and Human Capital Development." *Journal of Economic Literature* 47 (1): 87–122.

———. 2011. "Inequality at Birth: Some Causes and Consequences." *American Economic Review: Papers and Proceedings* 101: 1–22

Currie, Janet, and Duncan Thomas. 2000. "School Quality and the Longer-Term Effects of Head Start." *The Journal of Human Resources* 35 (4): 755–74.

Dearden, Lorraine, Steve Machin, and Howard Reed. 1997. "Intergenerational Mobility in Britain." *The Economic Journal* 107 (440): 47–66.

Ferreira, Francisco H. G., and Jérémie Gignoux. 2011. "The Measurement of Educational Inequality: Achievement and

Opportunity." Policy Research Working Paper 5873, World Bank, Washington, DC.

Fields, Gary S. 1996. "Accounting for Income Inequality and Its Change: A New Method, with Application to the Distribution of Earnings in the United States." In *Research in Labor Economics*, ed. S. Polachek. Bingley, U.K.: Emerald Group Publishing Limited.

Fiszbein, Ariel, Norbert Schady, Francisco H. G. Ferreira, Margaret Grosh, Nial Kelleher, Pedro Olinto, and Emmanuel Skoufias. 2009. "Conditional Cash Transfers: Reducing Present and Future Poverty." Policy Research Report, World Bank, Washington DC.

Gallegos, Francisco. 2002. "Competencia y Resultados Educativos: Teoría y Evidencia para Chile." *Latin American Journal of Economics (formerly Cuadernos de Economía)* 39 (118): 309–52.

Gertler, Paul, Harry Patrinos, and Eduardo Rodríguez-Oreggia. 2012. "Parental Empowerment in Mexico: Randomized Experiment of the *Apoyo a La Gestion Escolar* (AGE) Program in Rural Primary Schools in Mexico." Research report, Society for Research on Educational Effectiveness, Evanston, IL.

Hanushek, Eric A., and Ludger Woessmann. 2006. "Does Educational Tracking Affect Performance and Inequality? Differences-in-Differences Evidence across Countries." *Economic Journal* 116 (510): C63–C76.

———. 2011. "How Much Do Educational Outcomes Matter in OECD Countries?" *Economic Policy* 26 (67): 427–91.

Harbison, Ralph W., and Eric A. Hanushek. 1992. *Educational Performance of the Poor: Lessons from Rural Northeast Brazil*. Oxford, U.K.: Oxford University Press.

Haveman, Robert, and Barbara Wolfe. 1995. "The Determinants of Children's Attainments: A Review of Methods and Findings." *Journal of Economic Literature* 33 (4): 1829–78.

Henríquez, Francisco, Bernardo Lara, Alejandra Mizala, and Andrea Repetto. 2012. "Effective Schools Do Exist: Low-Income Children's Academic Performance in Chile." *Applied Economics Letters* 19 (5): 445–51.

Hertz, Tom, Tamara Jayasundera, Patrizio Piraino, Sibel Selcuk, Nicole Smith, and Alina Verashchagina. 2007. "The Inheritance of Educational Inequality: International Comparisons and Fifty-Year Trends." *The B.E. Journal of Economic Analysis and Policy* 7 (2).

Hoxby, Caroline M. 2003. "School Choice and School Competition: Evidence from the United States." *Swedish Economic Policy Review* 10 (2): 9–65.

Hsieh, Chang-Tai, and Miguel Urquiola. 2006. "The Effects of Generalized School Choice on Achievement and Stratification: Evidence from Chile's Voucher Program." *Journal of Public Economics* 90 (8–9): 1477–503.

Jäntti, Markus. 2012. *Family Associations in Economic Status in Developed Countries: A Review of Approaches*. Washington, DC: World Bank.

Justino, Patricia, and Arnab Acharya. 2003. "Inequality in Latin America: Processes and Inputs." Working Paper 22, Poverty Research Unit, University of Sussex, U.K.

Keane, Michael, and Kenneth I. Wolpin. 2001. "The Effect of Parental Transfers and Borrowing Constraints on Educational Attainment." *International Economic Review* 42 (4): 1051–103.

Krugman, Paul. 1992. "The Rich, the Right, and the Facts." *The American Prospect* 11: 19–31.

Lugo, Maria Ana, and Julian Messina. 2012. "Student Achievement: Correcting for Selection into School Using Non-Parametric Bounds." Unpublished background paper for the current volume of *Economic Mobility and the Rise of the Latin Middle Class*, World Bank, Washington, DC.

Manski, Charles. 1994. "The Selection Problem." In *Advances in Econometrics, Sixth World Congress, vol. 1*, ed. C. Sims, 143–170. Cambridge, U.K.: Cambridge University Press.

Manski, Charles, and John Pepper. 2000. "Monotone Instrumental Variables: With Application to the Returns to Schooling." *Econometrica* 68 (4): 997–1010.

McIntosh, Steven, and Anna Vignoles. 2001. "Measuring and Assessing the Impact of Basic Skills on Labour Market Outcomes." *Oxford Economic Papers* 53 (3): 453–81.

Mizala, Alejandra, and Pilar Romaguera. 2000. "School Performance and Choice: The Chilean Experience." *Journal of Human Resources* 35 (2): 392–417.

Neal, Derek A., and William R. Johnson. 1996. "The Role of Premarket Factors in Black-White Wage Differences." *Journal of Political Economy* 104 (5): 869–95.

OECD (Organisation for Economic Co-operation and Development). 2011. "PISA 2009

Technical Report (Preliminary Version)." OECD, Paris.

Patrinos, Harry A. 2012. "Private Education Provision and Public Finance: The Netherlands." In *Education Economics*, forthcoming. Online publication at http://www.tandfonline.com/doi/abs/10.1080/09645292.2011.568696.

Patrinos, Harry A., and Christos Sakellariou. 2011. "Quality of Schooling, Returns to Schooling, and the 1981 Vouchers Reform in Chile." *World Development* 39 (12): 2245–56.

Ponce, Juan, and Arjun S. Bedi. 2010. "The Impact of a Cash Transfer Program on Cognitive Achievement: The Bono de Desarrollo Humano of Ecuador." *Economics of Education Review* 29 (1): 116–25.

Rajkumar, Andrew S., and Vinaya Swaroop. 2008. "Public Spending and Outcomes: Does Governance Matter?" *Journal of Development Economics* 86 (1): 96–111.

Rodríguez, J. 1988. "School Achievement and Decentralization Policy: The Chilean Case." *Revista de Análisis Económico* 3 (1): 75–88.

Rodríguez-Oreggia, Eduardo. 2011. "Movilidad Social Intergeneracional de los Jóvenes Beneficiarios de Oportunidades Provenientes de Hogares en Zonas Rurales." Unpublished external evaluation, *Oportunidades*. http://evaluacion.oportunidades.gob.mx:8010/es/anuncios.php.

Rodríguez-Oreggia, Eduardo, and Freije, Samuel. 2008. "An Impact Evaluation of Oportunidades on Rural Employment, Wages and Intergenerational Occupational Mobility." In *External Evaluation of Oportunidades 2008: 10 Years of Intervention in Rural Areas (1997–2007)*. Mexico D.F.: Secretaria de Desarrollo Social.

Roemer, John E. 1993. "A Pragmatic Theory of Responsibility for the Egalitarian Planner." *Philosophy and Public Affairs* 22 (2): 146–66.

———. 1998. *Equality of Opportunity*. New York: Harvard University Press.

Roemer, John E., Rolf Aaberge, Ugo Colombino, Johan Fritzell, Stephen P. Jenkins, Arnand Lefranc, Ive Marx, Marianne Page, Evert Pommer, and Javier Ruiz-Castillo. 2003. "To What Extent Do Fiscal Regimes Equalize Opportunities for Income Acquisition among Citizens?" *Journal of Public Economics* 87 (3–4) 539–65.

Sapelli, Claudio, and Bernardita Vial. 2004. "Peer Effects and Relative Performance of Voucher Schools in Chile." Working Paper 256, Pontificia Universidad Católica de Chile, Santiago.

Schultz, T. Paul. 2004. "School Subsidies for the Poor: Evaluating the Mexican *Progresa* Poverty Program." *Journal of Development Economics* 74 (1): 199–250.

SEDLAC (Socio-Economic Database for Latin America and the Caribbean). 2011. Database of the Center for Distributive, Labor and Social Studies (CEDLAS), University of La Plata, Argentina, and World Bank, Washington, DC. http://sedlac.econo.unlp.edu.ar/eng/.

Skoufias, Emmanuel, and Susan W. Parker. 2001. "Conditional Cash Transfers and their Impact on Child Work and Schooling." *Journal of the Latin American and Caribbean Economic Association* 2 (1): 45–96.

Solís, Alex. 2011. "Credit Access and College Enrollment." Unpublished paper, University of California, Berkeley.

Solon, Gary. 1999. "Intergenerational Mobility in the Labor Market." In *Handbook of Labor Economics*, *vol. 3*, ed. O. Ashenfelter and D. Card, 1761–800. Amsterdam: North-Holland.

———. 2002. "Cross-Country Differences in Intergenerational Earnings Mobility." *Journal of Economic Perspectives* 16 (3): 59–66.

———. 2004. "A Model of Intergenerational Mobility Variation over Time and Place." In *Generational Income Mobility in North America and Europe*, ed. M. Corak, 38–47. Cambridge, U.K.: Cambridge University Press.

UNESCO (United Nations Educational, Scientific, and Cultural Organization). 2009. "Reporte técnico del segundo estudio regional comparativo y explicativo: los aprendizajes de los estudiantes en America Latina y el Caribe." Oficina Regional de Educación para América Latina y el Caribe/UNESCO, Santiago.

Woessmann, Ludger, Elke Luedemann, Gabriela Schuetz, and Martin R. West. 2009. *School Accountability, Autonomy and Choice around the World*. Cheltenham, U.K.: Edward Elgar.

Zimmerman, David. 1992. "Regression toward Mediocrity in Economic Stature." *American Economic Review* 82 (3): 409–29.

Mobility within Generations | 4

All mankind is divided into three classes: those that are immovable, those that are movable, and those that move.

—Benjamin Franklin

hapter 3 explored how mobility *across* generations has evolved in the region. In doing so, it asked whether children's opportunities have been improving over time relative to those of their parents. By contrast, this chapter explores how an individual can seize opportunities *within* his or her own lifetime—specifically focusing on long-term directional intragenerational mobility. As chapter 2 discussed, the concept of directional income movement in the intragenerational domain is of particular interest if we want to shed light on the microeconomic dynamics underpinning the growth process in Latin America.

For example, how does growth manifest itself at the individual or household level? How do the aggregate gross domestic product (GDP) growth figures translate into growing incomes for individuals and their families? Those are questions about income growth, or income movement, within a person's lifetime. On the other hand, as incomes grow at the lower end of the income distribution, raising millions of Latin Americans

out of poverty, where do those people go? Is it true that the middle class is growing across the continent? Who was already part of it, and who are the new entrants? Using the mobility measures and decomposition developed in chapter 2, we can explore the nature of social dynamics in the region and begin an investigation of their determinants and, in particular, of how public policy in various realms may have promoted or impeded upward mobility.

Of course, to do this entails studying the "gross" flow of movements for specific individuals over time, as opposed to the typical poverty analysis over time that focuses on "net" flows and trends of groups at different parts of the income distribution. In particular, panel data that follow individuals over time are needed. Although short-term panel data are widely available in Latin America as elsewhere, they rarely cover more than three to four years between rounds, making the study of long-term intragenerational mobility for the same individual (over 10 or even 20 years) impossible.

This is what we aim to do here. To overcome the lack of long-term panels, we apply a recently developed approach—validated in three Latin American countries—to construct synthetic panels for specific individuals, hence allowing the analysis of long-term dynamics. Specifically, the chapter aims to understand income dynamics during the past 20 years across Latin America by exploring three broad sets of questions:

1. How much directional intragenerational mobility has there been in the past 15 to 20 years?
2. Who benefited from upward mobility, and who suffered from downward mobility (for example, who exited poverty or joined the middle class, and who fell behind)?
3. What are the mechanisms behind observed results? (In other words, is there evidence, at least descriptive evidence, that different policy regimes are associated with different degrees of mobility—for example, as policy relates to macroeconomic performance, labor markets, or social policies?)

As the chapter shows, the answers to these three questions are telling:

1. The region has experienced high levels of intragenerational mobility during the past 20 years, especially upward mobility.
2. Those who are poor and or near poverty have benefited the most.
3. Growth (especially during the past decade) has played a big role in helping people move, especially upward, and other factors such as improvements in education, labor markets, and social policies may have also facilitated mobility.

The rest of the chapter explains how we arrive at these insights.

Using synthetic panels to study long-term mobility

With the proliferation of short-term panel data in the past decade or so, it is no surprise that recent years have seen the study of intragenerational mobility increasingly capture the attention of policy makers and researchers in developing countries.[1] Latin America is not the exception; a growing number of studies on intragenerational mobility have been developed in several countries in the region. Most of these studies are based on short-term panels or use pseudo-panel techniques.[2]

The existing literature in the region employs a variety of methods, time periods, data sets, and measures to gauge the notion of intragenerational mobility. Moreover, the measurement of mobility is based on several welfare aggregates, ranging from earnings to household total income. All of this, while useful, makes it difficult to synthesize the existing evidence on the magnitude of mobility in Latin America or to compare mobility levels across different countries in the region.[3] Despite these differences, the literature reveals certain commonalities. Box 4.1 summarizes the main findings of the literature on intragenerational mobility in Latin America.

When measuring intragenerational mobility, it is desirable to work with panel data sets that follow individuals or households over time. Unfortunately, such surveys pose at least four empirical challenges:

- In Latin America in particular and in the developing world in general, panels are usually limited to urban areas or to small samples and therefore they are not representative of the entire population of the country (Fields et al. 2007).
- Because they are typically costly and complex to administer, panel data sets that track individuals or households over long periods of time (10 to 20 years) are still rare in Latin America. This scarcity limits the generalization of results across the region (Fields et al. 2007).
- Connected to the previous point, it is usually difficult to revisit households that physically move or drop out from panel data surveys. As such, nonrandom attrition may significantly bias results, leading to an underestimation of the actual mobil-

ity in the general population (Antman and McKenzie 2007).

• Finally, measurement error will also introduce bias in the mobility estimates.

Although the existing literature may allow us to understand the correlates of short-term intragenerational mobility (which can be especially useful in a context of volatility and crises), short-term panel data do not help us

understand the long-term trends related to movements across economic classes. These limitations raise serious concerns regarding the validity of the policy implications drawn from the short-term panel literature.

Learning about the levels of long-term intragenerational mobility is crucial for the design of effective social policy interventions. The type of policies needed to attack long-term persistent poverty may be quite

---

BOX 4.1   Existing findings on intragenerational mobility in Latin America

Most of the earlier studies describe substantial directional mobility in terms of discrete welfare trajectories by which households in Latin America move across income classes and into and out of poverty and the middle class (see, for instance, Scott and Litchfield [1994] and Paredes and Zubizarreta [2005], both regarding Chile in the 1990s).

Apart from considerable mobility based on discrete welfare trajectories, many studies also find substantial mobility in terms of the *magnitude* of income changes. More important, these studies generally find that income changes are heterogeneous across income groups, the most disadvantaged being those who experienced in general the largest gains in the region. In this sense, Fields et al. (2007) present compelling evidence that, conditional on observable characteristics, households with the lowest initial incomes tend to gain relatively more (see, for instance, Duval Hernandez [2006] for the case of Mexico).

Because not many long-term panels are available in Latin America, it is difficult to study whether short-term transitory movements affect long-term positions in the income distribution. To answer this question, Fields et al. (2006) estimate two regressions using panels from Argentina, Mexico, and República Bolivariana de Venezuela. First, the authors regress earning changes on initial earnings. Then, they regress earning changes on predicted earnings, where predicted earnings come from regressing observed earnings on a set of time-invariant observable variables. The authors find non-

positive coefficients for both regressions in several years, suggesting that a convergence (or nondivergence) exists between the earnings of the rich and the poor. Moreover, the authors find that relatively more convergence exists when using initial earnings than when using predicted earnings. This result suggests that most of the observed changes in incomes are transitory and do not affect longer-term positions in the income distribution.

Comparisons of mobility levels between different country-specific studies are also difficult to gauge because of the differences in methodologies. However, a few studies provide cross-country mobility comparisons in Latin America as a region, showing that mobility differs between countries. For instance, Calónico (2006) uses pseudo-panels spanning 1992 to 2003 for eight countries and concludes that Argentina, Brazil, and Uruguay have very low levels of mobility, while Chile, Mexico, and República Bolivariana de Venezuela are among the most mobile countries on the continent. Ñopo (2011) estimates mobility for 14 countries, also using pseudo-panels for 1992 to 2003. The author finds low income mobility only in Brazil, Colombia, and Costa Rica; Chile and Argentina show modest levels of mobility; and the rest of the region is considered relatively mobile.

Finally, a large body of the literature studies the correlates of intragenerational mobility: gender, education, employment status, household composition, and the quality of housing systematically appear to be related to mobility in Latin America.[a]

a. Regarding gender, see, for instance, Ñopo (2011); Glewwe and Hall (1998); McKenzie (2004); and Corbacho, Garcia-Escribano, and Ichauste (2007). Regarding education, see, for example, Beccaria and Groisman (2006); Cruces and Wodon (2006); Beneke de Sanfeliu and Shi (2003); and Herrera (1999). Regarding employment, see, for instance, Cruces and Wodon (2006); Corbacho, Garcia-Escribano, and Ichauste (2007); McKenzie (2004); Duval Hernandez (2006); and Fields et al. (2003). Regarding household composition, see, for example, Beneke de Sanfeliu and Shi (2003); Glewwe and Hall (1998); Herrera (1999); and Fields et al. (2003). Finally, regarding the quality of housing, see for instance, Paredes and Zubizarreta (2005).

different from those required to address transient poverty; the former requires skills and asset creation, while the later must focus on social protection to cope with risks. Therefore, availability of longer-term panels is an indispensable tool for policy makers concerned about persistent poverty. Unfortunately, due to the lack of these types of data sets, no long-term income mobility estimates that are comparable across countries exist in Latin America.

Because of the growing concern that exists regarding the evaluation of long-term transitions into and out of poverty, an emerging body of the literature has developed techniques to overcome the major limitations of panel data sets by employing cross-sectional surveys. A vast array of the literature has mainly focused on what is commonly called the "pseudo-panel" approach, which tracks cohorts of individuals over several periods of time.[4] This methodology helps to overcome the main limitation of panel data sets; it can be used to understand long-term mobility across economic classes. However, studies that use pseudo-panels usually need to impose significant structural assumptions to yield mobility measures out of repeated cross-sectional surveys (Dang et al. 2011). In addition, by aggregating average trends for a given group (or cohort), this technique does not consider intragroup mobility, which may be equally or even more relevant than aggregate mobility.

Taking another route, Krebs, Krishna, and Maloney (2011) develop a framework linking individual income dynamics, social mobility, and welfare. In doing so, they define mobility as a composite of three elements: (a) "good" mobility, which is a convergence of individuals toward some appropriately defined level of income; (b) risk ("bad" mobility), corresponding to the variance of permanent shocks; and (c) transitory shocks and measurement error.

Based on this refinement, they offer a tractable analytical framework based on standard income processes that provides a closed-form link between the welfare theory and the empirics of income dynamic measurement.[5]

Mobility, measured in relation to the correlation of incomes over time,[6] can then be directly related to the parameters of the income process, which can then be estimated through standard econometric techniques.

This framework has the merit of drawing out the links between income volatility, income mobility, distribution, and social welfare in a simple and transparent manner, allowing for a clearer analytical and quantitative discussion of these interrelated concepts than has generally been possible in the past. The approach also permits a single measure of welfare, comparable across countries, that encompasses these interrelated phenomena and disaggregates measured income mobility into the three components above.

Their results from Argentina and Mexico offer some striking insights:

- More than half of measured mobility in these countries is estimated to be driven by transitory shocks to income.
- Approximately half of the residual (mobility in permanent income) is driven by social-welfare-reducing persistent income shocks.
- Finally, the share of measured mobility that corresponds to "good" mobility is fairly small.

Despite the potential of this approach, it relies on multiple rounds of panel data following specific individuals. These data requirements render it impractical for application to a large number of Latin American countries.[7]

In the absence of long-term panel data in the region, and to overcome these limitations, we employ an alternative approach to study directional intragenerational mobility. Specifically, we apply an innovative extension of poverty mapping techniques that construct "synthetic panels" using repeated cross-sectional data (Dang et al. 2011). The approach builds on an "out-of-sample" imputation methodology described in Elbers, Lanjouw, and Lanjouw (2002, 2003) for small-area estimation of poverty ("poverty maps").[8]

The method converts two or more rounds of cross-sectional data into a panel (of individuals or households) by predicting income for the same households in future (or past) periods. Because of the estimation involved, *lower-* and *upper-bound* estimates of income are constructed and can be used to subsequently estimate bounds of mobility measures. The bounds produced—the validation exercises by Cruces et al. (2011) in three countries in Latin America (Chile, Nicaragua, and Peru) also confirm this—are expected to sandwich *true* mobility estimates obtained from actual panel data sets. Focus note 4.1 at the end of this chapter provides a detailed technical note of this method and discusses both its advantages and limitations.

One important caveat: for the sake of simplicity, this chapter will focus on the lower-bound estimates (the story line is consistent when we look at the upper-bound results). One additional advantage beyond simplicity is that focusing on the lower-bound estimates allows us to provide conservative estimates of long-term intragenerational mobility because these estimates do not suffer from traditional measurement error. This decision is not without a drawback: the lower-bound estimates will underestimate upward mobility, painting a less-rosy picture in terms of welfare improvements. But focusing on the lower-bound estimates will also underestimate downward mobility and, as such, the role of risk and vulnerability will be inherently underplayed. The results should be interpreted accordingly. In fact, to reinforce this point—for the case of downward mobility—we also discuss the upper-bound results.

Although the technique is no substitute for having actual panel data, it has a number of advantages that enable great strides in both describing and understanding socioeconomic mobility in Latin America:

- It constructs a synthetic panel for every individual in the sample; therefore, it overcomes the attrition problem of actual panel data sets.
- Instead of constructing panels of cohort averages, as in the classical pseudo-panel

approach, the synthetic panel approach predicts the income of the same individual or household in different time periods.

- The same approach can be replicated for most Latin American countries for the same underlying period and using consistent concepts of income measures, data sets, and mobility measures, thus considerably enlarging the universe of estimates of mobility in the region.
- The biggest contribution of this methodology is that it allows for the estimation of long-term intragenerational mobility measures for the 18 Latin American countries we study, in some cases spanning 20 years.[9]

To do so, we use the Socio-Economic Database for Latin America and the Caribbean (SEDLAC) database of Latin American household surveys, compiled by the Universidad de la Plata in Argentina (CEDLAS) in partnership with the World Bank. The database consists of a set of harmonized surveys that include income, labor market, and other socioeconomic information spanning more than 20 years of nationally representative cross-sectional surveys, totaling more than 250 surveys for the region.[10] Data and periods used, by country, are presented in annex 4.1.

We focus on three measures of directional mobility for each country and the region (as chapter 2 discusses in more detail):

- *The proportion of people who move across thresholds* (poverty and the middle class), which provides an estimate of overall mobility (*how much*) as in traditional transition matrices.
- *Aggregate mobility as the sum of all income changes* (in levels and percentages), which gives us a sense of the magnitude (*how far*) of long-term mobility.
- *Transitions out of poverty* (US$4 purchasing power parity [PPP] per day) *and into the middle class* (US$10 PPP per day) in their own right. This allows us to study dynamics for each country related to these two thresholds and describe the types of groups that are more (or less) successful

in moving upward (or downward) and to explore the types of policies that may have contributed to the observed patterns.

The mobility estimates (as well as the decomposed measures in annex 4.2) permit us to identify how far the poor move out of poverty (or the vulnerable move into middle class) and whether these movements vary across the income distribution.

Income mobility in Latin America: The past two decades

Overall long-term mobility

Using synthetic panels as described above, we can estimate intragenerational mobility measures as in chapter 2 for each individual between two periods, from which we can obtain aggregate mobility measures for a country or the region as a whole. Table 4.1 presents an aggregate regional transition matrix for Latin America in terms of the three economic groups discussed earlier: the poor (those with incomes below US$4 PPP per day), the vulnerable (with incomes between US$4–10 PPP per day), and those in the middle and upper classes (with incomes above US$10 PPP per day). In this context, a measure of intragenerational mobility is the share of the total population that moved

across classes (the sum of the off-diagonal cells in the matrix).[11]

As the table 4.1 suggests, Latin America has experienced dramatic mobility in the past 15 years. A number of striking results emerge:

- Out of every 100 Latin Americans, 43 changed their economic status during the period.
- There is considerably more upward than downward mobility: out of the 43 people changing economic status, only two experienced a worsening of their status (into poverty or out of the middle class). Note that, as discussed above, these are lower-bound estimates (we come back to this point later).
- Despite the large levels of mobility, table 4.1 also suggests that a large part of the population is immobile. For example, more than one in five Latin Americans remained chronically poor throughout the whole period, while approximately the same proportion remained steadily in the middle class.

These trends vary across countries. For example, 50–60 percent of the population in countries such as Brazil, Chile, Colombia, and Costa Rica moved across one of the three economic groups during the past 15 years, as shown in figure 4.1). This compares

TABLE 4.1   **Intragenerational mobility in Latin America over past 15 years (circa 1995–2010)**
percentage of population

		Destination (c. 2010)			
		Poor	**Vulnerable**	**Middle class**	**Total**
Origin (c.1995)	**Poor**	22.5	21.0	2.2	45.7
	Vulnerable	0.9	14.3	18.2	33.4
	Middle class	0.1	0.5	20.3	20.9
Total		23.4	35.9	40.7	100.0

Source: Data from SEDLAC (Socio-Economic Database for Latin America and the Caribbean).
Note: "Poor" = individuals with a per capita income lower than US$4. "Vulnerable" = individuals with a per capita income of US$4–US$10. "Middle class" = individuals with a per capita income higher than US$10. Poverty lines and incomes are expressed in 2005 US$ PPP per day. PPP = purchasing power parity. Years vary across countries as follows: Argentina 1994 and 2009; Bolivia 1992 and 2007; Brazil 1990 and 2009; Chile 1992 and 2009; Colombia 1992 and 2008; Costa Rica 1989 and 2009; Dominican Republic 1996 and 2009; Ecuador 1995 and 2009; El Salvador 1991 and 2008; Guatemala 2000 and 2006; Honduras 1994 and 2009; Mexico 2000 and 2008; Nicaragua 1998 and 2005; Panama 1994 and 2009; Peru 1999 and 2009; Paraguay 1999 and 2009; Uruguay 1989 and 2009; and República Bolivariana de Venezuela 1992 and 2006. The table shows lower-bound mobility estimates using the Dang et al. (2011) technique. Results are weighted using country-specific population estimates of the last available period.

FIGURE 4.1   Sliders, climbers, and stayers: Intragenerational mobility in Latin America, by country

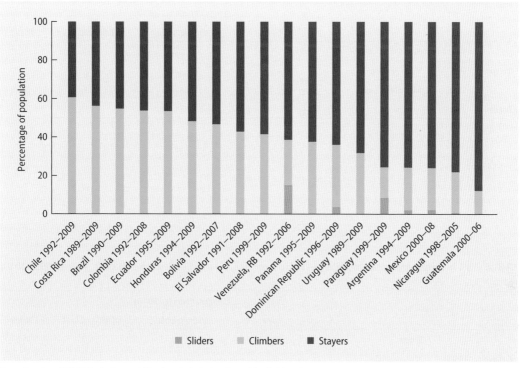

Source: Data from SEDLAC (Socio-Economic Database for Latin America and the Caribbean).
Note: The figure shows lower-bound mobility estimates using the Dang et al. (2011) technique. "Sliders" refers to those individuals who move downward. "Climbers" refers to those who move upward. "Stayers" refers to those who did not change status. "Poor" = individuals with a per capita income lower than US$4. "Vulnerable" = individuals with a per capita income of US$4–US$10. "Middle class" = individuals with a per capita income higher than US$10. Poverty lines and incomes are expressed in 2005 US$ PPP per day. PPP = purchasing power parity.

with significantly lower mobility (of around or less than 20 percent) in the populations of Argentina, Guatemala, Mexico, Nicaragua, and Paraguay. Although downward mobility ("sliders") is also part of the overall mobility measure, as the figure shows, upward mobility ("climbers") is driving the mobility results; downward mobility affects only a small number of countries (such as the Dominican Republic, Paraguay, and República Bolivariana de Venezuela).

The synthetic panels can allow us to estimate additional measures of directional mobility (described in chapter 2). For example, we may want to know *how much* individuals' incomes grew (in levels or percentages) over the period for the whole distribution or for specific groups.[12] Table 4.2 indicates that total mobility (as net income change for the whole region) was US$3.30 PPP per day per capita. In addition, the marginal distributions (last column of table 4.2) show that the net income change was different for different parts of the distribution: among those who escaped poverty (into vulnerability), income grew by US$2.80, while among the vulnerable who entered the middle class, income grew by US$6.90. Similarly, households that remained poor over the period experienced a small increase in median income of US$1 PPP, while those who remained in the vulnerable class saw their net incomes grow by US$2.60 PPP. Among the sliders, those who entered poverty experienced a net income decline of US$0.80, while those who fell out of the middle class saw a net income loss of US$1.80 PPP.

Table 4.3 presents similar trends in growth rates over the past 15 years. For the

TABLE 4.2   Intragenerational mobility in Latin America, by median income change, (circa 1995–2010)
US$ PPP per capita per day

		Destination (c. 2010)			
		Poor	**Vulnerable**	**Middle class**	**Total**
	Poor	1.0	2.8	8.4	1.8
Origin (c.1995)	**Vulnerable**	−0.8	2.6	6.9	4.9
	Middle class	−1.2	−1.8	11.6	11.3
Total		0.9	2.6	7.9	3.3

Source: Data from SEDLAC.
Note: SEDLAC = Socio-Economic Database for Latin America and the Caribbean. "Poor" = individuals with a per capita income lower than US$4. "Vulnerable" = individuals with a per capita income of US$4–US$10. "Middle class" = individuals with a per capita income higher than US$10. Poverty lines and incomes are expressed in 2005 US$ PPP (purchasing power parity) per day. Years vary across countries as follows: Argentina 1994 and 2009; Bolivia 1992 and 2007; Brazil 1990 and 2009; Chile 1992 and 2009; Colombia 1992 and 2008; Costa Rica 1989 and 2009; Dominican Republic 1996 and 2009; Ecuador 1995 and 2009; El Salvador 1991 and 2008; Guatemala 2000 and 2006; Honduras 1994 and 2009; Mexico 2000 and 2008; Nicaragua 1998 and 2005; Panama 1994 and 2009; Peru 1999 and 2009; Paraguay 1999 and 2009; Uruguay 1989 and 2009; and República Bolivariana de Venezuela 1992 and 2006. The table shows lower-bound mobility estimates using the Dang et al. (2011) technique. Results are weighted using country-specific population estimates of the last available period.

TABLE 4.3   Intragenerational mobility in Latin America, by median income change, (circa 1995–2010)
mecdian percentage income change

		Destination (c. 2010)			
		Poor	**Vulnerable**	**Middle Class**	**Total**
	Poor	86.6	110.0	269.8	99.5
Origin (c. 1995)	**Vulnerable**	−15.7	51.7	106.4	81.1
	Middle Class	−9.2	−15.4	65.1	63.5
Total		84.6	88.2	89.2	87.4

Source: Data from SEDLAC.
Note: "Poor" = individuals with a per capita income lower than US$4. "Vulnerable" = individuals with a per capita income of US$4–US$10. "Middle class" = individuals with a per capita income higher than US$10. Poverty lines and incomes are expressed in 2005 US$ PPP per day. PPP = purchasing power parity. SEDLAC = Socio-Economic Database for Latin America and the Caribbean. Years vary across countries as follows: Argentina 1994 and 2009; Bolivia 1992 and 2007; Brazil 1990 and 2009; Chile 1992 and 2009; Colombia 1992 and 2008; Costa Rica 1989 and 2009; Dominican Republic 1996 and 2009; Ecuador 1995 and 2009; El Salvador 1991 and 2008; Guatemala 2000 and 2006; Honduras 1994 and 2009; Mexico 2000 and 2008; Nicaragua 1998 and 2005; Panama 1994 and 2009; Peru 1999 and 2009; Paraguay 1999 and 2009; Uruguay 1989 and 2009; and República Bolivariana de Venezuela 1992 and 2006. The table shows lower-bound mobility estimates using the Dang et al. (2011) technique. Results are weighted using country-specific population estimates of the last available period.

period covering the study, incomes grew by an average of almost 90 percent (with an annualized rate of 6 percent). The results across groups show a progressive trend: much of this growth occurred among those originally poor or vulnerable. Specifically, while incomes among the originally poor doubled, the originally vulnerable experienced an increase in incomes of 81 percent, compared with 64 percent for those originally in the middle class (last column of table 4.3). As before, additional differences within specific groups exist. For the originally poor, incomes grew by 87 percent for those who remained

poor, compared with 110 percent for those who entered the vulnerable group and 270 percent for the few who made it into the middle class (2.2 percent of the total population, as in table 4.1). Among the "sliders," those originally vulnerable who fell into poverty saw an average income reduction of almost 16 percent.

These trends also vary across countries, as shown in figure 4.2. For example, Brazil, Chile, and Honduras have had the highest median income growth since the early 1990s (of almost 150 percent), while Guatemala, Paraguay, and República Bolivariana de

FIGURE 4.2   Intragenerational mobility in Latin America, by country
percentage median income change

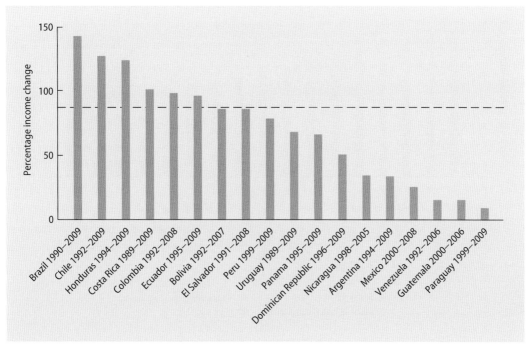

Source: Data from SEDLAC.
Note: Figure shows the synthetic panel median growth rate in incomes. Horizontal dashed line shows overall growth rates, weighted using country-specific population estimates of the last period from SEDLAC (Socio-Economic Database for Latin America and the Caribbean). Figure based on lower-bound mobility estimates using the Dang et al. (2011) technique.

Venezuela were among the worst performers (with median income growth over their respective periods of less than 10 percent).

In sum, these results suggest large income mobility in the region, driven by upward mobility out of poverty and into the vulnerable or middle classes. For these long-term mobility trends, the results suggest very little downward mobility. The next section explores these results further.

Unravelling the box: Exiting poverty and entering the middle class

Is this economic mobility similar across different parts of the distribution? The results above suggest that this is not the case. Focusing on initial economic status, table 4.1 suggests that out of the 43 people for each 100 in

Latin America who changed status during the period, 23 were originally poor who exited poverty, 18 were vulnerable who entered the middle class, while 2 fell into poverty or out of the middle class.

Again, this varies across countries. Among those countries with higher overall mobility (Brazil, Chile, Colombia, and Costa Rica), those exiting poverty contribute at least equally to overall mobility trends relative to those who were originally vulnerable and entered the middle class, as shown in figure 4.3. By contrast, mobility in countries with lower overall mobility is driven by people moving into the middle class from the vulnerable group (Argentina, Uruguay, and República Bolivariana de Venezuela). For countries such as Paraguay and República Bolivariana de Venezuela, downward mobility (into poverty) is also more pronounced.

FIGURE 4.3   Mobility for whom? Contribution to overall mobility of initial economic status in Latin America, by country

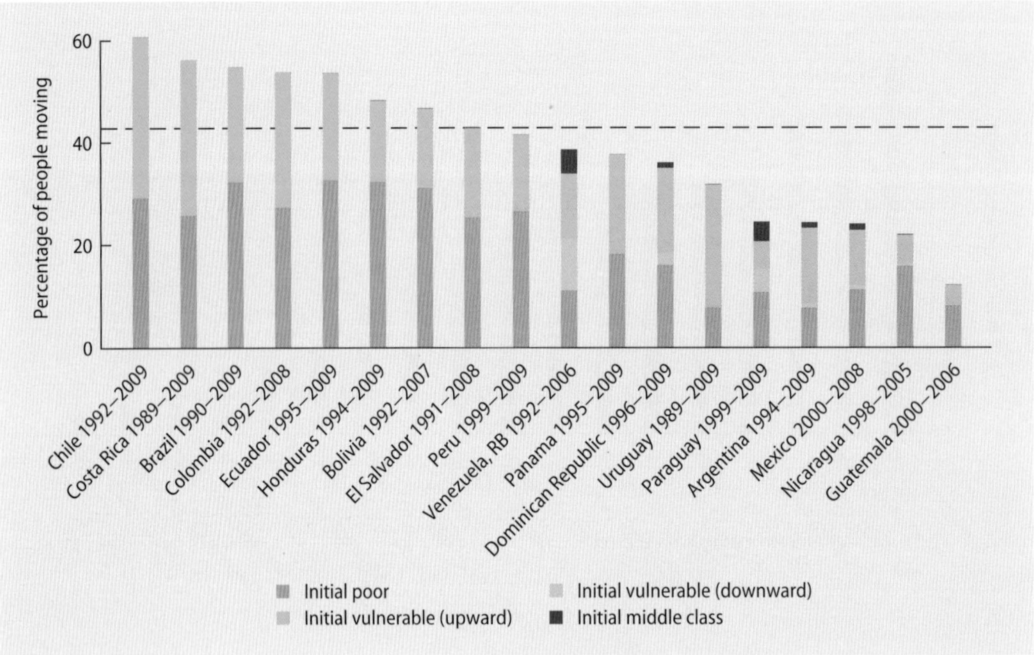

Source: Data from SEDLAC.
Note: The figure shows lower-bound mobility estimates using the Dang et al. (2011) technique. "Initial poor" refers to those who were poor in the first period. "Initial middle class" refers to those who belonged to the middle class in the first period. "Initial vulnerable (downward)" refers to those who were initially vulnerable in the first period and became poor in the second period. "Initial vulnerable (upward)" refers to those who were initially vulnerable in the first period and became middle class in the second period. "Poor" = individuals with a per capita income lower than US$4. "Vulnerable" = individuals with a per capita income of US$4–US$10. "Middle class" = individuals with a per capita income higher than US$10. Poverty lines and incomes are expressed in 2005 US$ PPP per day. PPP = purchasing power parity. The horizontal dashed line shows overall mobility in Latin America, weighted using country-specific population estimates of the last period from SEDLAC = Socio-Economic Database for Latin America and the Caribbean.

How large are these mobility changes? One way to answer this question is by looking at the initial and final income distribution among those who exited poverty or entered the middle class. This is summarized in figure 4.4 for the case of Uruguay. As can be seen, most of those who exited poverty between 1989 and 2009 were near the poverty line in 1989 in terms of income per capita (panel a). In addition, most of those who exited poverty hover above the poverty line with a median income of around US$6 PPP per day (panel b). Few households crossed the middle-class threshold. Indeed, most of the population who entered the middle class between 1989 and 2009 in Uruguay were near the middle-class line (US$10 PPP per day) in 1989 (panel

c). Once they entered the middle class, most of them were in the range of US$10–15 PPP per day (panel d).

These trends are generalized for most countries in the region, despite some differences. For example, those who exited poverty originally had a median income of between US$2 and US$3 PPP per capita per day as shown in figure 4.5, panel a. In most countries, the net income change was large enough to bring those individuals' median income up to around US$6 PPP per capita per day. This increase corresponds to more than double the per capita incomes of those exiting poverty in these countries (for their respective periods). And consistent with the earlier results, in none of the countries in the region did the

FIGURE 4.4   Upward mobility out of poverty: Origin and destination in Uruguay, 1989–2009

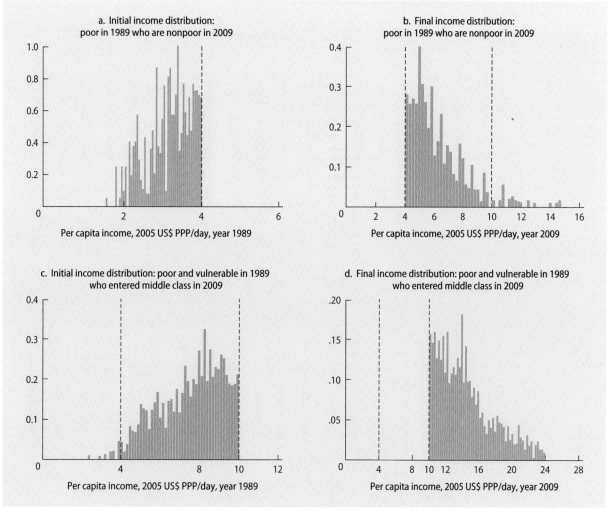

Source: Data from SEDLAC.
Note: The figure shows lower-bound mobility estimates using the Dang et al. (2011) technique. Panels a and b show the initial and final income distributions of those originally poor who escaped poverty, respectively. Panels c and d show the initial and final income distributions of those originally poor or vulnerable who entered middle class, respectively. "Poor" = individuals with a per capita income lower than US$4. "Vulnerable" = individuals with a per capita income of US$4–US$10. "Middle class" = individuals with a per capita income higher than US$10. Dashed vertical lines represent the US$4 poverty and the US$10 vulnerable poverty lines. Poverty lines and incomes are expressed in 2005 US$ PPP per day. PPP = purchasing power parity. SEDLAC = Socio-Economic Database for Latin America and the Caribbean.

income gains among the poor allow them to surpass US$10 PPP (median), thus putting them in the middle class. In other words, those who exited poverty in Latin America in the past two decades are neither poor nor in the middle class: they are vulnerable. Similarly, for those who entered the middle class, median incomes at the beginning of the

period were around US$6 PPP per capita as shown in figure 4.5, panel b. The net income change brought those individuals' median income up to around US$14 PPP, suggesting that the median person in this group doubled his or her per capita income.

Instead of looking at levels, one final exercise explores whether income growth differs

FIGURE 4.5 **Intragenerational upward mobility in Latin America: Origin and destination, by country**
median income, 2005 US$ PPP per capita per day

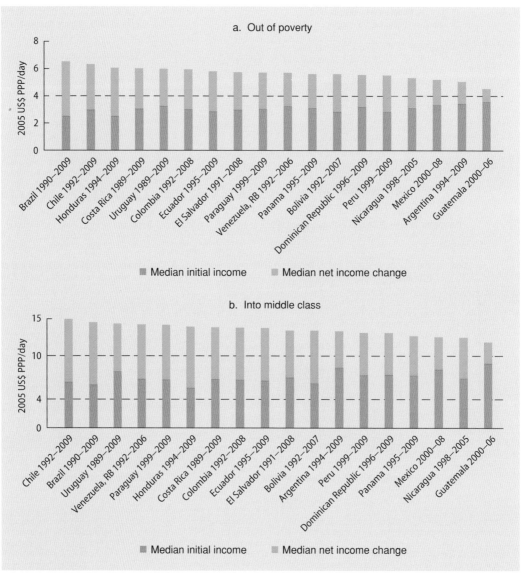

Source: Data from SEDLAC.
Note: The figure shows lower-bound mobility estimates using the Dang et al. (2011) technique. Panel a shows the median initial income and median income change of those originally poor who escaped poverty. Panel b shows the median initial income and median income change of those originally poor or vulnerable who entered the middle class. "Poor" = individuals with a per capita income lower than US$4. "Vulnerable" = individuals with a per capita income of US$4–US$10. "Middle class" = individuals with a per capita income higher than US$10. Poverty lines and incomes are expressed in 2005 US$ PPP per day. PPP = purchasing power parity. Horizontal dashed lines show overall mobility in Latin America, weighted using country-specific population estimates of the last period from SEDLAC = Socio-Economic Database for Latin America and the Caribbean.

across the income distribution. Figure 4.6 shows growth incidence curves (GIC) across deciles in two countries using two approaches: anonymous and non-anonymous:

- *For Costa Rica,* the traditional static GIC (anonymous as it looks at changes in mean incomes for a specific part of the distribution) indicates a regressive story

FIGURE 4.6   **Growth incidence curves for Costa Rica and El Salvador, using anonymous and non-anonymous information**

percentage income change, by decile

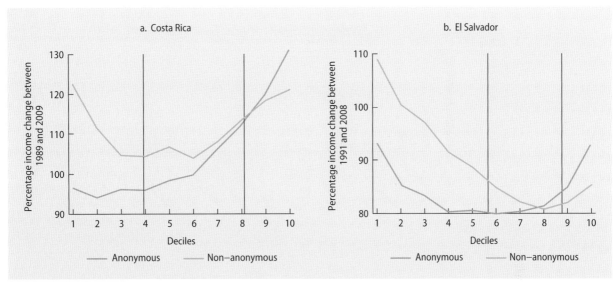

Source: Data from SEDLAC.

Note: All figures present the growth incidence curves (GICs), which show percentage income changes by decile of the per capita income distribution. First-round incomes are actual incomes in surveys, while second-round incomes come from lower-bound estimates using the Dang et al. (2011) technique. Anonymous GICs treat first and second round as if they were cross-sectional surveys, while non-anonymous estimates come from respecting the synthetic panel structure. The left vertical solid line represents the proportion of poor, while the right solid vertical line represents the proportion of vulnerable. "Poor" = individuals with a per capita income lower than US$4. "Vulnerable" = individuals with a per capita income of US$4–US$10. "Middle class" = individuals with a per capita income higher than US$10. Poverty lines and incomes are expressed in 2005 US$ PPP per day. PPP = purchasing power parity. SEDLAC = Socio-Economic Database for Latin America and the Caribbean.

where income growth was higher among the richer part of the distribution (the middle class). By contrast, the non-anonymous GIC (based on synthetic panels that follow the same households over time and look at mean changes in incomes for a specific part of the distribution) show that the poor actually had at least the same performance in income growth over the same period.

- *In El Salvador,* the non-anonymous results also suggest very progressive changes in the income distribution (the poorer parts of the distribution growing faster) relative to the conclusions one would reach from the anonymous trends.

Similar exercises in other countries reveal similar patterns. Taken together, the results suggest heterogeneity across countries in terms of mobility but also emphasize how the use of traditional incidence curves can hide the true nature of mobility trajectories

because one does not follow the same individual or household over time. If what we want to understand is an individual's welfare trajectory over time (true or synthetic), panel data are essential.

Downward mobility revisited

An additional insight from looking at the short-term mobility trends is in helping us understand one of the most striking results of long-term mobility in Latin America: the extremely low downward mobility, both in terms of the new poor as well as those who exit the middle class. As figure 4.7 summarizes, with the exception of the Dominican Republic, Paraguay, and República Bolivariana de Venezuela, the population that fell below their original class over the past 15-year period is small. Does this suggest that we should not care about interventions oriented to prevent people from falling into poverty or out of the middle class (such as

FIGURE 4.7   **Downward intragenerational mobility into poverty and out of middle class in Latin America, by country**

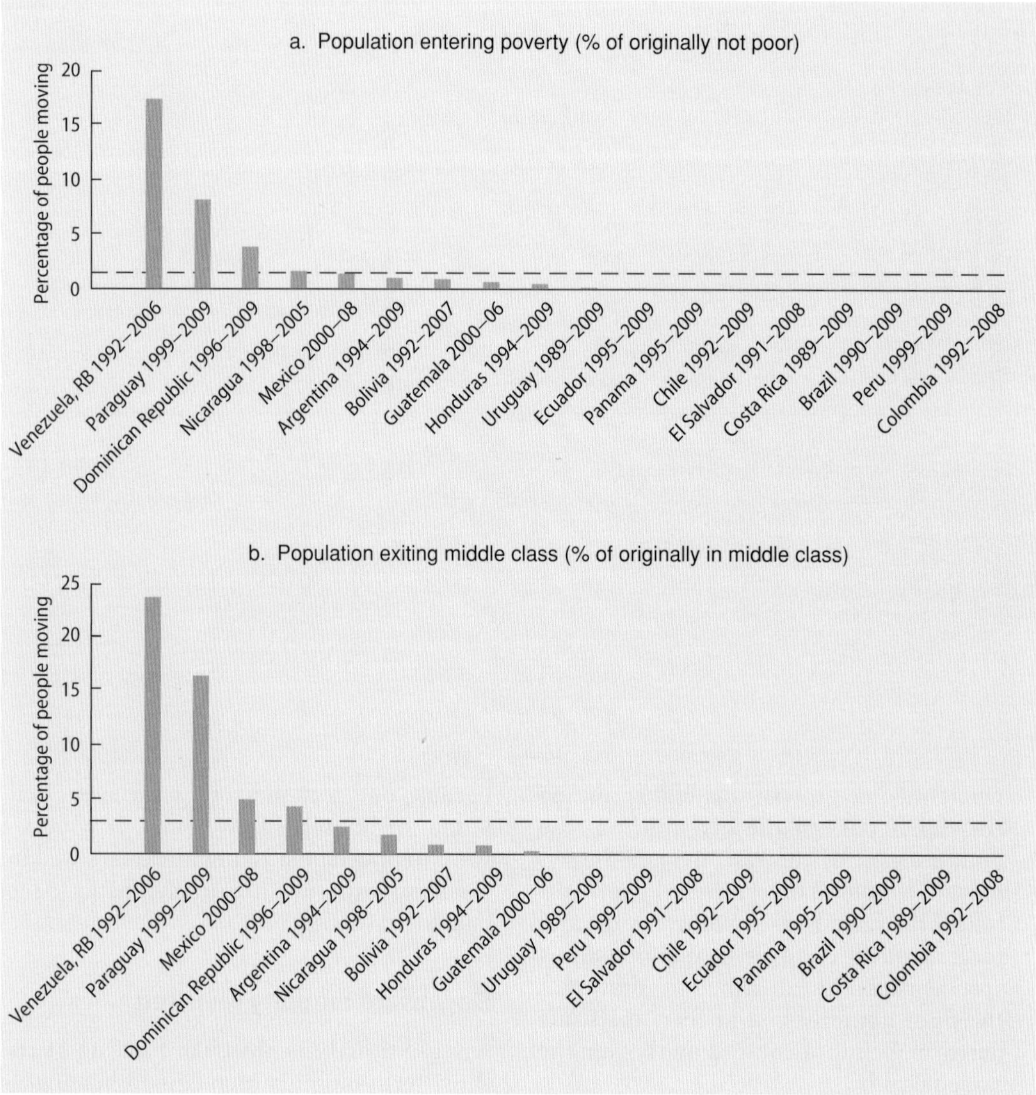

a. Population entering poverty (% of originally not poor)

b. Population exiting middle class (% of originally in middle class)

Source: Data from SEDLAC.
Note: The figure shows lower-bound mobility estimates using the Dang et al. (2011) technique. Panel a shows the proportion of those originally not poor who enter poverty. Panel b shows the proportion of those originally in the middle class who became poor or vulnerable. "Poor" = individuals with a per capita income lower than US$4. "Vulnerable" = individuals with a per capita income of US$4–US$10. "Middle class" = individuals with a per capita income higher than US$10. Both lines are expressed in 2005 US$ PPP per day. PPP = purchasing power parity. Horizontal dashed lines show overall mobility in Latin America, weighted using country-specific population estimates of the last period from SEDLAC = Socio-Economic Database for Latin America and the Caribbean.

social insurance or risk management policies)? There is reason to be cautious.

As was described earlier, the synthetic panel approach allows us to estimate lower and upper bounds for the mobility measures we discuss here. All the results presented in

this chapter use the lower bound. The choice was based on two reasons, as discussed earlier: (a) it is based on fewer technical assumptions (the strongest being that it does not include measurement error); and (b) by construction, it estimates a lower-bound estimate

FIGURE 4.8   Downward mobility into poverty in Latin American revisited, by country

percentage of those originally not poor

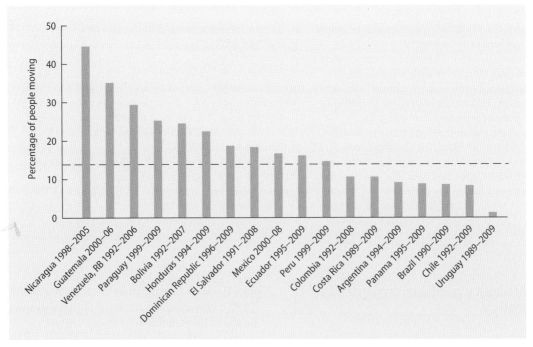

Source: Data from SEDLAC.
Note: The figure shows *upper*-bound mobility estimates using the Dang et al. (2011) technique. It presents the proportion of those originally not poor who enter poverty. "Poor" = individuals with a per capita income lower than US$4. The poverty line is expressed in 2005 US$PPP per day. PPP = purchasing power parity. The horizontal dashed line shows overall Latin American mobility, weighted using country-specific population estimates of the last period from SEDLAC (Socio-Economic Database for Latin America and the Caribbean).

that allows us to discuss the most conservative scenario of directional mobility (both upward and downward). In this sense, we expect the "true" mobility estimates to be higher.

Therefore, we also present the upper-bound estimates of downward mobility in figure 4.8. As can be seen, at the upper bound, there is considerable downward mobility into poverty. For countries such as Guatemala, Nicaragua, and República Bolivariana de Venezuela, there is a 30 percent probability of falling into poverty, while for Bolivia, Honduras, and Paraguay, it is 20 percent. At the other end, countries such as Brazil, Chile, and Uruguay still exhibit low rates of downward mobility (also see box 4.2). To the extent that the "true" mobility estimates are somewhere between the lower and upper bounds, these results do indicate that long-term downward

mobility is an important issue to consider from a policy point of view.

Using the upper bound to discuss downward mobility also suggests another interesting result: the overall average probability in Latin America of becoming poor is slightly higher than 10 percent. As discussed in more detail in chapter 2, we define the middle-class threshold at US$10 PPP per day using a vulnerability concept of the probability of falling into poverty (based on a 10 percent probability). As figure 4.8 shows, 10 percent turns out to be close to the average probability in the region, and in fact it is the prevailing probability for middle-class countries such as Argentina, Colombia, and Costa Rica. In this sense, this probability provides empirical validation of the justification of the "middle class" definition used in this volume.

BOX 4.2   The welfare costs of downward mobility in Nicaragua

Premand and Vakis (2010) use three rounds of panel data from Nicaragua between 1998 and 2005 to study downward mobility. They find that more than 25 percent of the vulnerable (using a definition comparable to that used in this chapter, based on consumption terciles) became poor over the period they studied, attributed partly to uninsured risks.

Using matching and double difference techniques, they also find causal evidence of the impact of past weather shocks in triggering downward mobility into poverty. Specifically, they find that a severe drought five years earlier increased the probability of the vulnerable (those in the second tercile) becoming poor

by 13 percent and increased the probability of falling out of the middle class (the top tercile) by 25 percent. A novel finding in the study is that weather shocks also increase the probability of poverty persistence: poor households affected by weather shocks have a 10 percent higher probability of staying poor in subsequent periods. This finding provides new evidence of how shocks can also prevent upward mobility and perpetuate poverty traps.[a]

Taken together, these results point to large potential gains from social risk management policies, targeting both the near-poor (vulnerable) and the extreme poor.

a. Cruces, Glüzmann, and López-Calva (2011) also find evidence that economic crises in Argentina have permanent impacts on increased mortality and long-term impacts through deteriorating health outcomes (low birth weight), with substantial consequences in terms of future income-generating capacity.

Mobility profiles: Insights for policy

How much do initial conditions matter?

Having established the long-term mobility trends and stylized facts in the Latin American region, we explore descriptively some of the potential channels that are associated with mobility. A first way to do this is to understand the correlates of upward mobility with household characteristics. Given the synthetic panel approach, one limitation is that we can only explain the extent to which socioeconomic characteristics *at the initial period* are correlated with mobility (as opposed to changes in those characteristics).

We first explore how today's households across the three economic classes (poor, vulnerable, and middle class) looked 15 years earlier (figure 4.9). The results, while not surprising, suggest that households that had better initial socioeconomic indicators are more likely to end up in a higher economic class 15 years later. For example, households that are today in the middle class were, on average, more educated than those in the vulnerable class who, in turn, had more education than the poor. In Ecuador, for example, a typical middle-class household head (today) already

had 10 years of education 15 years earlier (in 1995), compared with only 6 years among heads of households that today are poor.

And although the levels differ (also because the beginning and end of the period observed differ across countries), these trends are consistent across countries. Interestingly, there seems to be a general trend that today's middle-class households had twice the initial education levels of today's poor households, while the vulnerable class falls in between.

Similar trends emerge in other indicators. For example, today's middle class was more likely to have a household head working in the formal sector at the initial period relative to the other two classes. In the case of Brazil, 80 percent of household heads that are today in the middle class were already working in the formal sector in 1990, compared with only 40 percent among today's poor. Again, the vulnerable households fall in between, and the trends are consistent across countries. Similar trends for location of residence (middle-class households are more likely to have resided in urban areas earlier) and access to services like water and electricity (households in today's higher economic classes already had better access to basic services 15 years earlier). There is no difference, however, concerning the gender of household heads.

FIGURE 4.9   **Economic class (circa 2010) and initial characteristics (circa 1995) in Latin America, by country**

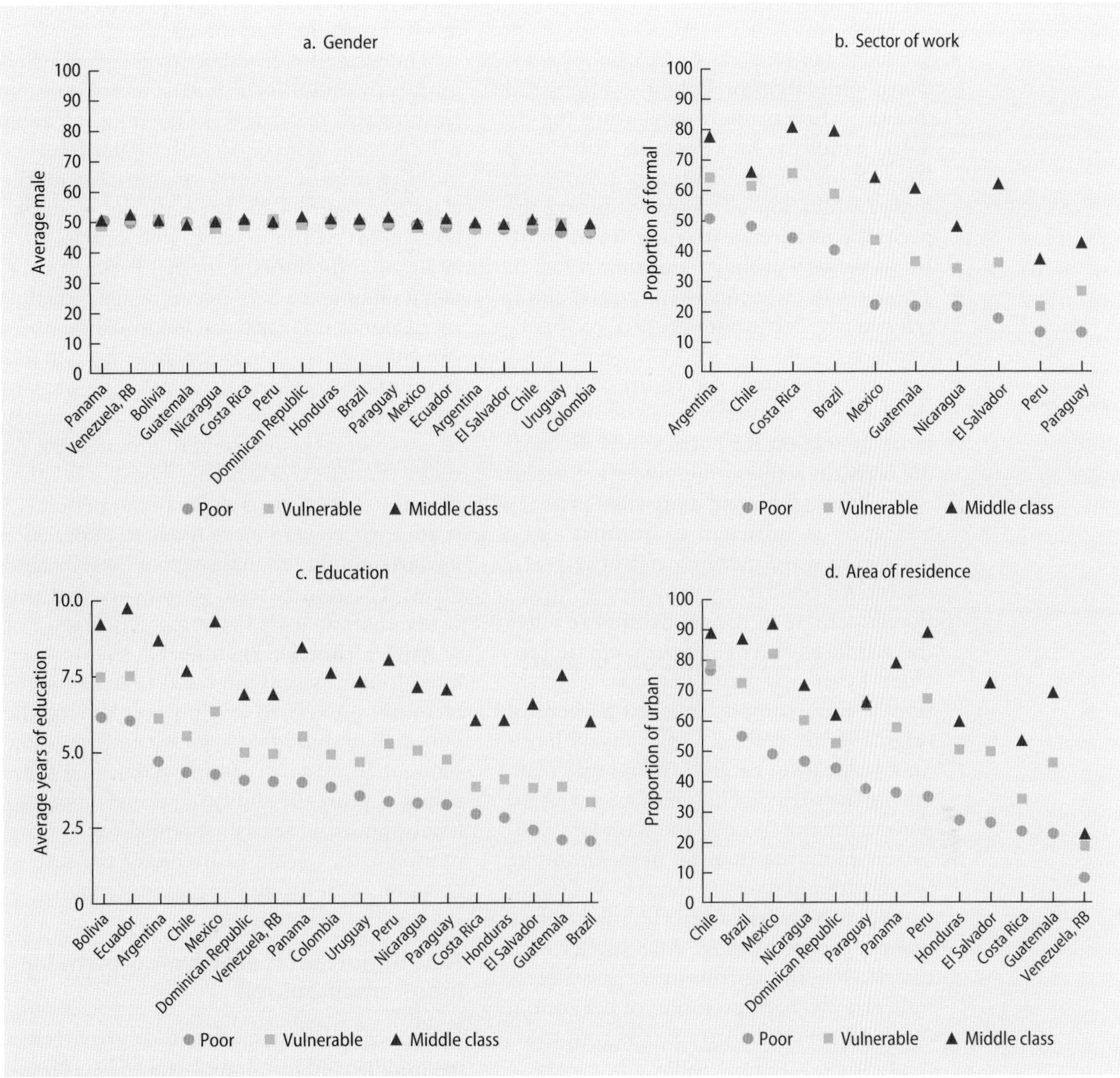

Source: Data from SEDLAC (Socio-Economic Database for Latin America and the Caribbean).
Note: The figure shows average characteristics (gender, sector of work, education, and area of residence) defined circa 1995 by economic status defined circa 2010 (poor, vulnerable, and middle class). "Poor" = individuals with a per capita income lower than US$4. "Vulnerable" = individuals with a per capita income of US$4–US$10. "Middle class" = individuals with a per capita income higher than US$10. Both lines and incomes are expressed in 2005 US$PPP/Per Day. PPP = purchasing power parity.

What drives upward mobility? To try and answer this question, we estimate conditional mobility measures out of poverty and into the middle class for various subpopulations using different initial characteristics. This allows us to say something about how much the initial levels of assets and endowments matter for upward mobility. A few insights stand out. For example, gender is not associated with different levels of mobility. As figure 4.10, panel a, indicates, the only variation regarding gender is across countries.

However, education strongly predicts upward mobility, both out of poverty and into the middle class. Specifically, three messages emerge on education:

- Secondary or university education is associated with larger probabilities of upward mobility than primary education (figure 4.10, panel b). For example, in Costa Rica, 8 out of 10 originally poor with higher education left poverty during the period, compared with only 6 out of 10 for those with primary education.
- These results are consistent across countries with different overall mobility trends.
- Even if suggestive, the figure also indicates that a university degree is much more important for entries into the middle class than to exiting poverty. Specifically, although having more than primary education is sufficient to improve one's odds of upward mobility out of poverty, university education provides an additional increase in the probability to enter the middle class (beyond the increase provided by primary and secondary education).[13] For example, only 20 percent of originally vulnerable Hondurans with primary education entered the middle class during the period. This compares with 40 percent among those with secondary education and more than 60 percent among those with a university degree. We might expect such returns from the steeper age-income profile of those with higher education, but the correlation nonetheless indicates the high premium of education. Again, these trends vary across countries.

A similar analysis can be done for characteristics relating to labor market access. For example, Figure 4.10, panel c, shows conditional mobility measures out of poverty and into the middle class based on the households head's sector of work. As the results indicate, with respect to poverty exits, having access to the formal work sector provides a small advantage over those in the informal sector in only a few of the countries, while for the rest there is not a difference. By contrast,

access to the formal sector is generally associated with slightly larger probabilities of upward mobility into the middle class.[14]

The results with respect to geography and long-term mobility are also interesting, at least for two reasons: Residing in urban areas is in general associated with higher levels of mobility out of poverty or into the middle class (see figure 4.10, panel d). For example, households exiting poverty in countries such as Brazil, Honduras, Panama, Peru, or Guatemala had up to 50 percent higher probability of doing it if they resided in urban areas (we find similar trends for those households that entered the middle class). The data in some countries also allow us to identify recent migrants from rural to urban areas. As such, we compare whether households that moved to urban areas at the initial period (15 years earlier) were more likely to experience upward mobility than those that lived in rural areas. The results seem to indicate that this is the case, at least for some countries. For example, households in Brazil, Guatemala, and Honduras that migrated to urban areas were more likely to exit poverty during the period than those that lived in rural areas (see figure 4.10, panel e). To the extent that these results capture the ability to take advantage of local opportunities as a channel for upward mobility, they seem to highlight the role of economic opportunities and geography.

How important is economic growth for long-term mobility?

Do countries that managed to grow faster over the period also have higher (directional) mobility? It turns out, yes. Although a complex analysis is difficult to do because of data requirements, some simple correlations are informative, even if they should be taken with a grain of salt. Figure 4.11 presents correlations between the conditional mobility out of poverty (left panel) and into the middle class (right panel) with annualized GDP growth rates across the region. For both poverty exit and middle-class entry, countries with higher growth rates are strongly associated

FIGURE 4.10   Upward mobility conditional on initial characteristics in Latin America, by country

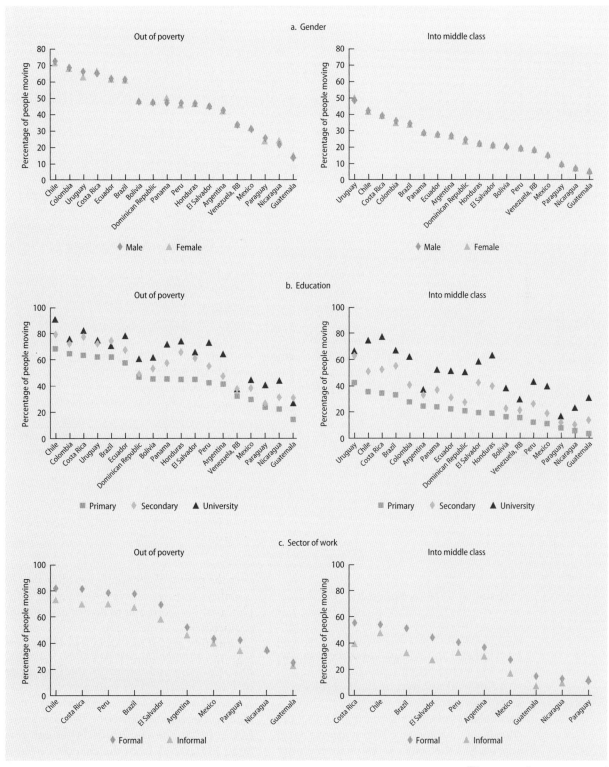

(Figure continues next page)

FIGURE 4.10 Upward mobility conditional on initial characteristics in Latin America, by country *(Continued)*

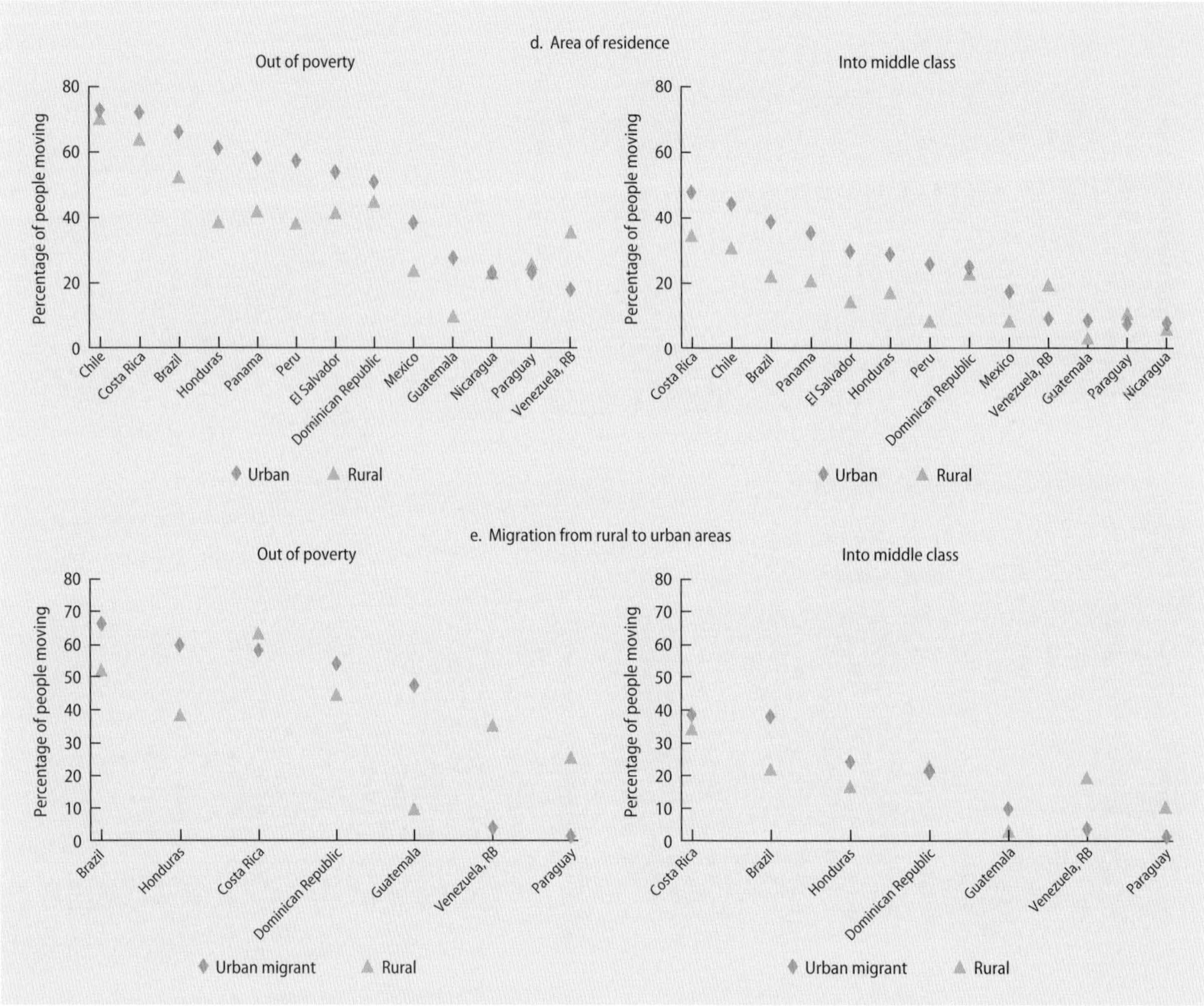

Source: Data from SEDLAC.
Note: The figure shows lower-bound mobility estimates using the Dang et al. (2011) technique. Left panels show the proportion of those originally poor who escaped poverty, while right panels show the proportion of those originally poor or vulnerable who entered the middle class. Mobility estimates are conditional on these initial characteristics of the household head and household: (a) gender (male versus female); (b) education (primary, secondary, or university); (c) sector of work (formal [that is, contributing to a pension] versus informal [that is, not contributing to a pension]); (d) area of residence (urban versus rural area); and (e) migration from rural to urban areas (recent migrants who are currently living in urban areas versus individuals living in rural areas). "Poor" = individuals with a per capita income lower than US$4. "Vulnerable" = individuals with a per capita income of US$4–US$10. "Middle class" = individuals with a per capita income higher than US$10. Poverty lines and incomes are expressed in 2005 US$ PPP per day. PPP = purchasing power parity. SEDLAC = Socio-Economic Database for Latin America and the Caribbean.

with higher mobility. Although this is only an association—and not unexpected—it is nevertheless an important finding.

Additional analysis of these results suggests that much of the correlation above is particularly linked to the roaring 2000s. Specifically, an advantage of the synthetic panel approach is that one can estimate mobility

for different periods and different year spans if cross-sectional data are available. Using the SEDLAC data and the fact that all countries in Latin America have had periodic cross-sectional surveys since the 1990s, we created synthetic panels covering five-year spans in the 1990s and the 2000s. Although this analysis deviates from the chapter's overall

FIGURE 4.11   GDP growth as a key correlate to upward mobility in Latin America

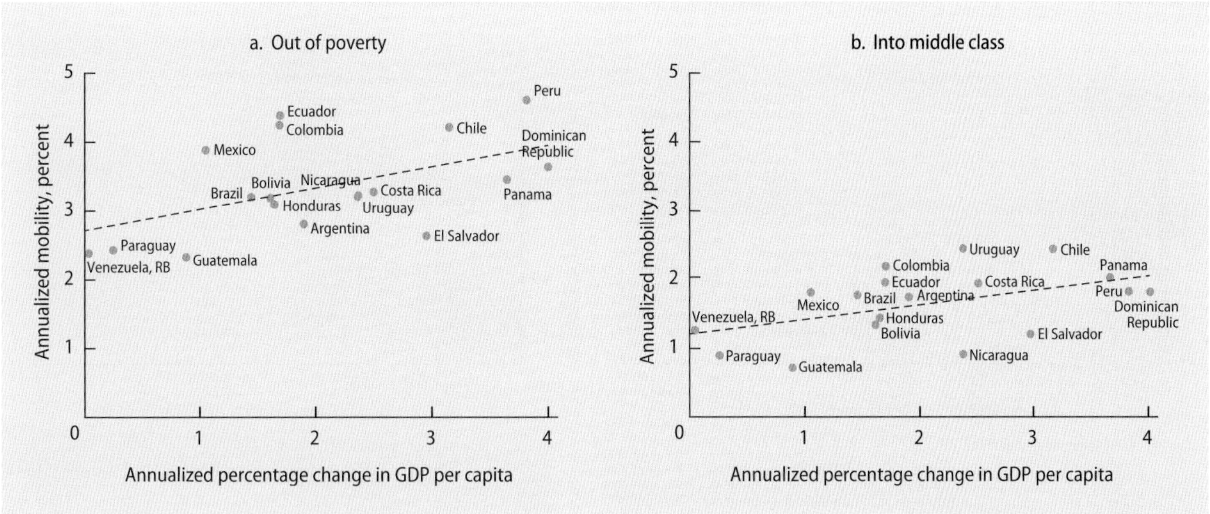

a. Out of poverty

Annualized mobility, percent (y-axis, 0 to 5)
Annualized percentage change in GDP per capita (x-axis, 0 to 4)

Peru, Ecuador, Colombia, Chile, Dominican Republic, Mexico, Bolivia, Nicaragua, Brazil, Honduras, Costa Rica, Uruguay, Panama, Argentina, El Salvador, Paraguay, Venezuela, RB, Guatemala

b. Into middle class

Annualized mobility, percent (y-axis, 0 to 5)
Annualized percentage change in GDP per capita (x-axis, 0 to 4)

Uruguay, Chile, Colombia, Panama, Ecuador, Costa Rica, Venezuela, RB, Mexico, Brazil, Argentina, Peru, Honduras, Dominican Republic, Bolivia, Paraguay, Guatemala, El Salvador, Nicaragua

Source: Data from SEDLAC and the World Bank's *World Development Indicators (WDI).*
Note: The figure shows lower-bound mobility estimates using the Dang et al. (2011) technique. Panel a shows the correlation between *annualized* GDP growth and the *annualized* proportion of those originally poor who escaped poverty. Panel b shows the correlation between *annualized* GDP growth and the *annualized* proportion of those originally poor or vulnerable who entered the middle class. "Poor" = individuals with a per capita income lower than US$4. "Vulnerable" = individuals with a per capita income of US$4–US$10. "Middle class" = individuals with a per capita income higher than US$10. Poverty lines and incomes are expressed in 2005 US$ PPP per day. GDP = gross domestic product. PPP = purchasing power parity. SEDLAC = Socio-Economic Database for Latin America and the Caribbean. Dashed lines show the ordinary least square estimation.

focus on long-term mobility, it allows us to compare mobility trends between the two decades.

Two results stand out. First, for the large majority of countries in Latin America, the 2000s was a decade with higher levels of mobility than the 1990s. For example, 30 percent of the people in Uruguay changed economic status in the 2000s, compared with only 10 percent in the 1990s (see figure 4.12). On the other end, countries like Nicaragua experienced similar mobility in each decade (about 20 percent in each).

Second, even among those countries where overall mobility is similar between the two decades, further distinguishing between downward and upper mobility suggests that the two decades were indeed different. As Figure 4.13 shows, the 2000s was a period of dramatic upward mobility (panels a and c) and very little downward mobility (panels b and d). By contrast, the 1990s exhibited much lower levels of upward mobility while higher downward mobility.

FIGURE 4.12   Mobility by decade in Latin America, 1990s versus 2000s

percentage of population changing economic status

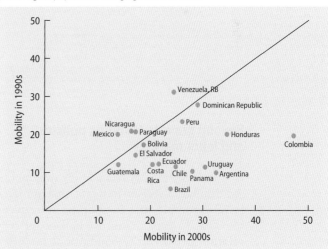

Source: Data from SEDLAC.
Note: Years vary across countries. The table shows lower-bound mobility estimates using the Dang et al. (2011) technique. Within each decade, periods span about five years. Economic status refers to poor, vulnerable, and middle class. "Poor" = individuals with a per capita income lower than US$4. "Vulnerable" = individuals with a per capita income of US$4–US$10. "Middle Class" = individuals with a per capita income higher than US$10. Poverty lines and incomes are expressed in 2005 US$ PPP per day. PPP = purchasing power parity. SEDLAC = Socio-Economic Database for Latin America and the Caribbean. The solid line represents the 45-degree line.

FIGURE 4.13   **Mobility over time in Latin America, 1990s versus 2000s**

percentage of population changing economic status

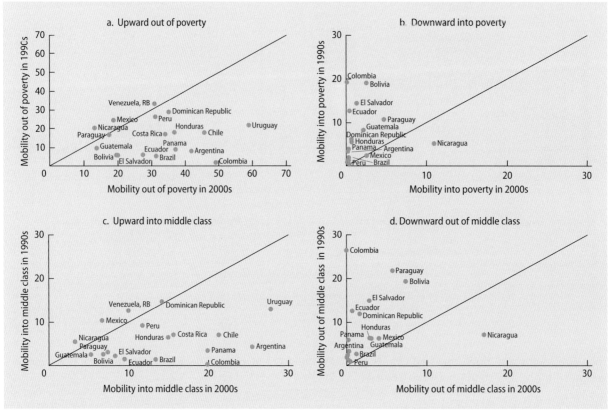

Source: Data from SEDLAC.
Note: Panels a and c show upward mobility out of poverty and into the middle class, respectively. Panels b and d show downward mobility into poverty and out of the middle class, respectively. Years vary across countries. The table shows lower-bound mobility estimates using the Dang et al. (2011) technique. Within each decade, periods span about five years. Economic status refers to poor, vulnerable, and middle class. "Poor" = individuals with a per capita income lower than US$4. "Vulnerable" = individuals with a per capita income of US$4–US$10. "Middle class" = individuals with a per capita income higher than US$10. Poverty lines and incomes are expressed in 2005 US$ PPP per day. PPP = purchasing power parity. SEDLAC = Socio-Economic Database for Latin America and the Caribbean. The solid line represents the 45-degree line.

Beyond growth: Mobility, policies, and labor markets

Is long-term mobility related only to growth? Additional exercises indicate that policies have an ample role in shaping long-term mobility. To explore this, we look at the correlation between the conditional mobility out of poverty and into the middle class with changes (over the same period) of key indicators and policies for each country. The analysis nets out the role of GDP growth—the idea being to explore, to the extent possible, whether changes in these conditional mobility probabilities are associated with changes

in policies and other relevant characteristics beyond the importance of growth.

For example, when we look at mobility and changes in inequality (measured by the income Gini coefficient), we find an interesting trend: Mobility out of poverty is strongly and negatively associated with increases in inequality, suggesting that mobility was higher among those countries that managed to reduce inequality (see figure 4.14). However, a rising inequality is weakly positively correlated with upward mobility into the middle class. Despite the caveats of these correlations, they suggest a potential trade-off of policies that reduce inequality because they

FIGURE 4.14   Upward mobility and inequality in Latin America: A trade-off?

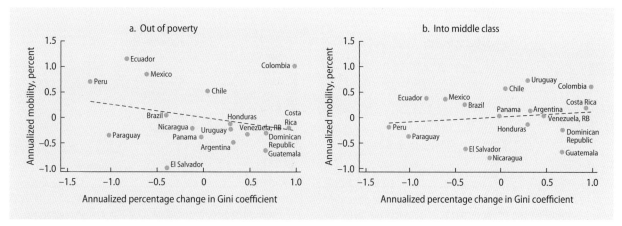

Source: Data from SEDLAC and the World Bank's *WDI.*
Note: The panels show the correlation between *annualized* changes in inequality (measured using the Gini coefficient), estimated from cross-sectional surveys matching the specific periods for each country used for the synthetic panels and (panel a) the *annualized* proportion of those originally poor who escaped poverty and (panel b) the *annualized* proportion of those originally poor or vulnerable who entered middle class. The figure shows lower-bound mobility estimates using the Dang et al. (2011) technique. All figures show regressions controlling for annualized GDP growth. "Poor" = individuals with a per capita income lower than US$4. "Vulnerable" = individuals with a per capita income of US$4–US$10. "Middle class" = individuals with a per capita income higher than US$10. Poverty lines and incomes are expressed in 2005 US$ PPP per day. GDP = gross domestic product. PPP = purchasing power parity. SEDLAC = Socio-Economic Database for Latin America and the Caribbean. Dashed lines show the ordinary least square estimation.

FIGURE 4.15   Educational expenditures and upward mobility in Latin America

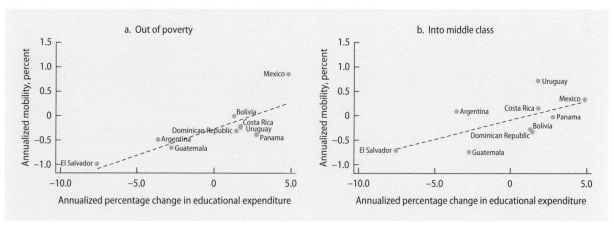

Source: Data from SEDLAC and the World Bank's *WDI.*
Note: The figure shows lower-bound mobility estimates using the Dang et al. (2011) technique. Panel a shows the correlation between *annualized* changes in public expenditures in education with the *annualized* proportion of those originally poor who escaped poverty. Panel b shows the *annualized* proportion of those originally poor or vulnerable who entered middle class. All figures show regressions controlling for annualized GDP growth. "Poor" = individuals with a per capita income lower than US$4. "Vulnerable" = individuals with a per capita income of US$4–US$10. "Middle class" = individuals with a per capita income higher than US$10. Poverty lines and incomes are expressed in 2005 US$ PPP per day. GDP = gross domestic product. PPP = purchasing power parity. SEDLAC = Socio-Economic Database for Latin America and the Caribbean. Dashed lines show the ordinary least square estimation.

could be affecting differentially distinct parts of the distribution.

In terms of policies, we explore whether different policies are correlated with higher levels of upward mobility. We proxy this by using the annualized changes in GDP shares of government spending for different types of expenditures. Again, these results control for GDP growth and, as such, they suggest the role of the changes in these policies beyond the GDP growth in these countries. For example, as figure 4.15 shows, countries

FIGURE 4.16 **Overall and targeted social protection expenditures and upward mobility in Latin America**

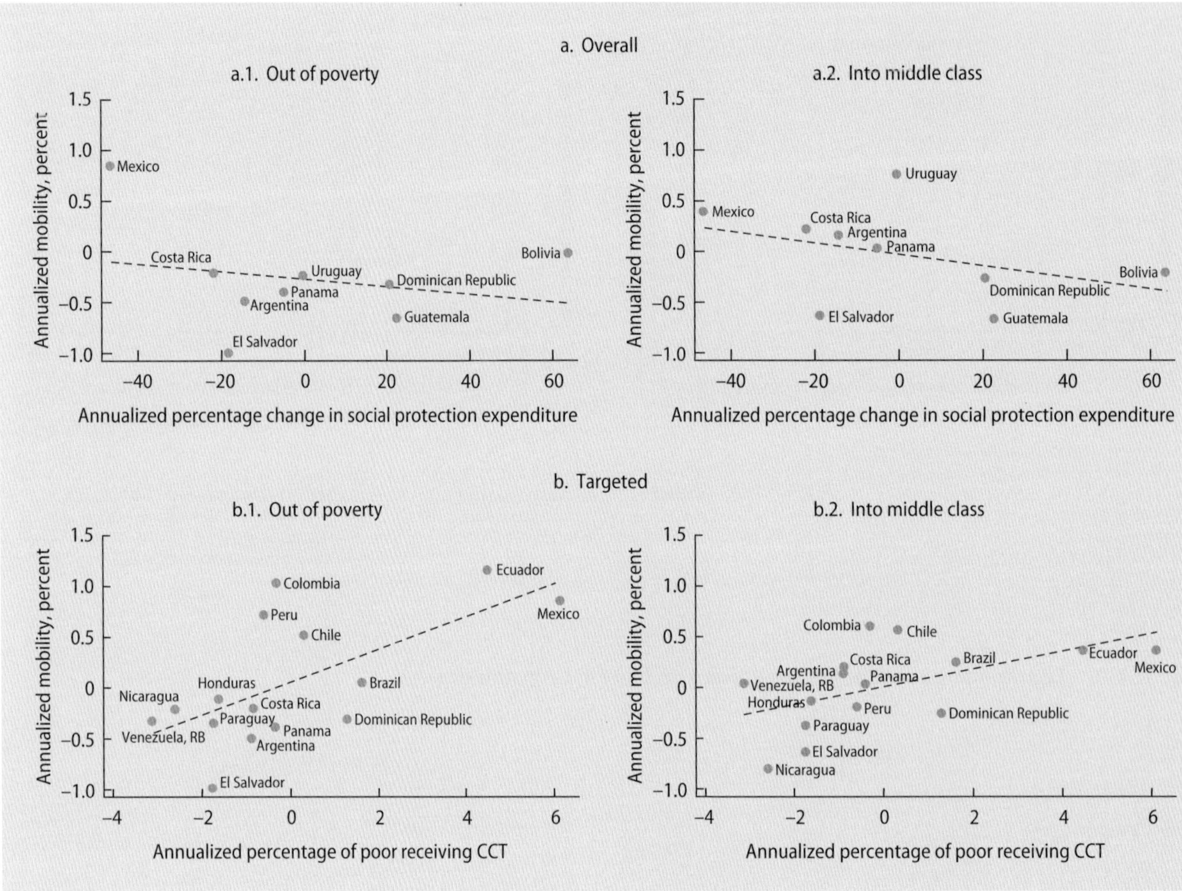

Source: Data from SEDLAC, the World Bank's *WDI*, and the International Food Policy Research Institute's (IFPRI) Statistics of Public Expenditure for Economic Development (SPEED) data sets.

Note: Panel a shows the correlation between the *annualized* social protection expenditure and the *annualized* upward mobility. Panel b shows the correlation between the *annualized* proportion of poor receiving conditional cash transfers and the *annualized* upward mobility. The figure shows lower-bound mobility estimates using the Dang et al. (2011) technique. All figures show regressions controlling for annualized GDP growth. "Poor" = individuals with a per capita income lower than US$4. "Vulnerable" = individuals with a per capita income of US$4–US$10. "Middle class" = individuals with a per capita income higher than US$10. Poverty lines and incomes are expressed in 2005 US$ PPP per day. CCT = conditional cash transfers. GDP = gross domestic product. PPP = purchasing power parity. SEDLAC = Socio-Economic Database for Latin America and the Caribbean . Dashed lines show the ordinary least square estimation.

that increased spending in education over the period exhibit higher levels of upward mobility for both poverty exits and entries into the middle class, confirming in a sense the important role of education investments.

The insights from the same analysis on social protection spending are particularly telling. When we look at changes in overall spending adding all the components of social protection (pensions, unemployment, and safety nets like conditional cash transfers), there is little correlation with upward

mobility (see figure 4.16, panel a). This is consistent with the fact that many social protection systems in the region, although they play a key role in supporting beneficiaries, are regressive in the sense that most of those receiving benefits (pensions, unemployment schemes, and so on) are in the formal sector. This makes it less likely for traditional social protection to reach the poor or the vulnerable classes (who tend to work in the informal sector). As such, although such schemes can be critical in reducing downward mobility,

FIGURE 4.17 **Female labor force participation and upward mobility in Latin America**

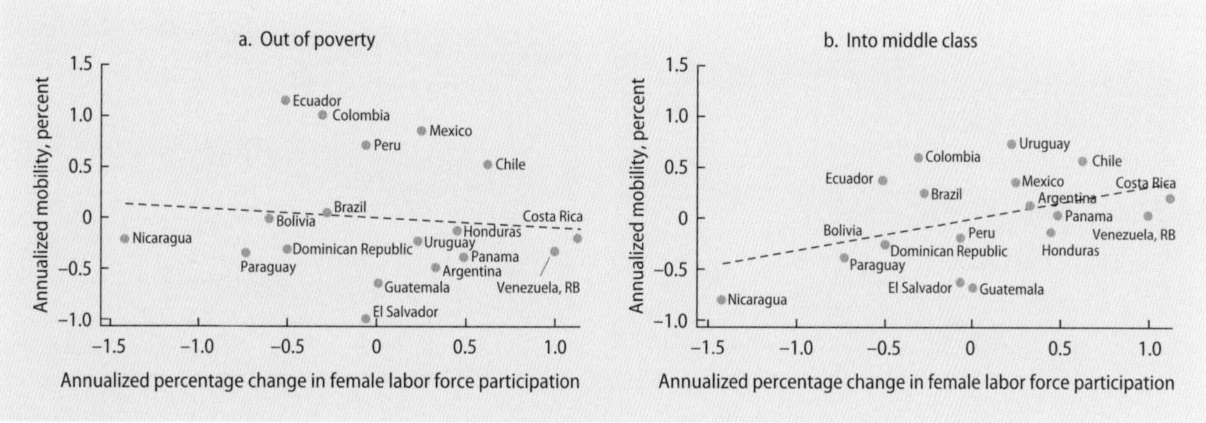

Source: Data from SEDLAC.

Note: The figure shows lower-bound mobility estimates using the Dang et al. (2011) technique. Panel a shows the correlation between *annualized* change in female labor force participation and the *annualized* proportion of those originally poor who escaped poverty. Panel b shows the correlation between *annualized* change in female labor force participation and the *annualized* proportion of those originally poor or vulnerable who entered middle class. All figures show regressions controlling for annualized GDP growth. "Poor" = individuals with a per capita income lower than US$4. "Vulnerable" = individuals with a per capita income of US$4–US$10. "Middle class" = individuals with a per capita income higher than US$10. Poverty lines and incomes are expressed in 2005 US$ PPP per day. GDP = gross domestic product. PPP = purchasing power parity. SEDLAC = Socio-Economic Database for Latin America and the Caribbean. Dashed lines show the ordinary least square estimation.

they do not seem to be conducive to upward mobility.

Interestingly, when the analysis focuses on targeted interventions (see figure 4.16, panel b)—and, specifically, conditional cash transfers (captured by the annualized change in the size of the programs as a share of the poor over the period we study)—we find a strong reversal of the results above: countries that increased their program coverage over the period are significantly more likely to have improved the probability of upward mobility, both out of poverty and into the middle class. Although, again, this is not a causal attribution, it suggests the potential role of targeted interventions in promoting upward mobility.

We also explore the role of labor markets in promoting mobility. Specifically, we focus on the role of female labor force participation and informality. In the case of female labor force participation, the past two decades have seen a significant entry of women in the labor force in the region. A recent study suggests that more than 70 million women entered the labor force since the 1980s (Chioda 2011). As such, we explore whether this is associated with mobility. The results are mixed. First,

with respect to moving out of poverty, there is no evidence of any correlation with women entering the labor market (see figure 4.17). By contrast, there seems to be (at least, less weak) support that the additional increases of women in the labor force are positively associated with middle-class entries. Finally, with respect to changes in country-level informality rates, the results do not show any correlation with mobility, suggesting that faster formal sector growth in some countries is not necessarily associated with higher long-term mobility (see figure 4.18).

Concluding remarks

This chapter explored directional intragenerational mobility. Because we are interested in long-term movements—and to overcome the problem of the lack of long-term panel data in the region—we construct synthetic panels that rely on two or more cross-sectional surveys. This allows the analysis of long-term dynamics and the calculation of mobility estimates for 18 countries in the region covering the past two decades. The main results are as follows:

FIGURE 4.18   **Informality and upward mobility in Latin America**

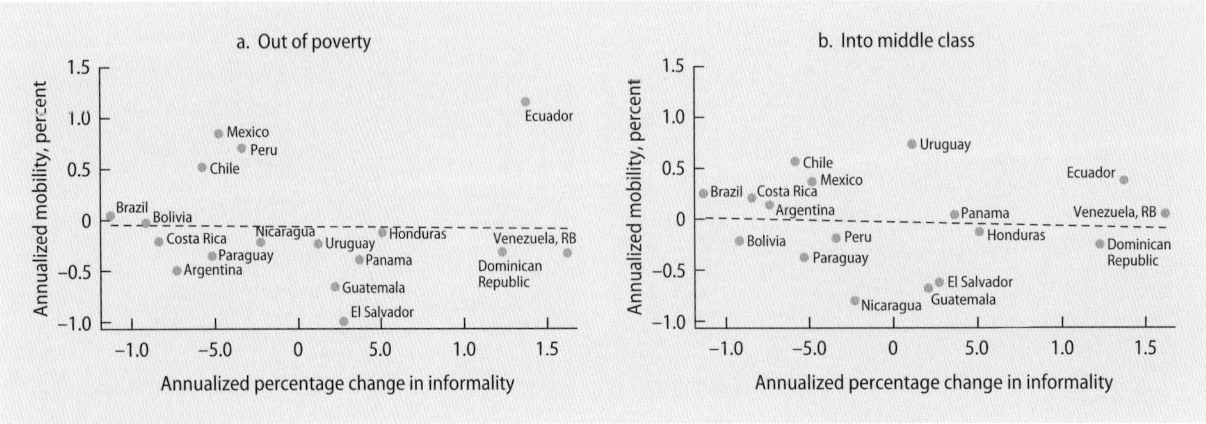

Source: Data from SEDLAC.

Note: The figure shows lower-bound mobility estimates using the Dang et al. (2011) technique. Panel a shows the correlation between *annualized* change in informality and the *annualized* proportion of those originally poor who escaped poverty. Panel b shows the correlation between *annualized* change in informality and the *annualized* proportion of those originally poor or vulnerable who entered middle class. All figures show regressions controlling for annualized GDP growth. "Poor" = individuals with a per capita income lower than US$4. "Vulnerable" = individuals with a per capita income of US$4–US$10. "Middle class" = individuals with a per capita income higher than US$10. Poverty lines and incomes are expressed in 2005 US$ PPP per day. PPP = purchasing power parity. SEDLAC = Socio-Economic Database for Latin America and the Caribbean. Dashed lines show the ordinary least square estimation.

- Latin America has experienced dramatic mobility in the past two decades. Out of every 100 Latin Americans, 43 have changed their economic status during the period. There is considerably more upward than downward mobility: out of the 43 people changing economic status, 23 exited poverty and 18 entered the middle class, while only 2 experienced a worsening of their status. And despite the large levels of mobility, more than 1 in 5 Latin Americans remained chronically poor throughout the whole period. These trends vary across countries.

- This mobility was especially pronounced at the bottom of the distribution. Although overall median incomes increased by US$3.3 PPP per day per capita (or almost 90 percent during this period) across the region, incomes among the originally poor doubled (an increase of US$1.8), compared with an 81 percent (US$4.9) increase among the originally vulnerable and a 64 percent (US$11.3) increase for those originally in the middle class.

- Although the poor are moving up (half of those who were originally poor have moved out of poverty), on average they do not enter the middle class but instead remain vulnerable to poverty. Only 5 percent of those exiting poverty entered the middle class. In fact, for every 10 people who entered the middle class, only one was originally poor. By contrast, the number of those who entered the middle class from the vulnerable was higher than the number who remained vulnerable—a trend that shows considerable upward mobility to the middle class.

- Despite the low levels of long-term downward mobility using the more conservative estimate, alternative (less conservative) estimates using the upper-bound synthetic panels suggest that downward mobility is of some concern, even in the long run. Using these estimates, the analysis suggests that up to 13 percent of those originally not poor fell into poverty. This supports the idea that exploring policy options to reduce long-term downward mobility for the vulnerable (but not poor) may be an important direction for further work.

- Various key correlates with mobility emerge at the individual level. Education,

BOX 4.3 "Calling in" long-term mobility: Did cell phones improve mobility in rural Peru?

Beuermann and Vakis (forthcoming) estimate the effects of mobile phone expansion over the past 15 years on poverty. They exploit the timing of the arrival of mobile phone coverage at the village level in rural Peru, which allows them to test causally whether extreme poverty in villages that received mobile coverage early on is lower. Their main findings are striking: mobile phone expansion increases household real consumption by 11 percent and decreases extreme poverty by more than 5 percentage points (see figure B4.3.1). These benefits increased over time: villages that received mobile coverage nine years earlier have extreme poverty rates that are almost 15 percentage points lower than those villages that did not receive mobile coverage. Equally important, those benefits appear to have been shared by all households in the villages, regardless of mobile ownership, suggesting strong spillover effects and equalizing opportunities.

FIGURE B4.3.1 **The effect of mobile phone coverage on extreme poverty in rural Peru**

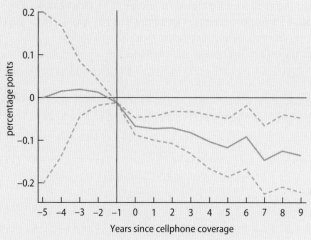

Source: Beuermann and Vakis, forthcoming.
Note: The figure shows double difference village-level estimates (and confidence intervals) of the additional extreme poverty reduction that can be attributed to the arrival of mobile phone coverage in a village as a function of the years since its arrival.

for example, strongly predicts upward mobility, both out of poverty and into the middle class. This is especially true for the correlation between university degrees and entries into the middle class—suggesting the high premium of education. With respect to labor market access, having access to the formal sector provides a small advantage over those in the informal sector in only a few of the countries, while for the rest there is not a difference. By contrast, access to the formal sector is generally associated with slightly larger probabilities of upward mobility into the middle class. Finally, households that moved to urban areas were more likely to experience upward mobility than those who lived (stayed) in rural areas, highlighting the role of economic opportunities and geography.

- Sustained economic growth matters for long-term mobility. For both poverty exit and middle-class entry, countries with higher growth rates over the period are strongly associated with higher mobility. This is particularly telling when one compares mobility in the 1990s (a period of mixed growth results) with that of the 2000s (a period of high sustained growth for much of the region). Growth was indeed pro-poor!

- Long-term mobility is not just about growth but also relates to macroeconomic stability and social policy. For example, countries that reduced inflation or income inequality are more associated with mobility out of poverty. Similarly, countries that increased spending in education over the period exhibited higher levels of upward mobility for both poverty exits and entries into the middle class. In social protection, although increases in overall social protection spending are not associated with mobility, increases in targeted interventions like conditional cash transfer programs are associated with upward mobility.

- With respect to labor market outcomes, the results are mixed. For female labor force participation, there is no evidence of any correlation between women entering the labor market and mobility among the poor. The analysis also shows no correlation between mobility and formal sector expansions, suggesting that countries where the formal sector grew faster are not necessarily associated with higher long-term mobility. By contrast, there seems to be (at least, less weak) support for the proposition that the additional increases of women in the labor force are positively associated with middle-class entries.

Synthetic panels using repeated cross-sectional data

This section summarizes the technique proposed by Dang et al. (2011) to estimate intragenerational mobility by converting two or more rounds of cross-sectional data into a synthetic panel. A model of income (or consumption) is estimated from cross-section data in year K, using a specification that includes only time-invariant covariates.[a] Parameter estimates from this model are then applied to the same time-invariant regressors in a cross-sectional survey from year L to predict an income estimate for households from year L in year K, thus creating a "synthetic panel." Analysis of mobility can then be done based on the households from year L, using their actual income observed in year L along with their predicted income from year K.

Formally, assume that we have two rounds of cross-sectional surveys (denoted as round 1 and round 2). Calling y_{it} round t household log per capita consumption or income (where $t = 1, 2$) of household i and z the poverty line, we are interested in estimating (a) the fraction of poor households in the first round of the survey that escaped poverty ($\Pr(y_{i2} > z | y_{i1} < z)$) or remained poor ($\Pr(y_{i2} < z | y_{i1} < z)$) in the second round of the survey; and (b) the fraction of nonpoor households in the first round of the survey who became poor ($\Pr(y_{i2} < z | y_{i1} > z)$) or remained nonpoor ($\Pr(y_{i2} > z | y_{i1} > z)$) in the second round of the survey. This task cannot be performed directly by using repeated cross-sectional surveys because all households are interviewed only once, in either in the first or second round of the survey.

However, we can straightforwardly estimate the relationship between income and time-invariant characteristics in each round:

$$y_{it} = \beta_t' x_{it} + \varepsilon_{it} \quad t = 1,2 \qquad \text{(F4.1a)}$$

where x_{it} is a vector of time-invariant characteristics (or characteristics that can be easily recalled from one round to the other one) of household i in round t of the survey and ε_{it} is an error term. Using observations from the second round, we can predict consumption in the first round ($\hat{y}_{i1}^2$) by means of the same observed vector of time-invariant or retrospective characteristics (x_{i1}^2) and the first round ordinary least squares

(OLS) estimates of parameters $\hat{\beta}_1$, where the superscript refers to observations of households surveyed in the second round. Because we do not know the empirical correlation between the error term between the two rounds, *lower-* and *upper-bound* estimates of mobility are derived using two different sets of assumptions about the correlation.

Specifically, Lanjouw et al. (2011) argue that the correlation between both error terms is likely to be non-negative.[b] Then, if we assume zero correlation between the first-round and second-round error terms, Lanjouw et al. (2011) propose to predict income in the first round by randomly drawing with replacement for each household i in the second round from the empirical distribution of first-round estimated residuals (denoted by $\tilde{\varepsilon}_{i1}^2$) as follows:

$$\hat{y}_{i1}^{2U} = \hat{\beta}_1' x_{i1}^2 + \tilde{\varepsilon}_{i1}^2. \qquad \text{(F4.1b)}$$

Equation (F4.1b) allows us then to compute estimates of movements in and out of poverty. For example, the fraction of poor households in the first round that escaped poverty in the second round is given by

$$\Pr(y_{i2}^2 > z | \hat{y}_{i1}^{2U} < z). \qquad \text{(F4.1c)}$$

Because we are randomly drawing from the empirical distribution of estimated errors, we need to repeat the procedure R times and take average of equation (F4.1c) to estimate movements in and out of poverty. In all likelihood, however, the correlation between error terms will be positive. By assuming no correlation, equation (F4.1c) will provide an upper-bound estimate of the mobility in and out of poverty. Dang et al. (2011) propose estimating also a lower bound on mobility by now assuming a perfect positive correlation between error terms. In this particular case, estimates of residuals from the second round ($\hat{\varepsilon}_{i2}^2$) can be directly used to predict income in the first round as follows:

$$\hat{y}_{i1}^{2L} = \hat{\beta}_1' x_{i1}^2 + \hat{\varepsilon}_{i2}^2. \qquad \text{(F4.1d)}$$

Equation (F4.1d) allows us to compute lower-bound estimates of movements in and out of poverty. For

a. The analysis presented in this chapter is based on the sample of households whose heads are between 25 and 65 years old. Results are then weighted using household-level survey sampling weights.
b. Correlation between error terms will be non-zero in two cases: (a) the error term includes an individual fixed effect, and (b) shocks to consumption persist over time. Lanjouw et al. (2011) argue that correlation between error terms will almost certainly be positive if the condition (b) holds. In their study using Vietnamese and Indonesian data, they present empirical support in favor of this assumption.

(Box continues next page)

| Focus Note 4.1 | *Synthetic panels using repeated cross-sectional data* *(continued)* |

example, the fraction of poor households in the first round that escaped poverty in the second time is given by

$$\Pr(y_{i2}^2 > z | \hat{y}_{i1}^{2L} < z). \qquad \text{(F4.1e)}$$

Because we are not drawing from the empirical distribution of estimated errors, we do not need to repeat the procedure R times as in the upper-bound approach. In fact, this last approach provides a clean underestimate of true mobility because we are using household-specific error terms (from the second round in this example). In other words, because mobility is estimated across two survey rounds in which the same disturbance term applies to both consumption measures, the lower-bound measure of mobility has been "purged" of classical measurement error and thereby provides a lower-bound estimate of "true" mobility. It is for this reason that we report these estimates in the report: it allows a more conservative estimate of mobility trends.

Any new methodology would make little sense without validating it, especially in a context of interest. Cruces et al. (2011) conduct a validation of this approach by implementing a wide range of sensitivity analyses and robustness checks in three countries in Latin America where different lengths of panel data are available (Chile, Nicaragua, and Peru). The authors show that the methodology performs well in predicting actual mobility in and out of poverty by means of two rounds of cross-sectional data; true mobility lies within the two bounds most of the time, and the results are robust to additional tests. Box F4.1 summarizes the paper's key findings.

BOX F4.1   Validating the approach for the case of Latin America

A recent paper by Cruces et al. (2011) validates the synthetic panel approach in three different settings in Latin America where panel data also exist (Chile, Nicaragua, and Peru). This allows the authors to compare true panel estimates of intragenerational mobility using the three panel data sets, with mobility estimates based on the Dang et al. (2011) synthetic panel approach. In the process, they carry out a number of refinements and test how well the procedure does.

The results are encouraging: the methodology performs really well in predicting a range of mobility measures in all three settings, especially in cases where richer model specifications can be estimated. For example, estimates for mobility transitions into and out of poverty or the middle class in general and for a diverse set of subgroups are impressively similar (such as female-headed households, households residing in urban areas, and household-head education levels). The results are also robust to alternative thresholds definitions (see box figure F4.1). More important, the technique does equally well in predicting short- and long-term mobility patterns and is robust to a broad set of additional "stress" and sensitivity tests. As such, the paper offers solid empirical validation to apply the approach to settings where panel data are absent by expanding this work to the 18 countries in Latin America as we do here.

Focus Note 4.1   *(continued)*

BOX FIGURE F4.1   **Poverty dynamics: Synthetic versus actual panel data for alternative poverty lines in Peru, 2008 and 2009**

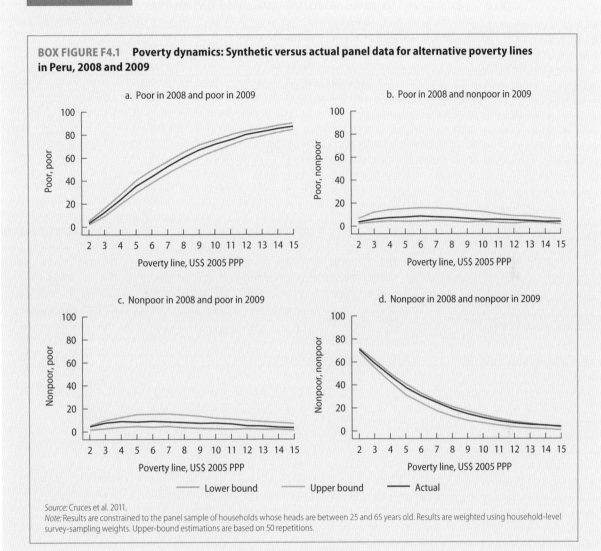

Source: Cruces et al. 2011.
Note: Results are constrained to the panel sample of households whose heads are between 25 and 65 years old. Results are weighted using household-level survey-sampling weights. Upper-bound estimations are based on 50 repetitions.

Annex 4.1

Data used for intragenerational mobility estimates

TABLE A4.1   Data sets used, years, and coverage, by country

Country	Data set	First year	Last year	Coverage
Argentina	Encuesta Permanente de Hogares	1994	2009	Urban: 31 cities
Bolivia	Encuesta Continua de Hogares	1992	2007	National
Brazil	Pesquisa Nacional por Amostra de Domicilios	1990	2009	National
Chile	Encuesta de Caracterización Socioeconómica Nacional	1992	2009	National
Colombia	Gran Encuesta Integrada de Hogares	1992	2008	National
Costa Rica	Encuesta de Hogares de Propósitos Múltiples	1989	2009	National
Dominican Republic	Encuesta Nacional de Fuerza de Trabajo	1996	2009	National
Ecuador	Encuesta de Empleo, Desempleo y Subempleo	1995	2009	National
El Salvador	Encuesta de Hogares de Propósitos Múltiples	1991	2008	National
Guatemala	Encuesta Nacional de Condiciones de Vida	2000	2006	National
Honduras	Encuesta Permanente de Hogares de Propósitos Múltiples	1994	2009	National
Mexico	Encuesta Nacional de Ingresos y Gastos de los Hogares	2000	2008	National
Nicaragua	Encuesta Nacional de Medición de Vida	1998	2005	National
Panama	Encuesta de Hogares	1995	2009	National
Paraguay	Encuesta Permanente de Hogares	1999	2009	National
Peru	Encuesta Nacional de Hogares	1999	2009	National
Uruguay	Encuesta Continua de Hogares	1989	2009	National
Venezuela, RB	Encuesta de Hogares Por Muestreo	1992	2006	National

Annex 4.2

Regional and country intragenerational mobility estimates and decomposition using synthetic panels

TABLE A4.2A   Regional weighted intragenerational mobility decomposition

median per capita income changes in levels (US$ PPP)

		Destination			
		Poor	**Vulnerable**	**Middle class**	**Total**
	Poor	0.22	0.60	0.18	0.99
Origin	**Vulnerable**	−0.01	0.37	1.26	1.62
	Middle class	0.00	−0.01	2.36	2.34
Total		0.21	0.95	3.79	4.96

Source: Data from SEDLAC.
Note: Years vary across countries. Years used are: Argentina 1994 and 2009; Bolivia 1992 and 2007; Brazil 1990 and 2009; Chile 1992 and 2009; Colombia 1992 and 2008; Costa Rica 1989 and 2009; Dominican Republic 1996 and 2009; Ecuador 1995 and 2009; Guatemala 2000 and 2006; Honduras 1994 and 2009; Mexico 2000 and 2008; Nicaragua 1998 and 2005; Panama 1994 and 2009; Peru 1999 and 2009; Paraguay 1999 and 2009; El Salvador 1991 and 2008; Uruguay 1989 and 2009; and República Bolivariana de Venezuela 1992 and 2006. The table shows lower-bound mobility estimates using the Dang et al. (2011) technique. Each cell shows median income changes in levels *weighted* using the proportion of the population in each cell. "Poor" = individuals with a per capita income lower than US$4. "Vulnerable" = individuals with a per capita income of US$4–US$10. "Middle class" = individuals with a per capita income higher than US$10. Poverty lines and incomes are expressed in 2005 US$ PPP per day. PPP = purchasing power parity. SEDLAC = Socio-Economic Database for Latin America and the Caribbean.

TABLE A4.2B   Regional weighted intragenerational mobility decomposition

percentage median income growth

		Destination			
		Poor	**Vulnerable**	**Middle class**	**Total**
	Poor	19.48	23.13	5.84	48.45
Origin	**Vulnerable**	−0.13	7.42	19.36	26.64
	Middle class	−0.01	−0.08	13.22	13.13
Total		19.34	30.47	38.42	88.22

Source: Data from SEDLAC.
Note: Years vary across countries. Years used are: Argentina 1994 and 2009; Bolivia 1992 and 2007; Brazil 1990 and 2009; Chile 1992 and 2009; Colombia 1992 and 2008; Costa Rica 1989 and 2009; Dominican Republic 1996 and 2009; Ecuador 1995 and 2009; Guatemala 2000 and 2006; Honduras 1994 and 2009; Mexico 2000 and 2008; Nicaragua 1998 and 2005; Panama 1994 and 2009; Peru 1999 and 2009; Paraguay 1999 and 2009; El Salvador 1991 and 2008; Uruguay 1989 and 2009; and República Bolivariana de Venezuela 1992 and 2006. The table shows lower-bound mobility estimates using the Dang et al. (2011) technique. Each cell shows median income changes in levels *weighted* using the proportion of the population in each cell. "Poor" = individuals with a per capita income lower than US$4. "Vulnerable" = individuals with a per capita income of US$4–US$10. "Middle class" = individuals with a per capita income higher than US$10. Poverty lines and incomes are expressed in 2005 US$ PPP per day. PPP = purchasing power parity. SEDLAC = Socio-Economic Database for Latin America and the Caribbean.

TABLE A4.2C   Country-specific intragenerational mobility in Latin America

percentage of population

		Argentina				Bolivia				Brazil			
		Destination				Destination				Destination			
		P	V	MC	Total	P	V	MC	Total	P	V	MC	Total
	P	10.6	7.6	0.1	18.3	34.0	28.1	3.1	65.2	20.8	27.8	4.5	53.1
Origin	V	0.8	22.6	14.7	38.2	0.3	10.8	15.1	26.3	0.0	4.8	22.5	27.3
	MC	0.0	1.1	42.4	43.5	0.0	0.1	8.4	8.5	0.0	0.0	19.6	19.6
Total		11.4	31.4	57.2	100.0	34.4	39.0	26.7	100.0	20.8	32.5	46.6	100.0

		Costa Rica				Chile				Colombia			
		Destination				Destination				Destination			
		P	V	MC	Total	P	V	MC	Total	P	V	MC	Total
	P	13.6	24.8	1.0	39.3	11.6	27.3	1.9	40.9	12.9	26.5	0.8	40.1
Origin	V	0.0	11.3	30.4	41.7	0.0	7.9	31.4	39.3	0.0	11.9	26.5	38.4
	MC	0.0	0.0	18.9	18.9	0.0	0.0	19.8	19.8	0.0	0.0	21.5	21.5
Total		13.6	36.0	50.4	100.0	11.6	35.3	53.1	100.0	12.9	38.4	48.7	100.0

		Dominican Republic				Ecuador				Guatemala			
		Destination				Destination				Destination			
		P	V	MC	Total	P	V	MC	Total	P	V	MC	Total
	P	17.8	14.8	1.2	33.8	20.5	30.2	2.4	53.1	50.2	8.1	0.0	58.3
Origin	V	2.4	23.3	16.6	42.3	0.0	11.5	20.9	32.5	0.3	24.9	3.8	28.9
	MC	0.1	0.9	22.8	23.8	0.0	0.0	14.4	14.4	0.0	0.0	12.7	12.8
Total		20.4	39.0	40.6	100.0	20.6	41.8	37.7	100.0	50.4	33.1	16.5	100.0

		Honduras				Mexico				Nicaragua			
		Destination				Destination				Destination			
		P	V	MC	Total	P	V	MC	Total	P	V	MC	Total
	P	37.3	28.4	4.0	69.7	24.9	11.1	0.2	36.2	54.3	15.5	0.4	70.1
Origin	V	0.1	6.1	15.7	22.0	0.9	27.9	10.7	39.5	0.5	16.8	5.6	22.8
	MC	0.0	0.1	8.3	8.4	0.0	1.2	23.1	24.3	0.0	0.1	7.0	7.1
Total		37.5	34.6	27.9	100.0	25.8	40.2	34.0	100.0	54.7	32.4	12.9	100.0

TABLE A4.2C *(continued)*

		Panama				Peru				Paraguay			
		Destination				Destination				Destination			
		P	V	MC	Total	P	V	MC	Total	P	V	MC	Total
	P	19.4	17.4	0.7	37.5	31.0	25.7	0.8	57.5	33.4	9.3	1.4	44.2
Origin	V	0.0	14.4	19.5	33.9	0.0	14.4	15.1	29.5	4.5	22.7	5.4	32.6
	MC	0.0	0.0	28.5	28.5	0.0	0.0	13.1	13.1	0.1	3.8	19.4	23.2
Total		19.4	31.9	48.7	100.0	31.0	40.1	28.9	100.0	38.0	35.8	26.2	100.0

		El Salvador				Uruguay				Venezuela, RB			
		Destination				Destination				Destination			
		P	V	MC	Total	P	V	MC	Total	P	V	MC	Total
	P	31.2	24.9	0.4	56.4	4.3	7.3	0.5	12.1	22.2	9.6	1.5	33.3
Origin	V	0.0	13.6	17.6	31.1	0.1	13.8	23.9	37.8	10.1	24.1	12.7	46.9
	MC	0.0	0.0	12.4	12.4	0.0	0.1	50.1	50.1	1.5	3.2	15.1	19.7
Total		31.2	38.4	30.4	100.0	4.5	21.1	74.4	100.0	33.8	37.0	29.2	100.0

Source: Data from SEDLAC.
Notes: P = poor. V = vulnerable. MC = middle class. Years vary across countries. Years used are: Argentina 1994 and 2009; Bolivia 1992 and 2007; Brazil 1990 and 2009; Chile 1992 and 2009; Colombia 1992 and 2008; Costa Rica 1989 and 2009; Dominican Republic 1996 and 2009; Ecuador 1995 and 2009; Guatemala 2000 and 2006; Honduras 1994 and 2009; Mexico 2000 and 2008; Nicaragua 1998 and 2005; Panama 1994 and 2009; Peru 1999 and 2009; Paraguay 1999 and 2009; El Salvador 1991 and 2008; Uruguay 1989 and 2009; and República Bolivariana de Venezuela 1992 and 2006. The table shows lower-bound mobility estimates using the Dang et al. (2011) technique. "Poor" = individuals with a per capita income lower than US$4. "Vulnerable" = individuals with a per capita income of US$4–US$10. "Middle class" = individuals with a per capita income higher than US$10. Poverty lines and incomes are expressed in 2005 US$ PPP per day. PPP = purchasing power parity. SEDLAC = Socio-Economic Database for Latin America and the Caribbean.

TABLE A4.2D   Country-specific intragenerational mobility decomposition in Latin America, by country

median per capita income changes in levels (US$ PPP)

		Argentina				Bolivia				Brazil			
		Destination				Destination				Destination			
		P	V	MC	Total	P	V	MC	Total	P	V	MC	Total
	P	0.03	0.12	0.01	0.16	0.33	0.75	0.30	1.38	0.31	1.04	0.38	1.72
Origin	V	−0.01	0.26	0.75	0.99	−0.01	0.34	1.03	1.36	0.00	0.17	1.99	2.16
	MC	0.00	−0.03	2.91	2.88	0.00	0.00	1.22	1.22	0.00	0.00	3.26	3.26
Total		0.02	0.35	3.66	4.03	0.32	1.09	2.55	3.96	0.31	1.21	5.62	7.14

		Costa Rica				Chile				Colombia			
		Destination				Destination				Destination			
		P	V	MC	Total	P	V	MC	Total	P	V	MC	Total
	P	0.15	0.73	0.09	0.97	0.15	0.89	0.15	1.19	0.16	0.77	0.06	0.99
Origin	V	0.00	0.40	2.18	2.59	0.00	0.29	2.78	3.07	0.00	0.44	1.91	2.36
	MC	0.00	0.00	3.15	3.15	0.00	0.00	4.94	4.94	0.00	0.00	3.58	3.58
Total		0.15	1.13	5.42	6.71	0.15	1.18	7.88	9.20	0.16	1.21	5.55	6.92

		Dominican Republic				Ecuador				Guatemala			
		Destination				Destination				Destination			
		P	V	MC	Total	P	V	MC	Total	P	V	MC	Total
	P	0.11	0.34	0.11	0.57	0.24	0.87	0.20	1.31	0.06	0.08	0.00	0.14
Origin	V	−0.05	0.40	0.93	1.29	0.00	0.37	1.47	1.85	0.00	0.24	0.11	0.35
	MC	−0.01	−0.04	1.91	1.86	0.00	0.00	2.17	2.17	0.00	0.00	0.58	0.58
Total		0.06	0.70	2.96	3.72	0.24	1.24	3.85	5.33	0.06	0.32	0.69	1.07

		Honduras				Mexico				Nicaragua			
		Destination				Destination				Destination			
		P	V	MC	Total	P	V	MC	Total	P	V	MC	Total
	P	0.38	0.96	0.36	1.70	0.11	0.21	0.01	0.32	0.20	0.34	0.03	0.58
Origin	V	0.00	0.17	1.29	1.46	−0.01	0.31	0.48	0.78	0.00	0.14	0.32	0.45
	MC	0.00	0.00	1.25	1.25	0.00	−0.02	0.83	0.81	0.00	−0.01	0.18	0.17
Total		0.38	1.13	2.91	4.41	0.10	0.50	1.32	1.92	0.20	0.48	0.53	1.20

TABLE A4.2D   *(continued)*

		Panama				Peru				Paraguay			
		Destination				Destination				Destination			
		P	V	MC	Total	P	V	MC	Total	P	V	MC	Total
	P	0.17	0.43	0.06	0.67	0.33	0.69	0.07	1.09	0.06	0.23	0.19	0.48
Origin	V	0.00	0.39	1.06	1.45	0.00	0.39	0.87	1.26	−0.07	−0.03	0.33	0.24
	MC	0.00	0.00	2.64	2.64	0.00	0.00	1.15	1.15	−0.01	−0.11	0.12	0.01
Total		0.17	0.82	3.77	4.77	0.33	1.08	2.09	3.49	−0.02	0.09	0.65	0.72

		El Salvador				Uruguay				Venezuela, RB			
		Destination				Destination				Destination			
		P	V	MC	Total	P	V	MC	Total	P	V	MC	Total
	P	0.28	0.69	0.03	1.00	0.03	0.19	0.04	0.26	0.02	0.22	0.20	0.44
Origin	V	0.00	0.33	1.15	1.48	0.00	0.30	1.55	1.84	−0.36	0.14	0.87	0.64
	MC	0.00	0.00	1.53	1.53	0.00	0.00	6.29	6.29	−0.18	−0.13	0.45	0.13
Total		0.28	1.02	2.71	4.01	0.03	0.49	7.87	8.39	−0.53	0.22	1.53	1.22

Source: Data from SEDLAC.
Note: P = poor. V = vulnerable. MC = middle class. Years vary across countries. Years used are: Argentina 1994 and 2009; Bolivia 1992 and 2007; Brazil 1990 and 2009; Chile 1992 and 2009; Colombia 1992 and 2008; Costa Rica 1989 and 2009; Dominican Republic 1996 and 2009; Ecuador 1995 and 2009; Guatemala 2000 and 2006; Honduras 1994 and 2009; Mexico 2000 and 2008; Nicaragua 1998 and 2005; Panama 1994 and 2009; Peru 1999 and 2009; Paraguay 1999 and 2009; El Salvador 1991 and 2008; Uruguay 1989 and 2009; and República Bolivariana de Venezuela 1992 and 2006. The table shows lower-bound mobility estimates using the Dang et al. (2011) technique. Each cell show median income changes in levels. "Poor" = individuals with a per capita income lower than US$4. "Vulnerable" = individuals with a per capita income of US$4–US$10. "Middle class" = individuals with a per capita income higher than US$10. Poverty lines and incomes are expressed in 2005 US$ PPP per day. PPP = purchasing power parity. SEDLAC = Socio-Economic Database for Latin America and the Caribbean.

TABLE A4.2E Country-specific weighted intragenerational mobility decomposition in Latin America, by country

median income growth in percentages

		Argentina				Bolivia				Brazil			
		Destination				Destination				Destination			
		P	V	MC	Total	P	V	MC	Total	P	V	MC	Total
	P	1.38	3.88	0.22	5.48	22.53	27.07	9.31	58.91	32.63	45.42	11.67	89.72
Origin	V	−0.23	4.48	9.78	14.03	−0.12	6.66	15.85	22.40	0.00	3.62	32.63	36.25
	MC	0.00	−0.25	17.22	16.98	0.00	−0.02	8.16	8.14	0.00	0.00	17.04	17.04
Total		3.88	0.22	0.00	36.49	22.42	33.70	33.33	89.45	32.63	49.05	61.34	143.02

		Costa Rica				Chile				Colombia			
		Destination				Destination				Destination			
		P	V	MC	Total	P	V	MC	Total	P	V	MC	Total
	P	11.43	25.29	2.82	39.55	10.09	32.63	4.47	47.19	10.38	27.26	1.58	39.23
Origin	V	0.00	8.42	33.21	41.62	−0.01	6.13	45.30	51.42	0.00	9.27	29.37	38.64
	MC	0.00	0.00	21.44	21.44	0.00	0.00	30.81	30.80	0.00	0.00	20.83	20.83
Total		11.43	33.71	57.47	102.61	10.08	38.76	80.57	129.41	10.38	36.53	51.78	98.69

		Dominican Republic				Ecuador				Guatemala			
		Destination				Destination				Destination			
		P	V	MC	Total	P	V	MC	Total	P	V	MC	Total
	P	6.67	10.70	3.54	20.91	16.94	31.56	5.97	54.47	3.77	2.39	0.00	6.15
Origin	V	−0.95	7.02	13.03	19.10	−0.01	7.88	22.17	30.04	−0.02	4.33	1.30	5.62
	MC	−0.08	−0.33	12.85	12.44	0.00	0.00	13.77	13.76	0.00	0.00	3.80	3.79
Total		5.64	17.39	29.42	52.45	16.93	39.44	41.90	98.26	3.75	6.71	5.10	15.57

		Honduras				Mexico				Nicaragua			
		Destination				Destination				Destination			
		P	V	MC	Total	P	V	MC	Total	P	V	MC	Total
	P	39.66	39.20	11.90	90.76	5.65	6.55	0.37	12.58	16.36	12.05	0.86	29.27
Origin	V	−0.05	3.17	21.59	24.71	−0.20	5.30	6.13	11.23	−0.07	2.72	4.76	7.42
	MC	0.00	−0.01	7.65	7.64	0.00	−0.19	4.20	4.02	0.00	−0.05	1.04	1.00
Total		39.61	42.36	41.15	123.11	5.45	11.66	10.71	27.82	16.29	14.73	6.66	37.68

TABLE A4.2E *(continued)*

		Panama				Peru				Paraguay			
		Destination				Destination				Destination			
		P	V	MC	Total	P	V	MC	Total	P	V	MC	Total
	P	15.00	14.34	2.28	31.62	29.21	25.71	2.01	56.94	5.17	7.90	9.79	22.86
Origin	V	−0.01	7.43	14.54	21.97	0.00	7.51	12.65	20.15	−1.45	−0.46	4.53	2.63
	MC	0.00	0.00	14.77	14.76	0.00	0.00	7.19	7.19	−0.05	−0.89	0.57	−0.37
Total		14.99	21.77	31.59	68.35	29.21	33.22	21.85	84.28	3.68	6.55	14.89	25.11

		El Salvador				Uruguay				Venezuela, RB			
		Destination				Destination				Destination			
		P	V	MC	Total	P	V	MC	Total	P	V	MC	Total
	P	25.33	26.26	0.91	52.50	1.47	6.37	1.03	8.87	0.84	7.19	7.05	15.08
Origin	V	0.00	6.12	18.71	24.83	−0.01	5.50	21.84	27.32	−6.28	2.45	14.16	10.33
	MC	0.00	0.00	9.75	9.74	0.00	-0.01	35.60	35.60	−1.43	−1.09	3.14	0.62
Total		25.33	32.38	29.36	87.07	1.46	11.86	58.47	71.79	−6.88	8.55	24.35	26.02

Source: Data from SEDLAC.
Note: P = poor. V = vulnerable. MC = middle class. Years vary across countries. Years used are: Argentina 1994 and 2009; Bolivia 1992 and 2007; Brazil 1990 and 2009; Chile 1992 and 2009; Colombia 1992 and 2008; Costa Rica 1989 and 2009; Dominican Republic 1996 and 2009; Ecuador 1995 and 2009; Guatemala 2000 and 2006; Honduras 1994 and 2009; Mexico 2000 and 2008; Nicaragua 1998 and 2005; Panama 1994 and 2009; Peru 1999 and 2009; Paraguay 1999 and 2009; El Salvador 1991 and 2008; Uruguay 1989 and 2009; and República Bolivariana de Venezuela 1992 and 2006. The table shows lower-bound mobility estimates using the Dang et al. (2011) technique. Each cell show median income growth in percentage *weighted* using the proportion of the population in each cell. "Poor" = individuals with a per capita income lower than US$4. "Vulnerable" = individuals with a per capita income of US$4–US$10. "Middle class" = individuals with a per capita income higher than US$10. Poverty lines and incomes are expressed in 2005 US$ PPP per day. PPP = purchasing power parity. SEDLAC = Socio-Economic Database for Latin America and the Caribbean.

Notes

1. This section benefits from the excellent review carried out in Fields et al. (2007).
2. Pseudo-panel methods construct panels of cohort averages, tracking these cohorts through multiple rounds of cross-section survey data.
3. As Fields et al. (2007) conclude, "While there is a vast array of results on mobility for Latin American economies, the large methodological disparities across studies limits their usefulness in contributing to a regional understanding."
4. Recent developments on pseudo-panel analysis include Bourguignon, Goh, and Kim (2004) and Antman and McKenzie (2007).
5. As is well known, general versions of such models are difficult to solve, and most work in the literature has therefore been computationally intensive (Hugget 1993; Krusell and Smith 1998). In contrast, this work relies upon an extended version of the incomplete-markets model recently developed and analyzed by Constantinides and Duffie (1996) and Krebs (2004) that is highly tractable but still rich enough to allow for tight links between the econometric framework and the welfare-theoretic model.
6. Specifically, the Hart index is used, which is the complement of the correlation between the logarithm of incomes over time (see Hart [1981]).
7. The results of Krebs, Krishna, and Maloney (2011) are based on five rounds of panel data spanning two years.
8. See Hoogeveen, Emwanu, and Okwi (2003) for an early application of the Elbers, Lanjouw, and Lanjouw (2002, 2003) approach to the construction of a "pseudo-panel" poverty map.
9. The validation exercises done by Cruces et al. (2011) show that the synthetic panel approach performs well in predicting both short- and long-term intragenerational mobility
10. For more information, see SEDLAC at http://sedlac.econo.unlp.edu.ar/eng.
11. To construct mobility measures for the whole region, we are constrained to use the respective periods of data from each country that are available. Because the start and end periods differ across countries, although we find these aggregate mobility results informative, they should be interpreted accordingly.
12. As chapter 2 discusses, these mobility measures can be decomposed linearly, which provides us with a number of additional insights (see annex 4.2 for the full set of results by country).
13. The population that was originally poor with a secondary degree is generally small (less than 10 percent, with some variations across countries).
14. Neri (2010) argues that the recent increase of the middle class in Brazil is directly linked to the equally large increase of the formal sector during the past decade.

References

Antman, Francisca, and David McKenzie. 2007. "Earnings Mobility and Measurement Error: A Pseudo-Panel Approach." *Economic Development and Cultural Change* 56 (1): 125–62.

Beccaria, Luis, and Fernando Groisman. 2006. "Inestabilidad, Movilidad y Distribución del Ingreso en Argentina." *Revista de la CEPAL* 89 (August): 133–52.

Beneke de Sanfeliu, Margarita, and Mauricio Shi. 2003. *Dinámica del Ingreso Rural en El Salvador.* San Salvador: Fundación Salvadoreña para el Desarrollo Económico y Social.

Beuermann, Diether, and Renos Vakis. Forthcoming. "Mobile Phones and Economic Development in Rural Peru." *Journal of Development Studies.*

Bourguignon, Francois, Chor-ching Goh and Dae Il Kim. 2004. "Estimating Individual Vulnerability to Poverty with Pseudo-panel Data." Policy Research Working Paper Series 3375, World Bank, Washington, DC.

Calónico, Sebastian. 2006. "Pseudo-Panel Analysis of Earnings Dynamics and Mobility in Latin America." Discussion paper, Inter-American Development Bank, Washington, DC.

Chioda, Laura. 2011. "Work and Family: Latin American and Caribbean Women in Search of a New Balance." Regional study, World Bank, Washington, DC.

Constantinides, George, and Darrell Duffie. 1996. "Asset Pricing with Heterogeneous Consumers." *Journal of Political Economy* 104 (2): 219–40.

Corbacho, Ana, Mercedes Garcia-Escribano, and Gabriela Inchauste. 2007. "Argentina: Macroeconomic Crisis and Household Vulnerability." *Review of Development Economics* 11 (1): 92–106.

Cruces, Guillermo, Pablo Glüzmann, and Luis F. López-Calva. 2011. "Economic Crises, Maternal and Infant Mortality, Low Birth Weight and Enrollment Rates: Evidence from Argentina's Downturns." Working Paper 121, Center for Distributive, Labor and Social Studies: Universidad de La Plata, Argentina.

Cruces, Guillermo, Peter Lanjouw, Leonardo Lucchetti, Elizaveta Perova, Renos Vakis, and Mariana Viollaz. 2011. "Intragenerational Mobility and Repeated Cross-Sections: A Three-Country Validation Exercise." Policy Research Working Paper 5916, World Bank, Washington, DC.

Cruces, Guillermo, and Quentin Wodon. 2006. "Risk-Adjusted Poverty in Argentina: Measurement and Determinants." Financiamiento del Desarrollo Paper 182, United Nations Economic Commission for Latin America and the Caribbean, Santiago.

Dang, Hai-Anh, Peter Lanjouw, Jill Luoto, and David McKenzie. 2011. "Using Repeated Cross-Sections to Explore Movements in and out of Poverty." Policy Resarch Working Paper 550, World Bank, Washington, DC.

Duval Hernández, Robert. 2006. "Dynamics of Labor Market Earnings and Sector of Employment in Urban Mexico, 1987–2002." PhD dissertation, Cornell University, Ithaca, NY.

Elbers, Chris, Jean O. Lanjouw, and Peter Lanjouw. 2002. "Micro-Level Estimation of Welfare." Policy Research Working Paper 2911, Development Research Group and World Bank, Washington, DC.

———. 2003. "Micro-Level Estimation of Poverty and Inequality." *Econometrica* 71 (1): 355–64.

Fields, Gary S., Paul Cichello, Samuel Freije, Marta Menéndez, and David Newhouse. 2003. "For Richer or Poorer? Evidence from Indonesia, South Africa, Spain, and Venezuela." *Journal of Economic Inequality* 1 (1): 67–99.

Fields, Gary S., Robert Duval Hernandez, et al. 2006. "Earnings Mobility in Argentina, Mexico, and Venezuela: Testing the Divergence of Earnings and the Symmetry of Mobility Hypothesis." Cornell University, Ithaca, NY.

Fields, Gary S., Robert D. Hernández, Samuel Freije, and Maria L. Sánchez. 2007. "Intragenerational Income Mobility in Latin America." *Journal of the Latin American and Caribbean Economic Association* 7 (2): 101–54.

Glewwe, Paul, and Gillette Hall. 1998. "Are Some Groups More Vulnerable to Macroeconomic Shocks Than Others? Hypothesis Tests Based on Panel Data from Peru." *Journal of Development Economics* 56 (1): 181–206.

Hart, Peter E. 1981. "The Statics and Dynamics of Income Distributions: A Survey." In *The Statics and Dynamics of Income*, ed. N. A. Klevmarket, J. A. Lybeck, and C. Tieto, 108-25. Clevedon, U.K.: Tieto.

Herrera, Javier. 1999. "Ajuste Económico, Desigualdad, y Movilidad." In *Pobreza y Economía Social: Análisis de una Encuesta ENNIV-1997*, ed. Richard Webb and Moises Ventocilla, 101–42. Lima: Instituto Cuanto, United Nations Children's Fund and U.S. Agency for International Development.

Hoogeveen, J., T. Emwanu, and P. Okwi. 2003. "Updating Small Area Welfare Indicators in the Absence of a New Census." Unpublished manuscript, World Bank, Washington, DC.

Huggett, Mark. 1993. "The Risk-Free Rate in Heterogeneous-Agent Incomplete-Market Economies." *Journal of Economic Dynamics and Control* 17 (5–6): 953–69.

IFPRI (International Food Policy Research Institute). Online database. Statistics of Public Expenditure for Economic Development (SPEED). IFPRI, Washington, DC. http://www.ifpri.org/book-39/ourwork/programs/priorities-public-investment/speed-database.

Krebs, Tom. 2004. "Testable Implications of Consumption-Based Asset Pricing Models with Incomplete Markets." *Journal of Mathematical Economics* 40 (1–2): 191–206.

Krebs, Tom, Pravin Krishna, and William Maloney. 2011. "Income Dynamics, Mobility and Welfare in Developing Countries." Discussion Paper, World Bank, Washington, DC.

Krusell, Per, and Anthony A. Smith. 1998. "Income and Wealth Heterogeneity in the Macroeconomy." *Journal of Political Economy* 106 (5): 867–96.

McKenzie, David J. 2004. "Aggregate Shocks and Urban Labor Market Responses: Evidence from Argentina's Financial Crisis." *Economic Development and Cultural Change*, 52 (4): 719–58.

Neri, Marcelo. 2010. *The New Middle Class: The Bright Side of the Poor*. Rio de Janeiro: Fundação Getulio Vargas Press.

Ñopo, Hugo. 2011. "Using Pseudo-Panels to Measure Income Mobility in Latin America."

Discussion Paper 5449, Institute for the Study of Labor, Bonn.

Paredes, Ricardo, and José Ramos Zubizarreta. 2005. "Focusing on the Extremely Poor: Income Dynamics and Policies in Chile." Working Paper 183, Departamento de Ingeniería Industrial y Sistemas, Pontifica Universidad Católica de Chile, Santiago.

Premand, Patrick, and Renos Vakis. 2010. "Do Shocks Affect Poverty Persistence? Evidence Using Welfare Trajectories from Nicaragua." *Well-Being and Social Policy* 6 (1): 95–129.

Scott, Christopher D., and Julie Litchfield. 1994. "Inequality, Mobility, and the Determinants of Income among the Rural Poor in Chile, 1968–1986." Discussion Paper 53, London School of Economics and Political Science, Suntory and Toyota International Centers for Economics and Related Disciplines, London.

SEDLAC (Socio-Economic Database for Latin America and the Caribbean). Center for Distributive, Labor and Social Studies (CEDLAS) of Universidad de La Plata, Argentina, and World Bank, Washington, DC. http://sedlac .econo.unlp.edu.ar/eng.

World Bank. Online database. *World Development Indicators*. Washington, DC: World Bank. http://data.worldbank.org/indicator/.

The Rising Latin American and Caribbean Middle Class | 5

In the past two decades, most of Latin America was characterized by a considerable degree of upward income movement. Such dynamics helped move a large number of families into the middle class, although many others stayed in a vulnerable condition. What did this process mean for the size and composition of different income groups or classes in the region?

Chapter 4 has documented that the transition from poverty into the middle class was not automatic. There are characteristics associated with class transitions, such as education, job stability, and area of residence. And as the poor move upward, in most cases, they do not jump all the way into the middle class. Instead, they remain vulnerable to poverty, and it may take time for them to accumulate assets or reach a combination of characteristics that allows them to move into the middle class. Thus, despite the dramatic movements out of poverty, the "new" middle classes may not be that different from the "old" ones.

The first part of this chapter documents the size and growth of the Latin American and Caribbean middle class, which, after an impressive growth spurt in the early 2000s, now represents a third of the region's population. It shows that where economic growth was able to translate into higher household incomes, it was the principal source of the middle-class expansion, reinforced by a reduction in income inequality. Nevertheless, despite impressive growth in the ranks of the middle class in most of the region's countries (on average, by 10 percentage points in less than a decade), Latin America and the Caribbean remains for the most part a "vulnerable" society, with many households that escaped poverty facing a nonnegligible risk of falling back into it. Social protection policies aimed at the poor are thus likely to remain crucial in the medium term. In fact, given the nonnegligible likelihood of the vulnerable to fall back into poverty, it may be worth exploring how best to address the vulnerabilities of this class, which currently is likely to be excluded from social assistance programs targeted to the poor but, at the same time, may not be able to fully benefit from social insurance programs designed for the middle class.

The second part of the chapter profiles the region's middle class. Although the synthetic panels discussed in chapter 4 allow us to identify time-invariant characteristics associated with class transitions, the absence of panel datasets still makes it difficult to profile "new" members of the middle class as opposed to "old" ones. To cope with this challenge, we conclude instead by reviewing how much the profile of the middle class has changed over the past 20 years.

The definition of middle-class status used in chapters 5 and 6 echoes the concept of *economic security*, which translates into the income thresholds discussed in chapter 2 (per capita income between US$10 and US$50 a day). In some analyses, because of data constraints, we shall, however, group the middle and upper classes together. At the end of this chapter, focus note 5.1 discusses how class levels and trends change under alternative definitions. It shows that middle-class definitions ought to be *context-specific* and that, for the purposes of this review, the absolute definition we have adopted appears to perform better than relative ones. The analysis in this chapter is mostly based on harmonized survey data from the Socio-Economic Database for Latin America and the Caribbean (SEDLAC), a collaboration between the Universidad Nacional de La Plata's Center for Distributive, Labor and Social Studies (CEDLAS) in Argentina and the World Bank.

The middle class in Latin America and the Caribbean

In 2009, for the first time in history, one out of three individuals in Latin America and the Caribbean was living with a per capita income above US$10 a day, joining the ranks of the middle class. This achievement notwithstanding, being middle class in Latin America is still, in relative terms, a privileged status.

Income distribution

Figure 5.1 shows the distribution of income in 2009 for the region. To construct figure 5.1, we merged available household surveys from Latin America and the Caribbean, weighting each observation by a country's population. We also converted per capita household income from local currencies to 2005 U.S. dollars in purchasing power parity (PPP) terms. The resulting income distribution includes 15 out of 41 countries (including overseas territories) in Latin America and the Caribbean, covering 86 percent of the region's population.

Figure 5.1 shows that *both* the poverty and middle-class lines (US$4 per capita or less and US$10 per capita or more per day, respectively) intersect the region's income distribution close to its mode. This is part of the reason why, as we shall document, we are observing both dramatic decreases of poverty and increases of the middle class: any small shift in the mean of the income distribution is accompanied by many people exiting poverty and entering the middle class—much more movement than occurs, say, at the upper middle-class threshold of US$50 dollars a day. Corroborating the evidence discussed in chapter 2, the figure also shows that the middle class in Latin America and the Caribbean remains relatively wealthy: the middle class starts at the 68th percentile, way above the median, and what we define as the upper class (which, for a family of three, corresponds to a monthly household income of approximately US$4,500) represents around 2 percent of the region's population.

In fact, about two-thirds of the region's population remains concentrated in the poor and vulnerable classes. This suggests that, despite positive trends, the region is not yet a "middle-class society" where most people earn a sufficiently high income to consume, live, and behave like middle-class citizens. Although people leaving poverty status represents a positive trend, vulnerability to poverty remains a serious concern for the majority, and social policies will continue to play an important role in the lives of many households for the foreseeable future. The large proportion of people who escaped poverty but did not join the ranks of the middle class is so high, in fact, that it may be worth exploring the extent to which the vulnerable

FIGURE 5.1   Income distribution in Latin America and the Caribbean, selected countries, 2009

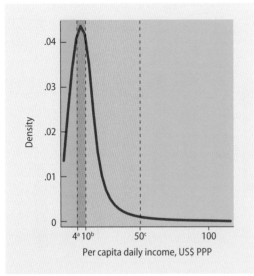

Source: Data from SEDLAC (Socio-Economic Database for Latin America and the Caribbean).

are adequately protected. Unfortunately such analyses, to reach a good level of accuracy, would require the use of "true" household panel data and fall beyond the scope of this report. But future advances in the analysis and design of social protection programs will likely require dynamic studies of poverty patterns.

Regional heterogeneity of income distribution

The regional distribution of income in figure 5.1 hides strong heterogeneities within the region. Although in Uruguay, for instance, more than 50 percent of society is of middle-class status, the proportion drops to around a third for countries such as Brazil and Panama, and to less than a fifth in El Salvador and Honduras, as figure 5.2 illustrates. Almost symmetrically, more than half of the population still lives in poverty (per capita income of less than US$4 a day) in Honduras. And even in wealthier countries such as Colombia, Mexico, and Panama, the proportion of those in poverty is about a third of the population.

GDP and other drivers of heterogeneity

Although the size of the middle class does relate to overall economic development, the relationship is far from perfect: the correlation between the size of the middle class and gross domestic product (GDP) per capita in PPP terms is in fact only equal to 0.65 for the region. Other factors, such as income inequality, are also important determinants of the size of the middle class: for example, in 2009, the size of the middle class differed between Brazil and Peru by only 7 percentage points despite GDP per capita being 20 percent higher in Brazil, partly because of higher income inequality there.

Recent middle-class growth trends

The appearance of a strong middle class is, for many countries, a relatively new phenomenon. Between 2003 and 2009, the Latin American middle class grew at an annualized rate of 6.7 percent, from slightly above 100 million people to more than 150 million (see figure 5.3). In 2008, for the first time, there were almost as many people in the middle class as in poverty (152 million and 158 million, respectively). Despite the global financial crisis, the trend reverted only minimally in 2009. This dramatic increase in the middle class contrasts strongly with the lagging performance of the 1990s—a "lost decade" for the middle class, during which its size fluctuated at around 21 percent of the population for most of the decade, barely keeping pace with population growth.

Heterogeneity of trends

As with the magnitudes (see figure 5.2), the overall class-related trends also hide heterogeneities across countries. In Argentina, Chile, and Peru, the middle class increased by more than 10 percentage points between 2000 and 2010, while in the Dominican Republic, El Salvador, and Uruguay, it actually shrank (as shown in figure 5.4). Overall, however, most

FIGURE 5.2   Class composition in Latin America by income percentile, selected countries, 2009

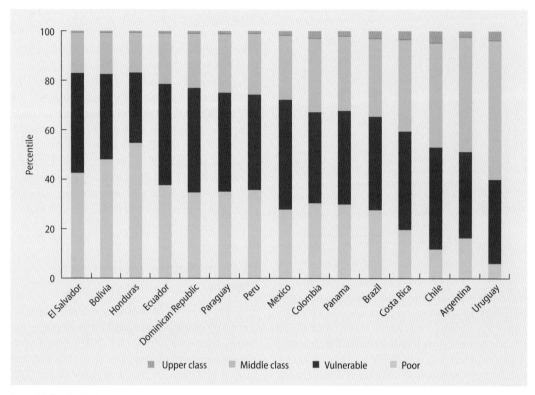

Source: Data from SEDLAC.
Note: Class composition in Bolivia is for 2008, and in Mexico is for 2010. "Poor" = individuals with a per capita daily income lower than US$4. "Vulnerable" = individuals with a per capita daily income of US$4–US$10. "Middle class" = individuals with a per capita daily income of US$10–US$50. "Upper class" = individuals with a per capita daily income exceeding US$50. Poverty lines and incomes are expressed in 2005 US$ PPP per day. PPP = purchasing power parity. SEDLAC = Socio-Economic Database for Latin America and the Caribbean.

countries experienced a large surge in their middle classes, so that the aggregate trend for Latin America observed in figure 5.3 did not hinge only on the massive increase of the Brazilian middle class, which alone contributed more than 40 percent of the overall increase in the region (see also box 5.1).

Influential factors in middle-class growth

Although important, as previously mentioned, economic growth is not the only driver of the increase in middle class: figure 5.4 shows that countries with similar growth rates at times differed significantly in terms of middle-class growth. The Dominican

Republic, for instance, experienced a higher growth rate than Ecuador between 2000 and 2010, but its middle class shrank, while Ecuador's grew by more than 15 percentage points. This difference clearly indicates that several other factors influence the growth of the middle class.

A purely mechanical factor that is often overlooked concerns differences in initial conditions (Bourguignon 2002). How much the middle class increases for each percentage point of growth depends on where the middle class threshold of US$10 per capita per day crosses each country's income distribution. By simple "mechanics," in poorer countries such as Honduras, 1 percentage point of growth will bring smaller growth of the middle class than it will in wealthier countries such as Uruguay, where the middle class threshold crosses the income distribution nearer the mode (where population density is higher and, thus, more people change class for the same growth performance). Similarly, initial levels of income inequality also influence the extent to which the size of the middle class responds to economic growth.

In addition to initial conditions, changes in the size of the middle class are influenced by redistributive policies. Using a methodology based on Datt and Ravallion (1992), Azevedo and Sanfelice (2012) have decomposed changes in the shares of population in each class between 1995 and 2010 into those that can be attributed to (a) growth in average per capita income, or (b) changes in the shape of the income distribution (that is, inequality). They find that per capita income growth and redistributive policies play different roles across classes. On average, across the sample of countries in figure 5.5, redistributive policies played a substantial role in decreasing poverty: 34 percent of the decrease in poverty can be attributed to redistributive policies, against 66 percent attributable to growth in average per capita income.

The high contribution of falling inequality to falling poverty corroborates the effectiveness of the dramatic expansion of social programs in most Latin American and Caribbean countries during the 2000s. Lustig, López-Calva, and Ortiz-Juarez (2011), for instance, do an in-depth analysis of the causes underlying the decline in inequality in Argentina, Brazil, Mexico, and Peru—a representative sample of the region's diversity in terms of initial inequality and economic growth. They find that policy interventions in the social sector played a key role. In Brazil, the authors estimate, the *Benefício de Prestação Continuada* and *Bolsa Família* programs explain more than 20 percent of the decline in household income inequality. In Mexico, the *Oportunidades* social assistance program accounts for 18 percent of the change in the

FIGURE 5.3 Middle class, vulnerability, and poverty trends in Latin America, 1995–2009

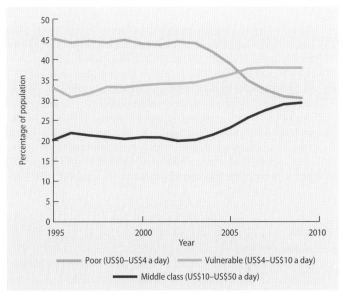

Source: Data from SEDLAC.
Note: Covered countries include Argentina, Bolivia, Brazil, Chile, Colombia, Costa Rica, the Dominican Republic, El Salvador, Ecuador, Guatemala, Honduras, Mexico, Nicaragua, Panama, Paraguay, Peru, Uruguay, and República Bolivariana de Venezuela. Poverty lines and incomes are expressed in 2005 US$ PPP per day. PPP= purchasing power parity. SEDLAC = Socio-Economic Database for Latin America and the Caribbean.

FIGURE 5.4 Middle class versus economic growth in Latin America, selected countries, 2000–10

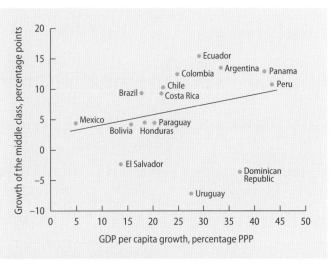

Source: Data from SEDLAC and *WDI.*
Note: "Middle class" = individuals with a per capita daily income of US$10–US$50 in 2005 US$ PPP per day. GDP = gross domestic product. PPP = purchasing power parity. SEDLAC = Socio-Economic Database for Latin America and the Caribbean.

BOX 5.1 The (sustainable?) rise of the Brazilian middle class

The rise of the Brazilian middle class is receiving increased attention of both academics and policy makers. According to Neri (2010), the middle class now represents more than half of the population in Brazil. It rose thanks to strong economic performance but also because the workforce became more educated, which commands higher wages. The rise in households with strong purchasing power is spurring a consumption boom, which, given the continued entrance of a more educated workforce in the labor market and the expansion of formal labor, is expected to continue.

Our analysis broadly confirms these trends, albeit with cautionary notes. Neri (2010) classifies households into five classes (from A, the richest, to E, the poorest).[a] The large size of the middle class (class C) stems in part from the fact that, with lower- and upper-income thresholds of approximately US$6.1 and US$26.2 a day per capita, class C comprises many of *both* our vulnerable and middle-class households (see figure B5.1a). Under the definition of Neri (2010), many middle-class households therefore remain close to poverty, and, in addition to facing

idiosyncratic risks that may draw them back into poverty, would also be at risk under a worsening of macroeconomic conditions.

The second cautionary note regards the sustainability of the current consumption boom. Although middle-class households do have stronger purchasing power, in Brazil many households finance a disproportionate share of their consumption through credit, and the current consumption boom is as much driven by the large demand of households joining the middle class as by the rapid growth in consumer credit due to microeconomic reforms that have facilitated credit-risk screening and the provision and recovery of collateral.

A question remains about the extent to which the new middle classes have the financial literacy needed to avoid getting themselves into excessive debt. Figure B5.1b shows trends in consumer and mortgage credit relative to gross domestic policy (GDP). It compares Brazil with the other six largest Latin American economies (in aggregate) as well with an international benchmark that takes into account GDP and other factors that are exogenous

FIGURE B5.1A **The Brazilian middle class under alternative definitions, 1990–2009**

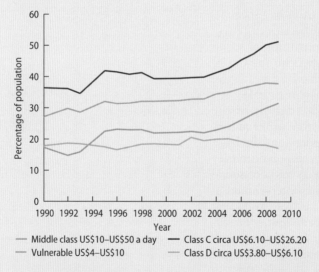

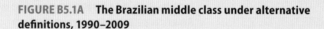

Source: Data from SEDLAC and the World Bank's *World Development Indicators (WDI)*; Class C and D definitions from Neri 2010.
Note: Poverty lines and incomes are expressed in 2005 US$ PPP per day. PPP= purchasing power parity. SEDLAC = Socio-Economic Database for Latin America and the Caribbean.

BOX 5.1   The (sustainable?) rise of the Brazilian middle class   *(continued)*

to economic performance, such as demography and country size. The figure shows that Brazil is an outlier: countries of similar characteristics tend to have half the consumer credit of Brazil and twice the mortgage credit (Didier and Schmukler 2011; De la Torre, Ize, and Schmukler 2012). Although Brazil managed to foster consumer finance, it lags in

generating finance that leads to asset accumulation. Brazilian middle-class households may thus be over-indebted and investing too little in asset accumulation, which may pose relatively few risks under the current high-growth scenario but could be a source of vulnerability in the long term.

FIGURE B5.1B   Consumer and mortgage credit relative to GDP in Brazil, 2001–09

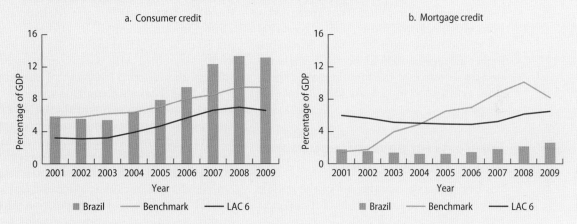

Sources: Adapted from Didier and Schmukler 2011; De la Torre, Ize, and Schmukler 2012.
Note: LAC 6 = Argentina, Brazil, Chile, Colombia, Mexico, and Peru. The international benchmark is based on regressing the variable of interest on country structural characteristics.
a. Neri's (2010) classification is close to the more widely known "Brazil Criterion," which uses access to and number of durable goods, as well as the education of the household head, to classify households into income categories (for more details, see Neri 2010).

pre- and post-transfers difference in the Gini coefficient. Observe that pro-poor targeting went beyond targeted cash transfers: spending on health, education, nutrition, and basic infrastructure also became more pro-poor.

In contrast, the new generation of social programs had a lower incidence in middle-class households. Growth in average household income played a more important role in inflating the ranks of the middle class: for the same set of countries, 74 percent of the growth in the middle class (shown in the bottom panel of figure 5.5) can be attributed to growth in average income, while reductions in inequality accounted for only 26 percent of middle-class growth. Observe, also, that

both redistributive policies and growth in average income affected the vulnerable class to a lesser extent. This is because the vulnerable class faced both strong entry and exit flows. Thus, while that segment's absolute size may have remained relatively unchanged, people belonging to the vulnerable class nowadays are not the same people who belonged to it 15 years ago.

Observe that GDP growth does not necessarily translate into higher household income. The Dominican Republic and Uruguay, for instance, saw the size of their middle classes decline despite sustained economic growth (figure 5.4). In-depth, country-specific analyses fall beyond the scope of this report. One should not forget, however, that to the extent that capital, rather than labor, may benefit disproportionately from economic growth, incomes of the lower and middle classes may not rise as much. It could also be that the incomes of many poor and vulnerable grew, but not enough to lead to a class transition. Moreover, household surveys substantially fail to capture incomes at the top. Thus, they are not informative in assessing how much the very rich (as opposed to households captured by the survey) benefited from the growth spurt of the past decade. Our findings therefore do not imply that growth was necessarily inclusive; rather, they suggest that where economic growth trickled down into higher average household incomes, it was the principal source of the middle-class expansion, reinforced by a reduction in income inequality.

Forecasts for poverty reduction and middle-class growth

Poverty reduction and the rise of the middle class are expected to continue for the next two decades, albeit at a slower pace. Bussolo and Murard (2011) forecast poverty and middle-class levels in 2030 for both Latin America and the emerging world. They base their forecasts on two tools developed by the Development Economic Prospects Group of the World Bank: (a) a LINKAGE global computable general equilibrium (CGE) model that feeds into a (b) Global Income Distribution Dynamics (GIDD) simulation.

New forecasting tools

At its core, the LINKAGE CGE model is essentially a neoclassical growth model, with aggregate growth predicted on assumptions regarding the growth of the labor force, savings and investment decisions (and therefore capital accumulation), and productivity. Unlike simpler growth models, however, LINKAGE has considerably more structure:

- It is multisectoral, which allows for differentiating productivity growth between agriculture, manufacturing, and services.

- It is linked across regions, which allows for the influence of openness (through trade and finance) on domestic variables such as output and wages.
- It has a more diverse set of productive factors, including land, natural resources, and skilled and unskilled labor.

On the other hand, the GIDD simulation is based on microsimulation methodologies developed in recent literature (Bourguignon and Pereira da Silva 2003; Ferreira and Leite 2003, 2004; Ravallion and Chen 2003; and Bussolo, Lay, and Van der Mensbrugghe 2006, among others). The authors' starting point is the global income distribution in 2000, assembled with data from household surveys that cover 91 percent of the world population. They then combine a set of price and volume changes from the LINKAGE model with expected changes in demographic structure to create a simulated distribution of income in 2030. Notably, they apply three main changes to the initial distribution: demographic changes (including aging and shifts in the skill composition of the population); shifts in the sectoral composition of employment; and economic growth (including changes in relative wages across skills and sectors).

Outlook for 2030 in Latin America

By 2030, 42 percent of Latin Americans are expected to be in the middle class, up from 29 percent in 2009 (as shown in figure 5.6). However, almost a fifth (18 percent) will remain in poverty. Over the next two decades, poverty is thus expected to fall by approximately 14 percentage points—a slower decline than the recent one, where poverty fell by more than 10 percentage points during the 2000s. Lower rates of poverty reduction are expected, both because the poverty gap remains relatively high in the region (hence, some of the remaining poor are far from the poverty line of US$4 per capita a day), and because of lower long-term growth forecasts with respect to the recent boom. Observe, also, that the proportion of people in the vulnerable group is expected to remain at current levels until at least 2030.

FIGURE 5.5 **Decomposition of class growth attributable to income growth versus redistributive policies in Latin America, by country, circa 1995–2010**

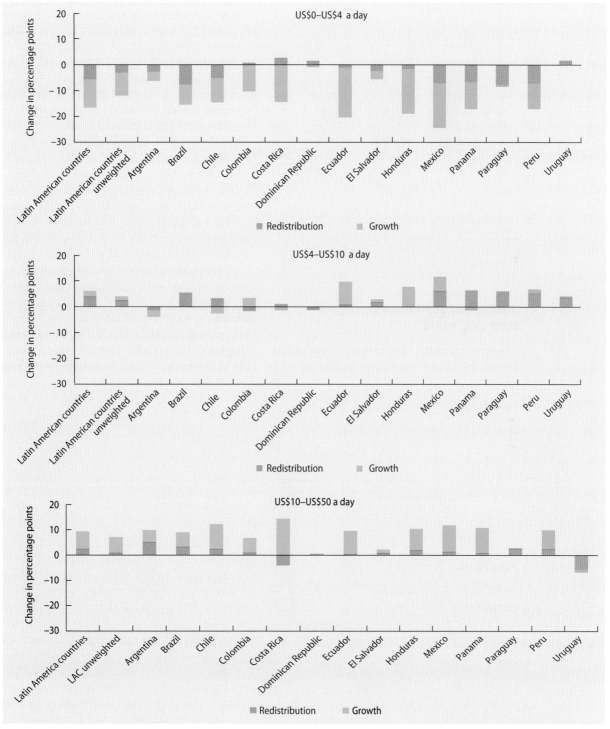

Source: Azevedo and Sanfelice 2012, using data from SEDLAC.
Note: "Poor" = individuals with a per capita daily income lower than US$4. "Vulnerable" = individuals with a per capita daily income of US$4–US$10. "Middle class" = individuals with a per capita daily income of US$10–US$50. Poverty lines and other income thresholds are expressed in 2005 US$ PPP per day. PPP= purchasing power parity. SEDLAC = Socio-economic Database for Latin America and the Caribbean.

FIGURE 5.6 **Middle-class growth forecasts for Latin America, 2005–30**

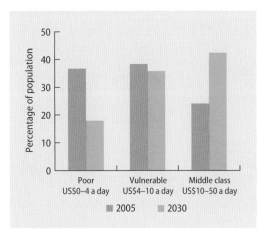

Source: Bussolo and Murard 2011.
Note: Poverty lines and incomes are expressed in 2005 US$ PPP per day. PPP = purchasing power parity. SEDLAC = Socio-Economic Database for Latin America and the Caribbean.

Outlook for 2030 throughout the emerging world

The steady growth of the middle class is not specific to Latin America; it can be observed all around the emerging world, especially in countries that have faced long spells of sustained economic growth. Figure 5.7 shows the evolution of the middle class in Latin America as a whole relative to the BRIC countries (Brazil, the Russian Federation, India, and China), both as a percentage of the population and in absolute terms.

In Brazil, China, and Russia, the middle class has gained dramatic relevance in just the past 10 to 15 years. Around 2009, the middle class consisted of 61 million people in Brazil, 83 million in China, and 75 million in Russia. When measured as a percentage of the population, however, the same countries appear to be at different stages. In Brazil, the emergence of a middle class is not an entirely new phenomenon: already in the early 1980s, the middle class consisted of more than 15 percent of the population, although now it consists of almost a third. The same can be said for Russia, where the middle class currently comprises more than half of the population. In contrast, in India, with 8.8 million people, the middle class still remains fairly modest in both absolute and relative terms. The

FIGURE 5.7 **Middle-class growth in the BRICs, circa 1980–2010**

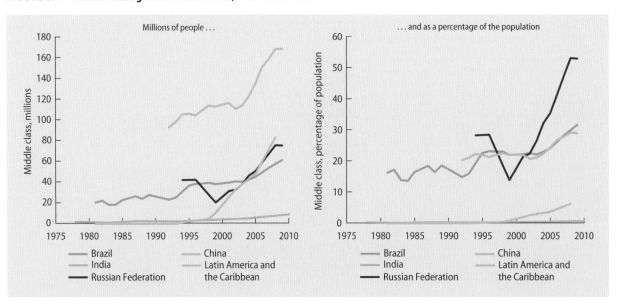

Sources: Data from PovcalNet, SEDLAC, and nationally representative household surveys.
Note: BRICs = Brazil, the Russian Federation, India, and China. Covered Latin American countries include Argentina, Bolivia, Brazil, Chile, Colombia, Costa Rica, the Dominican Republic, El Salvador, Ecuador, Guatemala, Honduras, Mexico, Nicaragua, Panama, Paraguay, Peru, Uruguay, and República Bolivariana de Venezuela. "Middle class" = individuals with a per capita daily income of US$10–US$50, expressed in 2005 US$ PPP per day. PPP = purchasing power parity. SEDLAC = Socio-Economic Database for Latin America and the Caribbean.

largest contributor to the growth of the middle classes in emerging countries, however, is China, where sustained economic growth led to a stunning eightfold increase of the middle class in the past decade, surpassing both Brazil and Russia.

Observe, however, that the middle class in China still represents a mere 6.3 percent of its population; hence its growth potential remains enormous. Accordingly, Bussolo and Murard (2011) predict that most of the growth of the emerging world's middle class in the next two decades will stem from China (see figure 5.8), where they forecast that the middle class will grow from 54 million people in 2005 to more than 1 billion in 2030.

In contrast, although still growing in absolute terms, the Latin American and Caribbean middle classes will gradually lose predominance. In 2005, the region's middle classes represented more than 40 percent of the entire middle class in low- and middle-income countries, but given the dramatic rise of China, that share is expected to drop to less than 20 percent in 2030.

Overall, the growth of the emerging world's middle classes will extend beyond China and Latin America. The next two decades will be characterized by a massive increase of middle-class households throughout emerging countries, from around 300 million households in 2005 to almost 1.9 billion in 2030—approximately six times the current population of the United States. Of course, as with any projections about an uncertain future, these numbers should be taken with a grain of salt. Forecasting is as much an art as a science, and in two decades many factors could affect, in one way or another, the parameters underlying the forecasts. In particular, an average Chinese economic growth rate of 7 percent between 2005 and 2030 is a key driving assumption behind these results.

Who is middle class in Latin America and the Caribbean?

Do members of the Latin American and Caribbean middle class have a sense of

FIGURE 5.8   **The emerging world's middle-class growth forecasts, 2005 versus 2030**

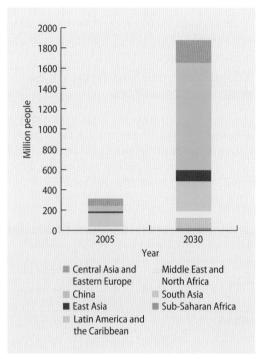

Source: Bussolo and Murard 2011.
Note: "Middle class" = individuals with a per capita daily income of US$10–US$50, expressed in 2005 US$ PPP per day. PPP = purchasing power parity.

shared identity? If so, is such an identity warranted in terms of economic and political interests, as opposed to ethnic, racial, or religious interests?

Profiles of the middle class across countries and over time can help address some relevant questions. They tell us how middle-class households differ from both poorer and richer households in terms of education, employment, and other characteristics. They help us assess whether middle-class people have particular attributes beyond their place in the income distribution. The extent of commonality across countries in middle-class household characteristics, beyond the association with income, is also worth exploring: Does a middle-class household in Honduras look the same as a middle-class household in Chile? And have the characteristics of the middle class in Latin America and the Caribbean changed over time? This section, which draws on Birdsall (2012), describes the middle classes of eight Latin American countries: Brazil, Chile, Colombia, Costa Rica, the Dominican Republic, Honduras, Mexico, and Peru.

Broad class profiles from three exemplar countries

Before plunging into the detailed country-specific profiles, we summarize the broader regional profiles of poor, vulnerable, and middle-class households as well as the main trends arising from the analysis. Without

claiming statistical representativeness, we shall begin by looking at average characteristics of a poor household in El Salvador, a vulnerable household in Panama, and a middle-class household in Argentina (see table 5.1). The countries, which differ from the eight receiving a more comprehensive analysis below, are chosen to some extent because of the preponderance of the respective classes in these countries. We find marked differences in households' profiles across classes.

Poor households in El Salvador

An average poor household in El Salvador earns a daily income, for the whole family, of US$10.30 a day in PPP terms (US$3,760 per year). It has 4.6 members, and the household head has 3.9 years of education. Only 40 percent of working-age women (ages 25–65) are in the labor force. Workers from poor households are roughly equally split between wage work and self-employment (around 40 percent of the workers in each employment category). Few are employers, and unemployment rates remain high, although the latter may reflect, in part, structural characteristics of the country. Almost no poor worker is employed by the public sector, and most work in agriculture.

Vulnerable households in Panama

With a household income of US$26.50 a day in PPP terms (US$9,670 per year), the average vulnerable household in Panama is richer. It has 3.9 members, and the household head has 7.8 years of education. Female labor-force participation is slightly higher (around 50 percent), and wage employment is now much higher than self-employment (64 percent and 27 percent, respectively). Among vulnerable workers, 12 percent are employed by the public sector, and only a few work in agriculture (although this feature also reflects structural characteristics of the country).

Middle-class households in Argentina

Finally, at US$54.30 a day (US$19,820 per year), the average household income of a

TABLE 5.1 Average class characteristics in El Salvador, Panama, and Argentina, 2009/10

	Poor	Vulnerable	Middle class
	El Salvador (2009)	Panama (2010)	Argentina (2010)
Household characteristics			
Household income (daily US$)	10.3	26.5	54.3
Household income per capita (daily US$)	2.3	6.8	20.9
Household size	4.6	3.9	2.8
Age of household head	46.9	49.0	52.5
Number of children	2.2	1.5	0.5
Years of education (household head)	3.9	7.8	11.3
Female labor participation (25–65)	0.40	0.49	0.72
Labor force characteristics (25–65)			
Employer (%)	2	2	6
Employee (%)	40	64	75
Self-Employed (%)	43	27	16
Unpaid worker (%)	5	2	0
Unemployed (%)	10	6	3
Employment sector			
Private sector (%)	99	88	79
Public sector (%)	1	12	21
Primary (%)	81	15	1
Health, education, and services (%)	11	14	26
Manufacturing (%)	5	11	14
Construction (%)	2	14	6

Source: Data from SEDLAC.
Note: "Poor" = individuals with a per capita daily income lower than US$4. "Vulnerable" = individuals with a per capita daily income of US$4–US$10. "Middle class" = individuals with a per capita daily income of US$10–US$50. Poverty lines and incomes are expressed in 2005 US$ PPP per day. PPP = purchasing power parity. SEDLAC = Socio-Economic Database for Latin America and the Caribbean.

middle-class family in Argentina is twice as much as the income of a vulnerable household in Panama, and five times as much as the income of a poor household in El Salvador. Household size is also smaller (2.8), and the household head is much more educated (11.3 years). In the middle-class labor force, 6 percent are employers, 75 percent are wage workers, and only 16 percent are self-employed. At 72 percent, female labor-force participation is significantly higher. The likelihood of working for the public sector is also higher (21 percent), and only 1 percent of middle-class workers work in agriculture.

Middle-class characteristics, selected countries

To be sure, it could be rightly objected that these differences may reflect different stages of economic development in the countries we examine. Yet, at least for the middle classes, profiles differ surprisingly little across the eight countries we investigate below. This is partly because PPP income thresholds are applied across countries to categorize households as middle class. Once income has been controlled for, however, marked differences could still subsist. Instead, the profiles reveal that, with a few exceptions, being middle class in Latin America and the Caribbean carries common characteristics.

In addition to differing little across countries, the profile of the middle class also seems to change little over time. Table 5.2 looks at trends in middle-class characteristics for the pooled middle classes of Brazil, Chile, Costa Rica, Honduras, and Mexico. Between 1992 and 2009, schooling rose by less than a year. The average age of the household head rose by five years; average household size fell by slightly less than 0.5 people, and average children per household fell by 0.3. Although we do observe changes that reflect the major ongoing economic and demographic shifts in the region, these changes tend to remain relatively modest compared with changes in characteristics of other groups: during the same period, for instance, years of schooling

TABLE 5.2 **Trends in middle-class characteristics in Latin America (pooled), 1992–2009**

	1992	2000	2009
Middle class (% population)	15.5	21.2	29.9
Daily household income per capita (2005 US$ PPP)	18.9	19.6	19.3
Years of education, adults 25–65	9.4	9.8	10.1
Age of household head	45.5	47.2	50.3
Age of children 0–17	8.7	9.3	9.4
Household size	3.3	3.1	2.9
Children per household	0.9	0.8	0.6

Source: Based on Birdsall 2012.
Note: Pooled, population-weighted averages for Brazil, Chile, Costa Rica, Honduras, and Mexico. "Middle class" = individuals with a per capita daily income of US$10–US$50, expressed in 2005 US$ PPP per day. PPP = purchasing power parity.

among the poor increased by 1.9 and 2.2 years in Brazil and Mexico, respectively.

Overall, the impressive changes at the country and regional levels do not concern class characteristics but rather the massive movements of households along the income scale, leading to dramatic increases in the middle class. Although the middle class of today may remain similar to the middle class of 20 years ago, many more households have reached the standards that enable them to belong to it. The rise of the middle class raises important questions for policy making: Has anything changed in the socioeconomic structure of society? And what are the implications of the strengthening of the middle classes for the political process? We explore these questions in chapter 6. Before doing so, however, we end this chapter by discussing country-specific middle-class profiles.

Demographics

Middle-class households tend to have about three to four people (more in poorer Honduras, fewer in richer Brazil and Chile) and an average of less than one child per household, as shown in table 5.3. Brazilian households have an average of just 2.7 people and 0.3 children. The average age of all middle-class adults is 39 (younger in Honduras; older in Chile and Brazil), approaching age 40.

As we would expect, the countries' house-hold characteristics tend to vary monoton-ically by class. Household size drops by one to two individuals between the poor and the upper class, and the average adult age increases by four to seven years (with the exception of Honduras). The proportion of elderly, in contrast, remains fairly constant. The differences in average household size and number of children accumulate across households in the different groups in a way that adds up: in Brazil, for instance, half of all children live in households that are below the US$4-per-day poverty line, and another 30 percent live in vulnerable households;

therefore, 80 percent of Brazilian children are growing up in households that are not middle or upper class.

Education

The average years of schooling of adults (ages 25–65) increase with income class, as shown in figure 5.9. The poor have not completed, on average, the basic curriculum, while, in virtually every country, the average adult in a middle-class household has attended at least some secondary school. At the other extreme of the spectrum, adults from the upper classes are far more likely to have attended, and even

TABLE 5.3   Average household characteristics, selected Latin American countries, circa 2009

	Poor					Vulnerable				
	Household size	Children 0–12	Children 13–18	Adults over 70	Age of adults 18+	Household size	Children 0–12	Children 13–18	Adults over 70	Age of adults 18+
Brazil	3.8	1.4	0.5	0.04	35	3.1	0.6	0.4	0.2	38
Chile	4.2	1.2	0.6	0.1	37	3.8	0.8	0.5	0.3	38
Colombia	4.2	1.5	0.6	0.2	37	3.8	1.0	0.5	0.1	37
Costa Rica	4.0	1.3	0.6	0.2	37	3.8	0.9	0.5	0.2	37
Dominican Republic	4.5	1.5	0.7	0.2	36	3.7	0.8	0.5	0.2	36
Honduras	5.0	1.8	0.8	0.2	36	4.5	1.2	0.7	0.2	35
Mexico	4.6	1.6	0.6	0.2	36	4.2	1.1	0.6	0.2	36
Peru	5.0	1.9	0.7	0.2	37	4.3	1.1	0.6	0.2	37

	Middle class					Upper class				
	Household size	Children 0–12	Children 13–18	Adults over 70	Age of adults 18+	Household size	Children 0–12	Children 13–18	Adults over 70	Age of adults 18+
Brazil	2.7	0.3	0.2	0.2	40	2.2	0.2	0.1	0.2	42
Chile	3.2	0.5	0.3	0.3	40	2.6	0.3	0.1	0.1	41
Colombia	3.0	0.5	0.3	0.2	38	2.3	0.3	0.2	0.1	42
Costa Rica	3.3	0.5	0.3	0.1	38	2.5	0.2	0.1	0.1	41
Dominican Republic	3	0.5	0.3	0.2	37	2.2	0.2	0.1	0.2	41
Honduras	4.0	0.8	0.6	0.1	36	3.1	0.5	0.4	0.2	38
Mexico	3.4	0.5	0.4	0.2	38	2.4	0.2	0.2	0.2	42
Peru	3.4	0.5	0.4	0.3	39	2.4	0.2	0.2	0.3	42

Source: Based on Birdsall 2012.
Note: "Poor" = individuals with a per capita daily income lower than US$4. "Vulnerable" = individuals with a per capita daily income of US$4–US$10. "Middle class" = individuals with a per capita daily income of US$10–US$50. "Upper class" = individuals with a per capita daily income exceeding US$50. Poverty lines and incomes are expressed in 2005 US$ PPP per day. PPP = purchasing power parity.

completed, university. Three points about education are noteworthy:

- Among middle-class adults, average years of schooling vary little across countries; there is thus constancy in the crude relationship between income (US$10–50 a day) and schooling of adults throughout the region.
- Apart from Chile, the average schooling years of the middle class are about 30–50 percent higher than the schooling of the vulnerable, and 80–250 percent higher than the schooling of the poor.
- Within each category, however, there is considerable variation, suggesting that even if the association between class and years of schooling is strong, other factors influence class status as well.

Geography

Figure 5.10 shows the percentage of households living in urban areas, by country. Overall, the region is highly urbanized. Comparisons across countries are not possible, however, because the definition of "urban" varies, but within each country, the middle classes are more likely than poorer classes to live in urban areas, which is consistent with economic activity being concentrated in urban areas.

Overall, the region also shows a great deal of internal migration: even among the poor, around half of the adults (ages 25–65) migrated out of the municipality where they grew up (figure 5.11). The proportion of migrants tends to increase with income in all countries, especially for the upper class. But how much the middle class differs from the poor and vulnerable, in terms of migration, is very much country-specific.

Employment

Table 5.4 provides a breakdown of workers by class and employment sector. The categories aggregate across 17 sectors; "primary activities" include agriculture, mining, and

FIGURE 5.9   Average years of schooling (ages 25–65), selected Latin American countries, by income class, circa 2009

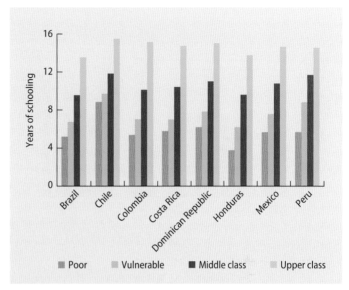

Source: Based on Birdsall 2012.
Note: "Poor" = individuals with a per capita daily income lower than US$4. "Vulnerable" = individuals with a per capita daily income of US$4–US$10. "Middle class" = individuals with a per capita daily income of US$10–US$50. "Upper class" = individuals with a per capita daily income exceeding US$50. Poverty lines and incomes are expressed in 2005 US$ PPP per day. PPP = purchasing power parity.

FIGURE 5.10   Percentage of households living in urban areas, by income class, selected Latin American countries, circa 2009

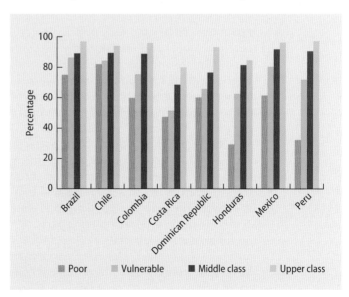

Source: Based on Birdsall 2012.
Note: "Poor" = individuals with a per capita daily income lower than US$4. "Vulnerable" = individuals with a per capita daily income between US$4–US$10. "Middle class" = individuals with a per capita daily income of US$10–US$50. "Upper class" = individuals with a per capita daily income exceeding US$50. Poverty lines and incomes are expressed in 2005 US$ PPP per day. PPP = purchasing power parity.

FIGURE 5.11   **Percentage of adults (25–65) living in a municipality other than place of birth, by income class, selected Latin American countries, circa 2009**

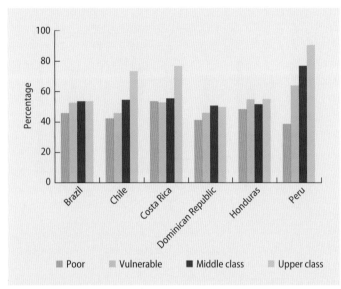

Source: Based on Birdsall 2012.
Note: "Poor" = individuals with a per capita daily income lower than US$4. "Vulnerable" = individuals with a per capita daily income of US$4–US$10. "Middle class" = individuals with a per capita daily income of US$10–US$50. "Upper class" = individuals with a per capita daily income exceeding US$50. Poverty lines and incomes are expressed in 2005 US$ PPP per day. PPP = purchasing power parity.

fishing, and "other" comprises mostly private activities such as real estate and hotels and restaurants. To be sure, within each category, there are more- and less-skilled jobs commanding more and less pay. Hence, it is not surprising that, for example, some workers in poor households work in the public sector and some in rich households work in primary activities.

At the same time, some broad patterns emerge: middle-class workers are less likely to work in the primary sectors and more likely to work in health, education, and public services (in both the public and private sectors) than their poorer counterparts. On this dimension, middle-class workers look far more like the typical "richer" worker than the typical "poorer" one. This finding is consistent with (a) our data on schooling, where differences are greater between the poorer and middle groups than between the middle and richer groups, and (b) the Latin American middle class's concentration in the top two or three income deciles.

The middle class also differs by employment status, as shown in table 5.5. Consistent with the reality that many middle-class workers benefit from a regular wage or salary, they are more likely than poor and vulnerable workers to be employees and less likely to be self-employed—though a considerable number of middle-class workers remain as such. Middle-class workers are also more likely to be employers. However, in that respect, they remain more similar to the poor and vulnerable than to the upper class, where the likelihood of being an employer is significantly higher.

Table 5.6 shows private and public employment by class. Casual observation might suggest that middle-class workers are concentrated in public sector jobs, including those in state-owned enterprises. That is true to some extent: between 9 percent (in Colombia) and 34 percent (in Honduras) of middle-class workers are in the public sector. On the other hand, in many countries, upper-class workers are as much or even more concentrated in the public sector. Among private firms' workers, the poor are more concentrated in small firms, the upper class in large firms. However, there is considerable variation across countries.

Female labor-force participation

Female labor-force participation is relatively high across the board (as shown in figure 5.12), which is consistent with rising levels of education and urbanization as well as with declining fertility. In middle-class households, 60–70 percent of women are in the labor force. This fits into a monotonic relation between female labor-force participation and income: for the most part, the higher the income per capita of the household, the more likely women are to be in the labor force.

This association may arise from a number of sources: Women's contributions to household incomes may move their households into higher income categories. Women in more-affluent households also tend to be more educated and may thus exhibit a higher likelihood of working. The notable exception is Peru, where female labor-force

TABLE 5.4   Employment sector by class, ages 25–65, selected Latin American countries, circa 2009
percentage

	Poor					Vulnerable				
	Primary activities	Health, education, and public services	Manu-facturing	Construction	Other	Primary activities	Health, education, and public services	Manu-facturing	Construction	Other
Brazil	35.6	7.2	9.4	9.5	38.3	16.1	12.0	14.6	9.5	47.9
Chile	22.6	9.1	10.8	13.2	44.4	17.8	11.7	11.8	11.8	46.9
Colombia	36.1	8.9	9.7	5.8	39.5	18.6	11.0	13.7	6.9	49.8
Costa Rica	23.0	7.6	9.6	8.0	52.0	15.5	10.1	13.6	8.1	52.8
Dominican Republic	22.3	14.5	7.7	6.1	49.5	14.2	15.5	11.2	6.7	52.5
Honduras	57.3	5.3	11.2	4.8	21.4	17.1	10.6	18.0	8.8	45.5
Mexico	34.6	4.4	14.4	8.8	37.7	9.5	9.7	18.5	10.6	51.7
Peru	67.1	4.5	6.5	2.6	19.3	23.4	11.7	11.2	6.0	47.7

	Middle class					Upper class				
	Primary activities	Health, education, and public services	Manu-facturing	Construction	Other	Primary activities	Health, education, and public services	Manu-facturing	Construction	Other
Brazil	8.1	20.0	15.4	6.2	50.3	4.0	29.2	10.0	2.5	54.4
Chile	11.1	19.8	10.3	7.3	51.5	7.2	28.2	6.2	7.1	51.3
Colombia	7.9	19.3	15.6	4.4	52.8	4.7	28.7	10.3	2.1	54.2
Costa Rica	5.8	20.7	11.8	5.7	56.0	2.7	29.5	7.1	2.8	58.0
Dominican Republic	7.0	20.5	11.4	7.1	54.1	6.9	29.8	6.5	3.5	53.3
Honduras	7.2	19.8	13.4	6.6	53.1	10.4	24.8	8.3	2.9	53.6
Mexico	4.2	22.9	14.6	6.5	51.8	6.7	26.9	11.2	4.7	50.6
Peru	8.6	19.6	12.2	5.2	54.4	7.6	15.2	14.8	3.5	58.9

Source: Based on Birdsall 2012.
Note: "Primary activities" include agriculture, mining, and fishing. "Other" comprises mostly private activities such as real estate and hotels and restaurants. "Poor" = individuals with a per capita daily income lower than US$4. "Vulnerable" = individuals with a per capita daily income of US$4–US$10. "Middle class" = individuals with a per capita daily income of US$10–US$50. "Upper class" = individuals with a per capita daily income exceeding US$50. Poverty lines and incomes are expressed in 2005 US$ PPP per day. PPP = purchasing power parity.

participation is not only among the highest but is also flat across classes. This could reflect both greater pressure to maintain high income and cultural differences.

Summing up: Is Latin America a middle-class society?

Although a third of the population in Latin America and the Caribbean is middle class, many people who left poverty are still in a condition of vulnerability and require policies that protect them from falling back.

Consistently, being more educated and into wage employment, the middle-class profile seems to be more stable, which suggests that people need to reach certain levels of socioeconomic characteristics to become less vulnerable to poverty and be considered as middle-class households.

Although Latin America is in the process of becoming a middle-class society, the transformation is not yet complete. Some of the social and political foundations for the sustainability of the current trends are the theme of the next chapter.

TABLE 5.5   Employment status by class, ages 25–65, selected Latin American countries, circa 2009

percentage

	Poor					Vulnerable				
Country	Employer	Employee	Self-employed	Working without salary	Unemployed	Employer	Employee	Self-employed	Working without salary	Unemployed
Brazil	1.2	46.8	25.2	12.9	13.9	2.2	65.3	21.4	5.6	5.6
Chile	1.4	54.0	15.6	0.5	28.4	0.8	74.2	14.9	0.3	9.8
Colombia	3.6	22.6	54.8	4.3	14.7	3.9	39.4	44.5	3.0	9.2
Costa Rica	6.0	48.5	27.5	1.0	17.0	5.6	66.1	21.8	1.2	5.3
Dominican Republic	2.2	43.0	48.6	0.8	5.4	3.8	50.5	42.8	0.7	2.1
Honduras	15.6	31.0	46.6	4.6	2.2	13.3	46.9	34.0	3.1	2.7
Mexico	5.1	51.2	31.1	7.0	5.6	3.8	71.5	18.6	3.3	2.8
Peru	4.1	18.8	51.7	23.1	2.3	5.7	44.2	39.6	7.5	3.1

	Middle class					Upper class				
	Employer	Employee	Self-employed	Working without salary	Unemployed	Employer	Employee	Self-employed	Working without salary	Unemployed
Brazil	7.4	66.7	20.0	3.4	2.5	20.9	60.0	16.4	1.3	1.4
Chile	3.0	70.7	21.9	0.4	4.0	15.0	60.0	21.5	0.2	3.4
Colombia	6.4	54.6	31.6	1.9	5.4	14.3	58.7	23.9	0.7	2.4
Costa Rica	8.6	72.5	16.0	0.9	2.0	17.6	73.6	7.4	0.3	1.0
Dominican Republic	8.2	52.8	36.0	1.1	1.9	17.2	46.8	34.5	0.0	1.6
Honduras	15.4	56.2	22.9	3.4	2.2	30.6	52.8	14.4	1.0	1.2
Mexico	6.9	76.3	12.9	2.2	1.8	21.1	65.0	8.7	3.5	1.6
Peru	8.6	56.3	28.1	4.2	2.8	20.5	63.8	12.3	0.6	2.8

Source: Based on Birdsall 2012.

Note: "Poor" = individuals with a per capita daily income lower than US$4. "Vulnerable" = individuals with a per capita daily income between US$4–US$10. "Middle class" = individuals with a per capita daily income of US$10–US$50. "Upper class" = individuals with a per capita daily income exceeding US$50. Poverty lines and incomes are expressed in 2005 US$ PPP per day. PPP = purchasing power parity.

TABLE 5.6 **Private and public employment by class, ages 25–65, selected Latin American countries, circa 2009**
percentage

| | Poor | | | Vulnerable | | |
| | Private firm | | | Private firm | | |
	Small	Large	Public firm	Small	Large	Public firm
Brazil	75.4	19.2	5.4	56.5	33.6	9.9
Chile	51.9	38.8	9.3	39.0	50.7	10.3
Colombia	87.2	11.5	1.3	71.9	26.3	1.8
Costa Rica	66.0	27.9	6.1	50.6	40.0	9.4
Dominican Republic	67.1	21.6	11.2	61.1	27.0	11.9
Honduras	68.8	26.4	4.9	29.4	54.7	15.9
Mexico	75.7	20.9	3.5	54.6	36.1	9.4
Peru	81.9	15.4	2.7	66.7	22.9	10.3

| | Middle class | | | Upper class | | |
| | Private firm | | | Private firm | | |
	Small	Large	Public firm	Small	Large	Public firm
Brazil	43.7	37.7	18.6	34.8	35.4	29.8
Chile	36.6	47.7	15.7	29.9	49.5	20.6
Colombia	48.8	42.0	9.2	28.7	51.5	19.9
Costa Rica	35.4	39.7	24.9	20.6	43.3	36.1
Dominican Republic	49.2	33.4	17.4	40.3	44.2	15.5
Honduras	11.6	54.3	34.2	2.2	50.1	47.7
Mexico	37.3	38.7	24.0	27.5	51.4	21.1
Peru	50.2	31.6	18.2	29.2	53.4	17.4

Source: Based on Birdsall 2012.
Note: Small firms have fewer than five employees. "Poor" = individuals with a per capita daily income lower than US$4. "Vulnerable" = individuals with a per capita daily income of US$4–US$10. "Middle class" = individuals with a per capita daily income of US$10–US$50. "Upper class" = individuals with a per capita daily income exceeding US$50. Poverty lines and incomes are expressed in 2005 US$ PPP per day. PPP = purchasing power parity.

FIGURE 5.12 **Female labor-force participation by class, ages 25–65, selected Latin American countries, circa 2009**

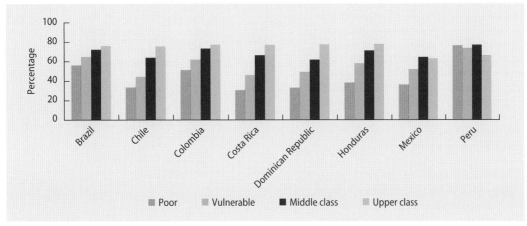

Source: Based on Birdsall 2012.
Note: Female labor-force participation is defined as the percentage of women between 25 and 65 who worked in a paid or unpaid job during the previous week (or month, for some surveys), provided a service, or looked for a job. "Poor" = individuals with a per capita daily income lower than US$4. "Vulnerable" = individuals with a per capita daily income of US$4–US$10. "Middle class" = individuals with a per capita daily income of US$10–US$50. "Upper class" = individuals with a per capita daily income exceeding US$50. Poverty lines and incomes are expressed in 2005 US$ PPP per day. PPP = purchasing power parity.

| Focus Note 5.1 | *The Latin American middle class under alternative definitions* |

There is no one unique definition of the middle class. Rather, because levels and trends of the middle class over time are likely to be sensitive to the concept behind them, the literature suggests that the concept of (middle) class to be used must be linked to the objective of the analysis (Sorensen 2005).

In what follows, we review how the main trends would vary for Latin America and the Caribbean under alternative definitions. In doing so, we explain why we believe that the definition of the middle class we have adopted is the most appropriate for the purposes of this report. We focus attention on three definitions:

- *An alternative, absolute definition* of the middle class that uses lower income thresholds (between US$2 and US$13 a day), following Ravallion (2009)
- *A relative definition* of the middle class by Cruces, López-Calva, and Battiston (2011)
- *A sociological definition* of middle-class status based on occupation, from Erikson and Goldthorpe (1992).

Absolute definitions

We begin by comparing absolute definitions. Figure F5.1a compares trends in the evolution of the middle class in Chile using the Ravallion (2009) definition, with trends using the definition of this report. The two measures show opposing trends: while, under our definition, the Chilean middle class has grown substantially in two decades; it *decreased* under the definition used in Ravallion (2009), which caps the middle class at relatively low levels (US$13 a day), given Chile's per capita income. Hence, with continued growth, more people leave the middle class to reach the upper-class level than extremely poor people join the ranks of the middle class.

The comparison presents two relevant lessons:

- *Middle-class measurements remain sensitive to the upper threshold*. When attempting to make international comparisons, therefore, it may be preferable to only use a common lower threshold

but no upper threshold because otherwise counterintuitive trends, such as those in figure F5.1a, may appear.

- *When possible, lower-income thresholds for the middle class ought to be adjusted to a country or region's level of economic development* by running, for instance, multiple vulnerability analyses along the lines of chapter 2. Although, for Latin America, US$10 a day seems to be an appropriate lower threshold (it distinguishes the middle class from the poor while also including a significant share of the population), the same amount does not provide the same resilience to poverty in Sub-Saharan Africa or Organisation for Economic Co-operation and Development countries. Even absolute measures of the middle class ought to depend, in part, on considerations about the *relative* position of the middle class, in full similarity with poverty lines in high-income countries being set higher than in low- and middle-income ones.

FIGURE F5.1A **Middle-class growth trends in Chile under two absolute definitions, 1992–2009**

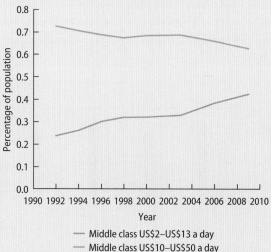

Source: Data from SEDLAC.
Note: Income ranges are expressed in 2005 US$ PPP per day. PPP = purchasing power parity. SEDLAC = Socio-Economic Database for Latin America and the Caribbean.

Relative definitions

We turn, next, to relative definitions of the middle class. Although we choose, as a point of comparison, the definition of Cruces, López-Calva, and Battiston (2011), other relative definitions tend to deliver similar results. Their definition draws from the polarization literature (in particular, the work of Esteban and Ray [1994] and Esteban, Gradín, and Ray [2007]) and relates the middle class to a measure of polarization of income. Specifically, income thresholds across classes are computed using a numerical procedure that maximizes income inequality (captured by the Gini coefficient) across classes while minimizing within-class inequality. Two interesting findings emerge:

- *Absolute and relative measures of the middle class do not necessarily overlap.* In fact, in poor countries, they may fail to overlap at all. Figure F5.1b shows the evolution of the middle class in Peru and Argentina, measured both in absolute terms (using the definition of this report) and in relative ones. Until 2005, there was no overlap in Peru, implying

that the two definitions were capturing totally different households. In contrast, the overlap in Argentina, a wealthier country, is much greater, although it dropped during the 2002 South American economic crisis. Absolute and relative concepts of the middle class thus remain substantially different, at times capturing fully different strata of the population. This is why the findings of our report may present marked differences from other studies (such as OECD [2010]) that have adopted a relative definition.

- *The relative definitions exhibit extreme stability.* The Latin American middle class, when measured in relative terms, has faced virtually no growth in the past two decades. It also did not signal any decline during the downturn in Argentina at the beginning of the 2000s. This stability occurs because the relative definition relates to the shape of the income distribution, which is much more persistent than its mean (to which the absolute definition relates). Because this report explores directional income movements across classes, the use of an absolute measure therefore seems more appropriate.

FIGURE F5.1B **Middle-class trends in Peru and Argentina under absolute and relative definitions, by income percentile, 1990s–2000s**

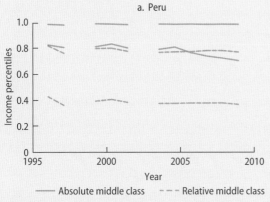

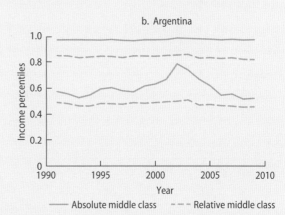

a. Peru

b. Argentina

——— Absolute middle class   - - - Relative middle class

——— Absolute middle class   - - - Relative middle class

Source: Data from SEDLAC.
Note: Pairs of solid and dotted lines in each figure panel represent the upper and lower end of the range covered by their respective definitions. Under the absolute definition (used throughout this volume), "middle class" = individuals with a per capita daily income of US$10–US$50. Incomes are expressed in 2005 US$ PPP per day. PPP = purchasing power parity. SEDLAC = Socio-Economic Database for Latin America and the Caribbean.

(Box continues next page)

| **Focus Note 5.1** | *The Latin American middle class under alternative definitions* *(continued)* |

Observe also, that the Cruces, López-Calva, and Battiston (2011) measure of the middle class suggests that Latin America is not only highly unequal but also highly polarized. Figure F5.1c shows the percentiles of the income distribution where the relative middle class starts and ends, using the polarization-based definition, compared with a more traditional measure that draws from the literature on inequality (specifically, people whose income is 75–125 percent of median income). It shows that although many Latin American and Caribbean countries do not have necessarily a much smaller relative middle class than do countries in other regions (with some exceptions, such as Chile and Colombia), most Latin American countries stand out for having a lower class extending until above the median (that is, consisting of half or more of the population), at the expense of a much narrower upper class.

A sociological definition

Finally, a comparison of our absolute definition with a sociological definition based on occupational status also shows marked differences. We base our comparison on the Goldthorpe class schema often used in sociological class analyses (Erikson and Goldthorpe 1992). According to its underlying theory, industrialized societies are stratified because of an increase in the differentiation of labor. Differentiation gave rise to a multiplication of scarce, yet desirable, technical and professional skills and to the emergence of a middle class. The diversification of occupations can be classified according to the relations they form with each other (see also Bergman and Joye 2005). Erikson and Goldthorpe (1992) identify 11 main categories: higher- and lower-grade professionals; administrators, officials, and technicians; routine

FIGURE F5.1C **Comparison of income polarization in selected countries of the world**

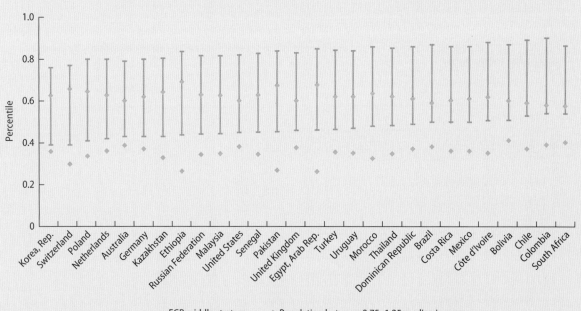

——— EGR middle stratum ◆ Population between 0.75–1.25 median income

Source: Data from SEDLAC.
Note: "EGR middle stratum" = approach to polarization in Esteban, Gradín, and Ray 2007. SEDLAC = Socio-Economic Database for Latin America and the Caribbean.

Focus Note 5.1 *(continued)*

nonmanual employees (higher and lower grades); small proprietors (with and without employees); farmers and smallholders; lower-grade technicians; skilled manual workers; semiskilled and unskilled manual workers; and workers in primary production.

Figure F5.1d shows the association between income and occupational class in Chile. The dots show average income for each occupation, while the bars show the standard deviation. Although there is some association between occupational status and income, the income within each category appears to vary dramatically. Part of the variation within categories can be attributed to difficulties in relating information from the survey about occupation to the Goldthorpe classification. But even within occupational categories defined by the survey, variation in income remains significant. Observe, also, that although they remain extremely informative, occupational definitions of middle-class status make comparisons across time challenging, and across countries almost impossible. They are thus poorly suited for the purposes of this report.

Summing up, although there is clearly no one unique ideal measure of middle-class status, one based on absolute income thresholds appears to be the most appropriate for this report for two main reasons:

- *It is fully consistent with our focus* on directional income movement in the analysis of economic mobility within generations.
- *It lends itself well to a comparison of trends* across a group of countries characterized by a reasonable degree of common cultural and economic identity (despite important income-level differences).

The adoption of an absolute measure also complements a predominant emphasis on relative measures in some of the recent academic and policy literature (OECD 2010).

FIGURE F5.1D **Average income by occupation type in Chile, 2009**

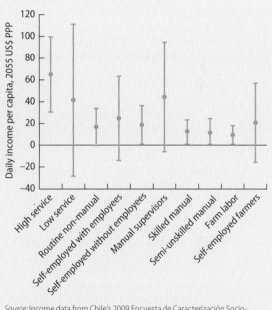

Source: Income data from Chile's 2009 Encuesta de Caracterización Socio-Económica Nacional (CASEN).
Note: Occupational categories are from the Goldthorpe Occupational Classification (Erikson and Goldthorpe 1992). Dots show average income for each occupation. Bars represent one standard deviation. PPP = purchasing power parity.

References

Azevedo, Joao P., and Viviane Sanfelice. 2012. "The Rise of the Middle Class in Latin America." Unpublished manuscript, World Bank, Washington, DC.

Bergman, Manfred M., and Dominique Joye. 2005. "Comparing Social Stratification Schemata: CAMSIS, CSP-CH, Goldthorpe, ISCO-88, Treiman, and Wright." Working paper, Cambridge Studies in Social Research 10, Social Science Research Group Publications, Cambridge, U.K.

Birdsall, Nancy. 2012. "A Note on the Middle Class in Latin America." Unpublished manuscript, Center for Global Development, Washington, DC.

Bourguignon, François. 2002. "The Growth Elasticity of Poverty Reduction: Explaining Heterogeneity across Countries and Time Periods." DELTA Working Paper 2002-03, DELTA (Ecole normale supérieure), Paris.

Bourguignon, François, and Luiz A. Pereira da Silva. 2003. *The Impact of Economic Policies on Poverty and Income Distribution.* Washington DC: World Bank; New York: Oxford University Press.

Bussolo, Maurizio, Jann Lay, and Dominique van der Mensbrugghe. 2006. "Structural Change and Poverty Reduction in Brazil: The Impact of the Doha Round." Policy Research Working Paper 3833, World Bank, Washington, DC.

Bussolo, Maurizio, and Elie Murard. 2011. "The Evolution of the Middle Class in Latin America: 2005–2030." Unpublished manuscript, World Bank, Washington, DC.

CASEN (Encuesta de Caracterización Socioeconómica Nacional), http://observatorio.ministerio desarrollosocial.gob.cl.

Cruces, Guillermo, Luis F. López-Calva, and Diego Battiston. 2011. "Down and Out or Up and In? Polarization-Based Measures of the Middle Class for Latin America." Working Paper 113, Center for Distributive, Labor and Social Studies, Universidad de La Plata, Argentina.

Datt, Gaurav, and Martin Ravallion. 1992. "Growth and Redistribution Components of Changes in Poverty Measures: A Decomposition with Applications to Brazil and India in the 1980s." Journal of Development Economics 38 (2): 275–96.

De la Torre, Augusto, Alain Ize, and Sergio L. Schmukler. 2012. *Financial Development in Latin America and the Caribbean: The Road Ahead.* World Bank Latin American and Caribbean Studies. Washington, DC: World Bank.

Didier, Tatiana, and Sergio L. Schmukler. 2011. "Financial Globalization: Some Basic Indicators for Latin America and the Caribbean." Background document, World Bank, Washington, DC.

Erikson, Robert, and John H. Goldthorpe. 1992. *The Constant Flux: A Study of Class Mobility in Industrial Societies.* Oxford: Clarendon Press.

Esteban, Joan, Carlos Gradín, and Debraj Ray. 2007. "An Extension of a Measure of Polarization, with an Application to the Income Distribution of Five OECD Countries." *Journal of Economic Inequality* 5 (1): 1–19.

Esteban, Joan, and Debraj Ray. 1994. "On the Measurement of Polarization." *Econometrica* 62 (4): 819–51.

Ferreira, Francisco H. G., and Phillippe G. Leite. 2003. "Meeting the Millennium Development Goals in Brazil: Can Microeconomic Simulations Help?" *Economía: Journal of the Latin American and Caribbean Economic Association* 3 (2): 235–79.

———. 2004. "Educational Expansion and Income Distribution: A Microsimulation for Ceará." In *Growth, Inequality, and Poverty: Prospects for Pro-Poor Economic Development,* ed. Anthony Shorrocks and Rolph van der Hoeven, 222–50. Oxford: Oxford University Press.

Lustig, Nora, Luis F. López-Calva, and Eduardo Ortiz-Juarez. 2011. "The Decline in Inequality in Latin America: How Much, Since When and Why?" Economics Working Paper 1118, Tulane University, New Orleans.

Neri, Marcelo. 2010. *The New Middle Class: The Bright Side of the Poor.* Rio de Janeiro: Fundação Getúlio Vargas Press.

OECD (Organisation for Economic Co-operation and Development). 2010. *Latin American Economic Outlook 2011: How Middle-Class Is Latin America?* Paris: OECD.

PovcalNet (database). Online poverty analysis tool. World Bank, Washington, DC. http://ire search.worldbank.org/povcalnet.

Ravallion, Martin, 2009. "The Developing World's Bulging (buy Vulnerable) "Middle Class"." Policy Research Working Paper Series 4816, World Bank, Washington, DC.

Ravallion, Martin, and Shaohua Chen. 2003. "Measuring Pro-Poor Growth." *Economics Letters* 78 (1): 93–99.

SEDLAC (Socio-Economic Database for Latin America and the Caribbean). Center for Distributive, Labor and Social Studies, Universidad de La Plata, Argentina, and World Bank, Washington, DC.

Sorensen, Aage B. 2005. "Foundations of a Rent-Based Class Analysis." In *Approaches to Class Analysis,* ed. Erik Olin Wright, 119–48. Cambridge, UK: Cambridge University Press.

World Bank. Various years. *World Development Indicators.* Washington, DC: World Bank.

The Middle Class and the Social Contract in Latin America | 6

The Marxian sociologist Erik Olin Wright tells the story of a heated debate on British Broadcasting Corporation radio after the new seven-category class scheme was introduced in the British census in 2001 (Wright 2005). A police inspector talked about being classified in class I, along with lawyers, doctors, and even executives of private companies. "Does it mean," he reportedly asked, "that now I have to wear tennis whites when I go out to do my gardening?" Professor David Rose from the University of Essex, the author of the new categories, was challenged by one person from the audience: "How can you have a sense of solidarity and consciousness when you are [category] 'five' or 'seven'? . . . Can you imagine the *Communist Manifesto* written by the University of Essex?"

Indeed, many people associate the concept of class with dimensions that go beyond its economic basis and link it to aspects such as identity, status, consumption patterns, and political beliefs. The middle class, specifically, has itself been associated in the literature with a sense of cohesion around a set of values that determine political attitudes. Since the times of the classic Greek philosophers, the debate on the values and virtues of the middle classes never lost momentum. Yet, despite all the hopes that have been placed on the middle class as an agent of stability and prosperity, and the attention the middle classes have received in both the academic and policy worlds (ADB 2010; OECD 2011; AfDB 2011), there is surprisingly little empirical evidence backing most assertions. The social, political, and economic implications of the rise of the middle classes in middle-income countries remain to be understood.

In this chapter, we explore the potential systemic implications of a larger middle class for the nature and quality of policy making in Latin America and the Caribbean. Although we do not aim at providing a comprehensive picture of these complex relationships, broad trends emerge that are relevant for the region. Using cross-country analyses that include countries beyond Latin America and the Caribbean, we find evidence of an association between larger middle classes and better governance, deeper credit markets, and greater spending on the social sectors, in particular, public health and education.

Such an association can have various roots. It has often been claimed that the middle classes carry specific beliefs and values that lead to political, economic, and social reforms. Middle classes, however, do not need to carry "good values" to push for these reforms. Their higher incomes may simply give them greater voice to push for reforms that are beneficial for them. The two views are not mutually exclusive but carry different implications for policy: if the middle classes have intrinsically "good values," their growth is unambiguously beneficial to society. On the other hand, if they push agendas that are beneficial for them, their growth is beneficial to society only to the extent that their needs are aligned with those of other classes. It could be imaginable, for instance, that growing middle classes may want to slow social spending targeted to the poor to limit the fiscal burden associated with it and, in turn, to push for more public expenditures in services from which they benefit.

To answer these questions, we look next at the relationship between class and values in seven Latin American countries. We fail to find values that distinguish the middle class from other classes in a particular way. With a couple of exceptions, values seem to associate monotonically with income. Moreover, income accounts for only a small fraction of the overall variation in values, while other factors, such as country effects, account for a much larger proportion.

But even if economic class does not relate significantly to values, is there a way to leverage the greater voice of the middle classes toward higher inclusion and better governance in the region? We argue, in a concluding section, that an important obstacle to social reforms is a historically fragmented social contract. Achieving a more inclusive social contract will require changing the framework in which the region thinks and operates—from a world of uncoordinated patchwork approaches, each aimed at addressing vulnerabilities and needs of specific groups, to a more inclusive social contract with which the poor, the vulnerable, and the middle class can all identify.

The chapter may raise more questions than it answers. In the process, however, we hope that the reader will acquire a clearer picture of which arguments are supported by empirical associations, and which arguments still remain wishful working hypotheses. The chapter has three parts:

- A review of the theory and evidence relating the middle classes to policy making
- A look at the values and beliefs of the Latin American middle classes
- An examination of the fragmentation of the Latin American social contract.

The middle class and the shaping of economic policy

The emergence of a class of consumers that has higher purchasing power is shifting demand from basic goods to more sophisticated ones, owing to larger incomes and, possibly, changing consumer preferences. Demand for cars, personal computers, household appliances, and international tourism is booming all over the middle-income world. But this mere economic effect is almost a tautology. Wealthier households not only consume more but also want different goods, and with sustained growth, consumption patterns in middle-income countries are bound to become closer to those of the rich developed world.

The more interesting, much speculated upon but less explored, aspect of growing middle classes pertains to their impact on the shaping of economic policy and the social contract. Despite the plethora of case and historical studies attributing to the middle classes the merits of social cohesion and economic growth—including persuasive theoretical arguments—the socioeconomic implications of a rising number of citizens with stronger economic means remains an open empirical question.[1]

Along the history of social and economic thought, the middle class has been assumed to positively affect growth through various channels. A first channel stresses how fixed costs in human and physical capital investments may give the middle class a greater ability to make investments that lead to greater long-term returns. Under imperfect credit markets, the poor may not earn enough income or own enough savings to overcome a fixed investment in the acquisition of human capital or productive physical capital. In this context, the larger the middle class, the more people who may be able to overcome these fixed investments and contribute to economic growth.[2]

A second channel highlights the importance of domestic markets for growth, which may be boosted by the middle classes' higher purchasing power and their demand for quality goods. Domestic markets may be particularly important when world trade is costly (Murphy, Shleifer, and Vishny 1989) and when middle-class consumers are able to play a catalytic role by providing a large market for innovation that helps lower the prices of new goods (Matsuyama 2002). From a global perspective, the growth of the middle classes in emerging countries (in particular, China) may also drive global consumption in the future and offset the falling trend in demand by American and European consumers (Kharas 2010).

The middle classes have not only been given a role as drivers of growth but have also often been perceived as agents of institutional change and democratization, as follows:

- Particular attention has been given to the "modernization theory" (Lipset 1959), which looks at the extent to which more affluent societies favor the creation and consolidation of democracies and, more generally, good institutions.
- Conceptually, higher incomes may reduce conflict over income distribution because preferences for democracy and stability may overcome the benefits from redistributive and expropriative activities (Benhabib and Przeworski 2006).
- Citizens with higher human capital may be more effective in sustaining good institutions (Glaeser et al. 2004).

In addition to higher income and human capital, the middle classes may also hold values that foster economic activity and the development of good institutions (Weber 1905 [2003]). How these values develop,

however, remains an open question. They may, for instance, be influenced by the occupations of middle-class workers, which require skills and experience and thus may help in developing work ethics and patience (Doepke and Zilibotti 2008). There is also a relevant literature that explores the links between inequality, political economy, and macroeconomic outcomes such as aggregate investment and growth rates (see box 6.1).

Data do show a clear correlation between gross domestic product (GDP) per capita, democracy, and good institutions, but there is an ongoing debate on the extent to which the relationship can be interpreted causally (Benhabib, Corvalan, and Spiegel 2011; Acemoglu et al. 2008, 2009; Epstein et al. 2006; Glaeser et al. 2004). Moreover, because of data constraints, most cross-country studies base their results on GDP per capita, a good proxy for overall development that, however, embeds too many factors to properly distinguish the impact of the middle class from other characteristics of the economy. Studies looking directly at the socioeconomic implications of growing middle classes remain thus more qualitative in nature. Among the few, Birdsall (2010) argues that, though the middle class is key for government accountability and to sustain good institutions, it may not benefit from the recent development of social policies targeting the poor, which raises political economy considerations on how best to sustain inclusive growth—an argument that we will further develop in this chapter.

In sum, despite a plethora of theoretical studies postulating that a strong middle class should bring stability and prosperity, rigorous statistical analyses remain scant. Next, therefore, we turn our attention to the data and investigate, by means of a newly developed data set, the extent to which middle classes may be associated with good institutions.

Despite the relevance and strong interest in understanding how the middle classes may shape institutions, data constraints have limited the ability to conduct robust statistical analyses. Only a handful of cross-country data sets report headcount indexes for income thresholds above US$4 a day, and

BOX 6.1   Inequality, growth, and institutions

A large literature investigates how lower inequality and a larger class that "sits in the middle" of the income distribution may bring social cohesion and institutional change. This literature relates more to a relative concept of the middle class and had a strong influence on the economic thought of the past two decades. Early studies postulated that, in democracies, "swing" voters who are at the median of the income distribution should drive redistributive decisions (Downs 1957; Roberts 1977; Meltzer and Richard 1981). The higher the income inequality (which implies a smaller middle class measured in relative terms), the more the income of the median voter moves away from average income; hence, the more demand there should be for redistribution, which, the studies postulated, may lower economic growth because of distortive taxation (Persson and Tabellini 1991; Alesina and Rodrik 1994). And even in nondemocratic regimes, income inequality, by exacerbating the distance between median and average income, may foster social conflict because pressure for redistribution increases (Benhabib and Rustichini 1996).

Although these channels have strong theoretical foundations, most studies fail in finding a causally clear-cut empirical relationship between inequality, redistribution, social conflict, and other variables of interest.[a] The biggest challenge facing empirical investigations are biases caused by omitted variables,

as variations in inequality are likely to be correlated with many unobservable factors associated with the variable of interest. Moreover, the relationship could also be nonlinear (Banerjee and Duflo 2003), and income inequality may be a poor predictor of some outcomes because other characteristics of society, such as ethnic and religious fractionalization and polarization, may be better related to outcomes such as instability and conflict (Esteban and Ray 2008; Esteban and Schneider 2008).

Accordingly, a few studies also attempt to look at how equality *and* group homogeneity may lead to greater stability and better institutions. Easterly (2001), for instance, looks at the extent to which a "middle class consensus" (defined as a high share of income in the hands of the middle three quintiles combined with low ethnic fractionalization) affects growth and socioeconomic outcomes. He finds that both the level and growth rate of per capita income are affected by the middle class consensus. He also looks at the extent to which the middle class consensus is related to human capital, a variety of public goods, and economic policies. Although the association with human capital and public goods tends to be generally positive, controlling for per capita income lowers the significance of many results. In a related paper, Easterly, Ritzen, and Woolcock (2006) also find that the middle class consensus affects institutional quality.

a. The advent of new cross-country data sets measuring income inequality has, in fact, spurred a plethora of studies looking at, among other things, the relationship between (a) inequality and growth (Persson and Tabellini 1991; Alesina and Rodrik 1994; Benhabib and Spiegel 1994; Forbes 2000; Barro 2000, 2008; Banerjee and Duflo 2003); (b) democracy (Barro 1999; Przeworski et al. 2000); (c) sociopolitical instability and conflict (Alesina and Perotti 1996; Perotti 1996; Esteban and Ray 2008; Esteban and Schneider 2008); and (d) corruption (You and Khagram 2005).

the ones that do exist span time periods that are too short to exploit both cross-country and time series variations. As a result, current analyses tend to use GDP per capita as opposed to actual household income, and they fail to investigate directly whether, as postulated by the literature, "critical masses" of people overcoming the middle-class income threshold can affect institutional outcomes.

To cope with some of these pitfalls, Loayza, Rigolini, and Llorente (2012) build a new cross-country panel data set spanning 672 yearly observations across 128 countries to revisit the relationship between the middle

classes and institutions, using better data (see box 6.2). The analysis focuses on the proportion of individuals in extreme poverty (below US$2.5 a day in purchasing power parity [PPP] terms) and the proportion of individuals who have reached middle-class status (above US$10 a day). The authors refrain from using an upper income ceiling because they pool together countries from all income levels; hence, an income ceiling may lead to strange measurements by which the middle class in rich countries may be artificially too small. The findings should, correspondingly, be interpreted as the impacts of a growing proportion of people with sufficient income

BOX 6.2   A new data set on the world's middle classes

Empirical analyses of the socioeconomic implications of growing middle classes suffer from a major challenge: data availability, particularly data that are comparable across countries. There is currently no data set that reports absolute measures of the middle class (which, for many economic implications, may be the most appropriate variable to use) and that also has large enough cross-sections and long-enough time series to perform meaningful cross-country comparisons.

To cope with this challenge, Loayza, Rigolini, and Llorente (2012) have developed a cross-country panel data set that contains information about the proportion of people living in extreme poverty (below US$2.5 a day in per capita purchasing power parity [PPP] terms), the percentage of the population that lives on more than US$10 a day, and overall income inequality as measured by the Gini coefficient. The data set spans 672 yearly observations across 128 countries, from 1967 to 2009. (Around 90 percent of the observations are, however, from the 1990s and 2000s.)

To compute the headcount indexes, the data set draws from (a) various World Bank collections of harmonized, nationally representative household surveys that contain information on income or expenditures, and (b) simulated distributions of income and expenditures from the World Bank's PovcalNet database.[a] The data set is fairly balanced across levels of economic development: 21 percent of the observations are from high-income countries, 37 percent from upper-middle-income countries, 30 percent from lower-middle-income countries, and 11 percent from low-income countries. Because of the nature of the primary data, 17 percent of the countries and 38 percent of the annual observations are, however, from Latin America. Because surveys tend to report information either for income or expenditures, the data set reports, for each country, only one of the two measures.

All income and expenditures data are in 2005 U.S. dollars PPP. For each survey, current units are first corrected for inflation using the national consumer price indexes and then converted into 2005 U.S. dollars PPP using the International Comparison Program PPP conversions. Where possible, the conversion, weights, and methodology are the same as those used to compute internationally comparable poverty data.

For the cross-country analysis, yearly observations are collapsed into five-year averages. Countries with populations of less than 2 million are also dropped. The final data set thus contains 343 observations over 110 countries. By taking averages, the proportion of observations from Latin America also is reduced to 24 percent.

a. PovcalNet is an online poverty analysis tool, available at http://iresearch.worldbank.org/povcalnet.

to undertake activities beyond constantly fighting poverty.

An attempt is made to correct for reverse causality and omitted-variable biases in the association between the size of the middle class and institutions. To do so, the cross-country comparison draws from the generalized method of moments (GMM) estimator for panel data developed by Arellano and Bond (1991) and Arellano and Bover (1995). The GMM estimator takes advantage of the panel nature of the data set in dealing with country-specific effects and endogenous explanatory variables. Unobserved country-specific effects are controlled for by differencing the regression equation and using instrumental variables based on previous observations of the explanatory variables.

Differencing the regression equation also controls for potential level effects caused by some countries reporting income data while others report expenditures. The method relies on similar instrumental variables to control for joint endogeneity (see also Loayza, Rigolini, and Llorente 2012). To be sure, GMM may not help in assessing causality under certain circumstances—for instance, if error terms suffer from higher order serial correlation. A Hansen-type test confirms the validity of the moment conditions and their underlying assumptions of the following analysis. But even if some skepticism may remain in interpreting the results causally, the mere associations we observe may be of interest.

The cross-country comparison suggests that looking at the association between GDP

TABLE 6.1 Relationship between economic development and institutions

Observations	Social policy		Economic structure		Governance	
	Public health expenditures (% GDP)	Public education expenditures (% GDP)	Mean applied tariff	Credit mkt liberalization	Polity score	Corruption
Output per capita	1.209***	0.717***	−2.179***	0.585***	2.727***	−0.656***
(Log of GDP per capita)	[6.447]	[3.183]	[−3.882]	[3.897]	[4.563]	[−4.423]
Observations (5 year averages)	269	192	265	294	318	285
Number of countries	107	97	103	100	106	92
Hansen Test – p value	0.0349	0.330	0.0340	0.308	0.230	0.0450

Source: Loayza, Rigolini, and Llorente 2012.
Note: z-statistics are in parentheses. GDP per capita is in PPP adjusted, constant 2005 prices. GDP = gross domestic product. PPP = purchasing power parity.
*** $p < 0.01$, ** $p < 0.05$, * $p < 0.1$.

and institutions, something commonly done, may deliver an overly simplistic picture. Controlling for the share of population below and above given income thresholds gives, in fact, a much richer picture and highlights the association of the middle class with institutional reforms.

For these purposes, we look first at the simple relationship between economic development and institutions (table 6.1). We also represent a country's economic development by its GDP per capita and divide policies and institutions into three broad categories: social policies (public expenditures in health and education), market-oriented economic structure (international trade and finance), and quality of governance (democratic participation and absence of official corruption). A clear result emerges: GDP per capita significantly and beneficially affects the indicators of social policy, economic structure, and governance. Specifically, an increase in GDP per capita induces a rise in public health and education expenditures, a reduction in tariff rates on international trade, a liberalization of credit markets, an improvement in democratic participation, and a reduction in official corruption.

The association found between GDP and institutions, however, may summarize more nuanced associations related to the distribution of income. From a statistical perspective, it is unlikely that a regression model with only GDP per capita as an explanatory variable is well specified. On conceptual considerations, we would like to know which aspect of the income distribution is most relevant: average output, income inequality, the prevalence of poverty, or, more specifically, the size of the middle class?

Table 6.2 presents the results of the set of regressions on the indicators of social policy, economic structure, and governance, considering as explanatory variables not only GDP per capita but also measures of poverty, inequality, and the middle class. When controlling for the size of the middle class, the coefficients corresponding to GDP per capita lose their significance, size, or even sign, depending on the regression. At the same time, the size of the middle class appears to now carry the coefficients' sign and significance that GDP per capita used to have when it was the only explanatory variable.

It is plausible, therefore, that the beneficial effect that had been attributed to changes in GDP per capita actually corresponds to the evolution of the middle class. An expansion of the middle class has a significant impact on social policy by inducing an increase of public health and education expenditures as a share of GDP. A larger middle class does not, however, necessarily mean a more state-driven economy. An increase in the size of the middle class reduces tariffs on international trade and liberalizes the financial sector. No less remarkable is the effect on the quality of governance. An expansion of

TABLE 6.2 **The middle-class effect on indicators of social policy, economic structure, and governance**

	Social policy		Economic structure		Governance	
	Public health expenditures (% GDP)	Public education expenditures (% GDP)	Mean applied tariff	Credit market liberalization	Polity score	Corruption
Middle class	2.054***	2.918**	−10,945***	1.357***	6.431***	−1.764***
(% of population with income above 10 USD)	[3.849]	[2.337]	[−3.072]	[2.799]	[4.068]	[−4.767]
Poverty	−0.019**	−0.042**	0.203***	0.047***	−0.042**	−0.011*
(US$2.5 a day poverty headcount)	[−2.411]	[−2.472]	[2.874]	[3.383]	[−2.345]	[−1.825]
Inequality	−3.716**	3.028	20.736***	−0.209	9.262**	4.083***
(Gini Index)	[−2.456]	[1.360]	[3.373]	[−0.165]	[2.164]	[3.866]
Output per capita	0.121	−0.922	5.485**	1.292***	0.280	−0.470**
(Log of GDP per capita)	[0.416]	[−1.310]	[2.439]	[3.009]	[0.334]	[−2.218]
Observations (5 year averages)	269	192	265	294	318	285
Number of countries	107	97	103	100	106	92
Hansen Test – p value	0.174	0.640	0.934	0.469	0.701	0.451

Source: Loayza, Rigolini, and Llorente 2012.
Note: z-statistics are in parentheses. GDP per capita is in PPP adjusted, constant 2005 prices. PPP = purchasing power parity.
***p < 0.01, **p < 0.05, *p < 0.1.

the middle class induces an improvement in democratic participation and a decline in official corruption.

The indicators of poverty and inequality are also relevant determinants for social policies, economic structure, and governance quality, but not always in the expected way or with the consistency shown by the middle-class measure. For instance, a decrease in income inequality seems to produce not only a decline in official corruption (as possibly expected) but also a reduction in democratic participation (which is hard to explain). Similarly, a decrease in the poverty headcount appears to induce not only a liberalization of international trade but also, surprisingly, a constriction of credit markets.

The findings suggest that growing middle classes have enough voice to exert pressure for reforms. When the size of the middle class increases, social policy on health and education becomes more active, and the quality of governance regarding democratic participation and official corruption improves.

These regressions, however, include countries from all over the world. Do the results

hold for Latin America? And if they do, what are the reasons behind these reforms? Is the middle class entrusted with specific values, or does it act based upon self-interest? Understanding well the reasons why the middle class is associated with more social expenditures, lower tariffs, more liberalized credit markets, better functioning democracies, and lower corruption is a challenging but essential exercise for sound policy analysis. For one thing, if the middle class intrinsically favors democracy and abhors corruption, it can be an agent of change and reforms that go beyond these specific issues. But it could also be the case that an "income effect" makes it simply more expensive to buy the votes and favors of the middle class. Under this alternative scenario, which has gained traction in recent years (Fukuyama 2012), the middle class may be a much less likely agent of change.

This report does not pretend to provide comprehensive answers to these difficult questions. It aims, however, to shed some light on how the growing Latin American middle class may influence social and economic policy along two dimensions: First, it looks at the extent to which the Latin American middle class may hold values that distinguish it from other classes and may favor institutional development. Second, it looks at the nature of the Latin American social contract and at how growing middle classes may affect it.

Values and beliefs of the Latin American middle classes

Theories of middle-class values and beliefs contrast with the scarcity of empirical research on the association between income (or occupation) and values, attitudes, and behavior. Yet even from a theoretical perspective, the relationship is not necessarily obvious. Even if higher wealth and specific occupations may lead to adopting a particular set of values—a hypothesis that is far from proven—cultural and societal factors also influence values, which may lead to tenuous differences in the values profile with respect to other classes. In this section, therefore, we review the association between income and values in Latin America.

Most empirical studies looking at middle-class values in emerging countries classify people based on self-perception of either status or position in the income distribution (PRC 2008; Amoranto, Chun, and Deolalikar 2010; OECD 2011), but self-reported status is a poor predictor of someone's income, education, or occupation. In addition, attempts to use income measures in values surveys, such as Cárdenas, Kharas, and Henao (2011), are limited by the lack of accurate income information, which is either absent or classified into broad categories. Many studies also fail to compare income effects with relevant individual characteristics that could affect values (such as education or occupation) and that could be in part captured by income.

The analysis in this section, based on a study by López-Calva, Rigolini, and Torche (2011)—whose approach is described in box 6.3—attempts to solve some of these conceptual and technical issues. It addresses, for Latin America, the following questions:

- How do political and social values vary across income and class?
- To what extent does class, as opposed to education and social origins, have a net association with values?
- Does the Latin American middle class hold specific values that distinguish it from both upper and lower classes, or is the relationship between social classes and values, if any, a monotonic one?

It is important to state at the outset that the analysis will not claim to assert causality in the relationship between class and values. If the middle class is found to hold a particular set of values, the analysis cannot establish that the level or sources of economic well-being that characterize this class are the cause of observed values, as implicitly suggested by theories on the role of the middle class in economic development or political stability. Endogeneity due to reverse causality or omitted-variable biases prevents such causal interpretation. But given the current status of research and the relevance of the question, documenting systematic variations in values and orientations across education, income, and occupation levels in Latin America represents a first, necessary step in understanding how the emergence of new middle classes may affect future growth and development prospects.

Figure 6.1 shows the association between values and beliefs, years of education, and income class in a regression that also controls for individual characteristics (age, gender, ethnicity) and country effects. To better compare the magnitude of the associations, the effects are all expressed in terms of the values' standard deviation, and the education coefficient is also multiplied by its standard deviation. In addition, because of the difficulties in including enough people from upper classes (those earning more than US$50 a day per capita), the authors investigate differences in values between "lower-middle classes" (with per capita incomes of US$10–US$20 a day) and "upper-middle classes" (with per capita incomes above US$20 a day). Observe also that the associations with income shown

BOX 6.3 Studying middle-class values

Middle-class values remain a challenging field for investigations. The first challenge to surmount is conceptual: what measure of class to use? Results are likely to differ significantly if the measure of class is based on income rather than, say, occupation. It is therefore important to clarify that values relate to a *specific* aspect of the middle class as captured by the measure that is used (in our case, absolute income).

The second challenge to surmount is statistical: analyses remain flawed by omitted-variable and reverse-causality biases. The latter can be quite worrying: Are values dictated by reaching a certain income, or did individuals manage to reach a certain income *because* they had specific values?

The third challenge regards the availability of good data. The sampling rigor of some values surveys has been questioned, and most of them do a poor job in capturing households' income. This is why many studies of middle-class values use self-reported status (PRC 2008; Amoranto, Chun, and Deolalikar 2010; OECD 2011) or peoples' perceived relative position in the income distribution (Fischer and Torgler 2007) as indicators. Both are, however, poor substitutes for actual income.

The analysis in López-Calva, Rigolini, and Torche (2011) does not resolve possible biases caused by omitted variables and, more important, reverse-causality effects. The findings thus only document *associations* between income and values without implying any causal link. On the other hand, the analysis makes a serious effort to address the challenge of poor income data in values surveys. The analysis draws on the 2007 Ecosocial values surveys. These values surveys were implemented by the Corporation for Latin American Studies (*Corporación de Estudios para Latinoamérica*; CIEPLAN), a Latin American think tank, in seven Latin American countries: Argentina, Brazil, Chile, Colombia, Guatemala, Mexico, and Peru. (However, the analysis does not use Argentinean data because of difficulties in imputing income). The surveys are representative of the adult population (18 years or older) living in large urban centers in each country. The authors choose to use the Ecosocial surveys because of their rigorous sampling methodology, the information they collect on a variety of values, and the information they collect about households' assets, which will allow them to construct a measure of households' permanent income.

Specifically, as in most values surveys, data on households' income are unavailable in Ecosocial surveys. Therefore, they use information about households' assets to construct a measure of households' permanent income—the long-term level of economic well-being, purged from short-term volatility and measurement error (Torche 2009). To do so, they match assets in Ecosocial with assets from an "external" household survey in each country that contains information on both assets and households' income. Using these external surveys, they run a regression model predicting the log of per capita household income by means of the set of household goods and assets (controlling for the household head's education) and the log of household size. The coefficients obtained for the household goods and assets are then used in Ecosocial to predict, using the same set of assets and household characteristics, (the log of) per capita income for each household. To achieve comparability across countries, they convert each income variable into 2005 U.S. dollar purchasing power parity terms.

Finally, to investigate the association between income and values, they create "values indexes," as follows. First, they select a series of survey questions capturing orientations that are plausibly related with each other. They then extract the weight of each variable in the first principal component (the linear combination that accounts for the largest proportion of the variance across all items) and compute predicted values of the principal component for each observation in the data set. These new, summary variables constitute the dependent variables of the analysis. (For example, the value index "trust in institutions" is based on five items, ascertaining trust in the following institutions: the national government, congress, political parties, the mayor, and the police.) This technique allows for substantive decision making in terms of the items selected to identify each value index, while at the same time preventing arbitrary combination of items that are only weakly correlated. Together, they investigate 11 dependent variables: trust in institutions; political alienation; perception of mobility and opportunity; support for individual rights under any circumstances; legitimization of political violence; voting; social tolerance; nationalism; political ideology; interpersonal trust; and interpersonal alienation. For a complete list of indicators and details on the methodology, see López-Calva, Rigolini, and Torche (2011).

FIGURE 6.1   Education, class, and values, selected Latin American countries, 2007

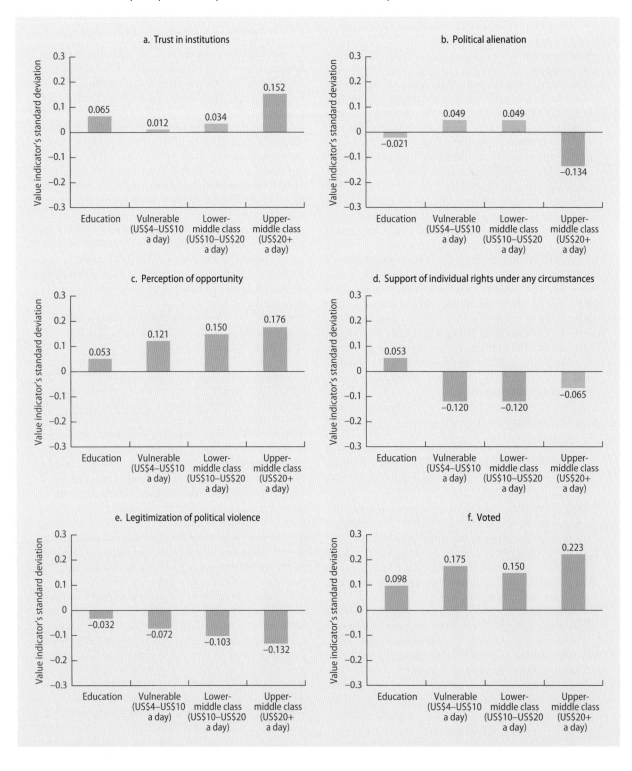

FIGURE 6.1   Education, class, and values, selected Latin American countries, 2007   *(continued)*

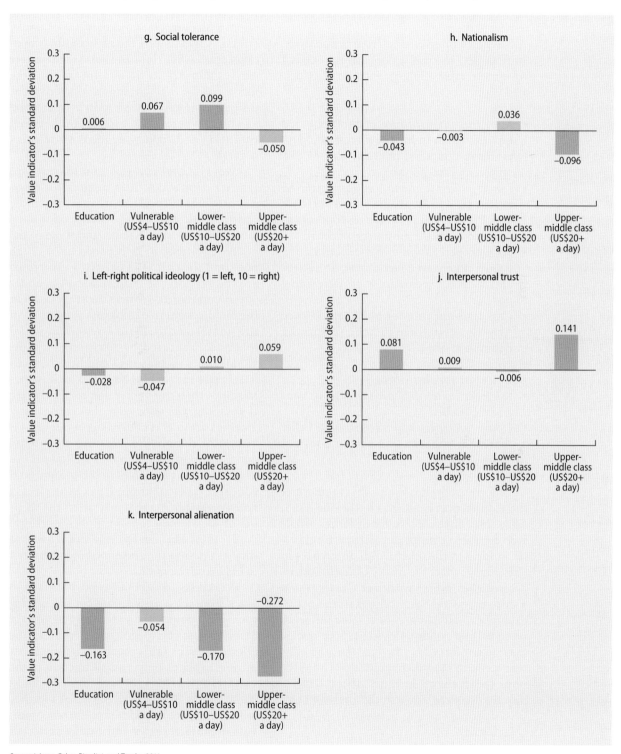

Source: López-Calva, Rigolini, and Torche 2011.
Note: Orange columns are statistically insignificant at the 10 percent level. Effects are all expressed in terms of the values' standard deviation. Education is multiplied by its standard deviation. Class dummies refer to the difference from the poor (per capita income of US$0–US$4 a day in 2005 PPP terms). PPP = purchasing power parity.

in figure 6.1 should be interpreted as the additional association of a given class with respect to the poor.

Several findings emerge from the analysis. Statistically, income is robustly associated with most values. Higher income is associated with

- *More trust in institutions* (an index based on how much individuals trust the government, congress, political parties, the mayor, and the police)
- *Lower political alienation* (the perceived extent to which people in power care about people similar to the respondents as opposed to taking advantage of them)
- *Stronger perception of opportunities* (the degree of perceived meritocracy in society and the perceived easiness of overcoming poverty)
- *Less legitimization of political violence* (the use of violence to achieve socially desirable goals)
- *Higher likelihood of voting*
- *Lower nationalistic beliefs*
- *Stronger belief that people can, in general, be trusted*
- *Lower interpersonal alienation* (a belief that what happens to a person does not count much).

Unfortunately, it is impossible to interpret these differences causally. On the one hand, values may drive success: for instance, people who believe in meritocracy may perform better in life. On the other hand, differences in values may reflect the reality of Latin American societies, where wealthier classes live in a different world that is closer to the political process and that may bear more influence on social and political decisions. Such a view may be reinforced by the fact that the class that seems to most distinguish itself from the poor (people with incomes below US$4 a day, the "omitted" class in the analysis) comprises people earning between US$20 and US$50 a day.

Observe that although, overall, income classes follow a pattern similar to that of education (although their association is controlling for it), they differ in a few important

dimensions. Higher education shows a positive association with support of individual rights under any circumstances (for example, criminals should have the same rights as honest people), while the association with income classes appears to be nonlinear. And the income-class variable shows a positive but insignificant association with a right-wing ideology, whereas the association between education and right-wing ideology remains negative.

Overall, the analysis summarized in figure 6.1 provides little support for theories attributing special merits to the middle classes. Most values and beliefs tend to vary monotonically with income, and those of the middle class tend to be between those of the poor and the rich. The only two exceptions are the support for individual rights under any circumstances—where the two classes in the middle seem to exhibit less support than the poorer and richer classes—and social tolerance (captured by tolerance for individual traits such as race and homosexuality), where the middle classes exhibit higher tolerance than the poorer and richer classes. If anything, the only value that consistently emerges from the analysis is *moderation*. Values of the middle class are repeatedly and consistently more moderate than those of people at the extremes of the income (and education) distribution. That in itself is a noteworthy finding that may affect the shaping of social and economic policies because moderation can indeed represent a force of social cohesion that intermediates between the rich and the poor.

Nonetheless, we should avoid inferring too much from these associations for several reasons. First, despite the statistically significant associations, the magnitude of the income effects remains fairly small, suggesting that income explains only a small fraction of the variation in values. In fact, even by looking at all the explanatory variables together (which include, in addition to income, individual characteristics and country effects), the proportion of the overall variation in values that is explained remains fairly small. The R-squared of the regressions—a measure of how much the regressions are able to "capture" the variation in values—remain overall very low, on the order of 2–15 percent. That means that 85 percent or more of the variation in values remains unexplained. This poor performance of income and education (and of other individual characteristics, such as age, gender, and ethnicity that are included in the regressions) suggests that other factors must also influence values. To address this possibility, the authors run the same regressions as in the baseline analysis, but adding people's occupation. Using occupational status available in Ecosocial, they classify occupations into unskilled jobs, self-employed, manual skilled, clerical (low), clerical (high), professional independents, high professional executives, workers in the home, students, and people not in the labor force. Although they do find that some occupations (in particular, high professional executives) show some association with values, the association for most categories (after correcting for individual characteristics, income, and education) remains *weaker* than the one for income. Moreover, adding occupation only marginally improves the R-squared. The exercise suggests, therefore, that *values are difficult to explain for many definitions of the middle class, not only income-related ones.*

Second, the variation in values that is driven by income and education remains significantly smaller than the variation in values across countries. Figure 6.2 compares, for selected values, the magnitude of their association with income and country effects. To ease the comparison, the income regression coefficient is multiplied by the standard deviation of income. It shows that income has a relatively small association with values such as trust in institutions, perceptions of opportunities, and social tolerance when compared with the variation across countries. The strong cross-country variation undermines further the supposition that the middle classes share common values across Latin America that can lead to greater social cohesion and economic prosperity. Values appear to be, to some extent, *circumstantial* and driven by changing challenges and socioeconomic environments. And while the values of the middle class show moderation, they do so only within boundaries dictated by society.

This should not be surprising at all. Over the past century, the middle class has been tolerating extremist movements as much as it supported reforms. For instance, an influential 1967 article about the relationship of middle classes and military regimes asserts that the middle class aspires to become part of the elite and is willing to abandon democratic values when it perceives a threat to its own class status (Nun 1967). The moderation of middle-class values may, therefore, reflect a pragmatic attitude. Using our indicators, for example, economic success may engender in the middle class more trust in institutions and a stronger perception of opportunities in life, but, at the same time, the middle classes are not ready to support individual rights of criminals that have undermined law and order, a necessity for prosperous economic activity.

The lack of strong values leading to greater stability and cohesion, however, may further undermine a Latin American social contract that appears to be already under stress. We conclude the chapter by looking at these issues in deeper detail.

Overcoming a fragmented social contract

The Latin American middle classes do not appear to hold exceptional values that may lead to greater stability and social cohesion. In fact, as this concluding chapter suggests, they appear to be rather pragmatic, supporting policies that are good for them, and, in some areas, may be opting out from a social contract from which they see little benefit. Many middle-class Latin Americans do not rely on the state for basic services such as education and health, and, in some cases, even for core public services such as the provision of electricity and security.

Although the middle classes may opt out from some basic services (see box 6.4), they also benefit disproportionately from other services. The middle classes, for instance, benefit disproportionately from

FIGURE 6.2 **Income versus country-specific values, selected Latin American countries, 2007**

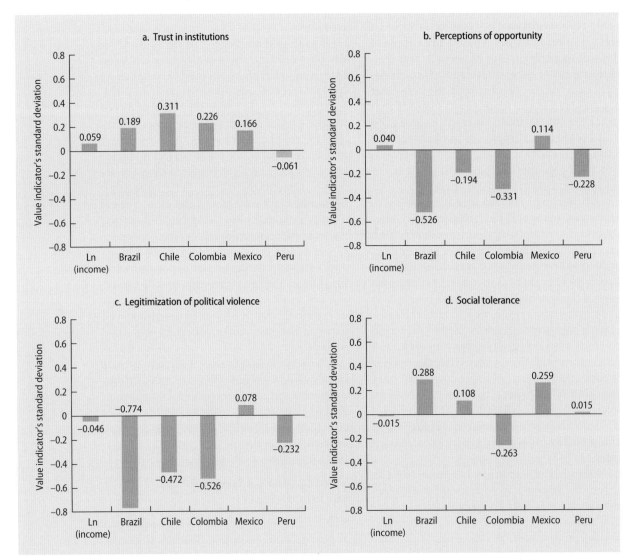

Source: Lopez-Calva, Rigolini, and Torche 2011.
Note: Ln(income) = natural logarithm of income. Orange columns are statistically insignificant at the 10 percent level. Effects are all expressed in terms of the values' standard deviation. Country dummies refer to the difference with respect to Guatemala. Income is multiplied by its standard deviation.

public tertiary education and subsidized social insurance schemes, which only marginally address the needs of the poor. The Latin American and Caribbean social contract is a fragmented one, with facets of it benefiting different classes and being only loosely connected with one another.

This section does not aim to provide a comprehensive picture of the Latin American social contract, which could be the subject of a report on its own. Rather, it wants to highlight some features that may affect the mobility prospects of the remaining poor and may prevent, at the same time, achievement of a more cohesive and stable contract. It shall do so by focusing attention on two areas of the welfare state that have received strong attention: cash transfers and education.

As with many institutions, the welfare state reflects the spirit and nature of a social contract. Rather than following a clear vision, however, most Latin American welfare states are the result of a buildup of features, each aimed at addressing specific challenges. Many welfare states thus remain highly fragmented, providing through various channels differentiated services to various population groups, often separated along the divide of labor formality (Ribe, Robalino, and Walker 2010). History may be the culprit. Traditionally, social security systems in Latin America were designed for middle-class, formal-sector workers under the belief that coverage would have expanded as the economies formalized. Once it became clear that labor informality was not disappearing, however, many countries began implementing parallel systems to fill the coverage gaps by offering protection to informal workers (Kaplan and Levy 2012; Antón, Hernández, and Levy 2012).

To be sure, the rapid developments of targeted cash transfer programs, combined with heavy investments in primary and secondary education, have borne fruit. Between 2000 and 2009, around 10 percent of the Latin American population was lifted out of moderate poverty (measured as the proportion of people with incomes below US$4 per capita per day; see World Bank 2010), and while this would not have been possible without sustained economic growth, the development of targeted cash transfer programs and the improvement in social spending toward more progressivity played an important role (López-Calva and Lustig 2010).

Yet although these efforts did contribute significantly to poverty reduction, they were for the most part built on top of existing welfare states, partly because it would have been politically difficult to introduce drastic overhauls of social protection systems. The result of this uncoordinated development is a quite heterogeneous picture of social policies across countries, with some having managed to achieve a fair amount of progressiveness in their social spending, while others still distribute benefits in a fairly flat manner. An analysis by Lustig (2011) suggests, for instance, that although, in countries such as Argentina and Peru, most cash transfers

programs are directed to the poor and vulnerable, in countries like Bolivia and Brazil, the middle class receives as much in cash transfers as the poor (see figure 6.3). The lack of progressiveness of cash transfers in these countries stems from either the introduction of universal benefits or the legacy of social insurance systems for the formal sector (often pensions and unemployment insurance) that were financed out of general taxation. These schemes may pose a challenge in expanding benefits for the poor because they consume large portions of the governments' budgets.

The fragmentation of the welfare state may pose several challenges:

- By having specific programs tailored to each class, it may contribute to promoting competition among classes for limited resources. These tensions can be particularly strong if needs differ across classes.
- It may distort labor markets. If the social insurance system is too generous, it may exacerbate the insiders-outsiders divide and hence the vulnerability of informal labor. On the other hand, as the study of *Seguro Popular* in Mexico seems to suggest, generous social assistance programs that compete with social insurance may stimulate informal labor and create an unjust situation, where formal workers are forced to pay to receive benefits that are similar to those given to informal workers for free (Levy 2008).
- It may also pose a challenge in providing effective protection because people are more prone to fall through the cracks (Ribe, Robalino, and Walker 2010).

Fragmentation and truncation also extend to education. On first impression, the region made significant efforts to increase education spending for the poor, which brought results: in Chile, Costa Rica, and Mexico, for instance, net secondary enrollment rates among children from the poorest income quintile rose by 24, 53, and 38 percentage points, respectively, between the 1990s and 2009 (SEDLAC 2011). These advances are

FIGURE 6.3   Class incidence of social policies, selected Latin American countries, circa 2007–10

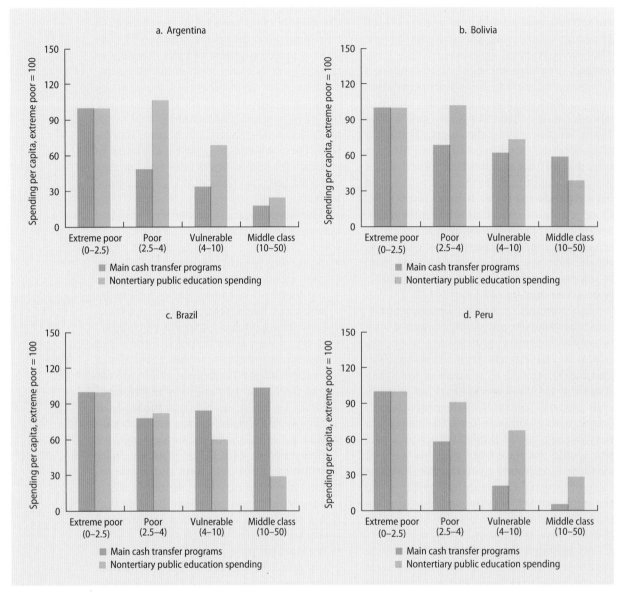

Source: Lustig 2011.
Note: Class status is based on net market income. Upper class is omitted. "Extreme poor" = per capita income of US$0–US$2.50. "Poor" = per capita income of US$2.50–US$4. "Vulnerable" = per capita income of US$4–US$10. "Middle Class" = per capita income of US$10–US$50. Poverty lines and incomes are expressed in 2005 US$ PPP per day. PPP = purchasing power parity. Main cash transfer programs include *Jefas y Jefes de Hogar, Familias,* unemployment insurance, scholarships, noncontributory pensions, food, and *Asignación Universal Por Hijo* (Argentina); *Bono Juancito Pinto,* school feeding, *PAN, Bono Sol,* lactation subsidy, *Bono de Natalidad,* and pensions (*Sistema de Reparto*) (Bolivia); *Bolsa Família,* other scholarships, *Benefício de Prestação Continuada,* unemployment benefits, special circumstances pensions from INSS, and other social programs (Brazil); and *Juntos* and food transfers (Peru).

reflected in the incidence of non-tertiary education spending, which also suggests quite a progressive picture (the right-side bars in figure 6.3): the ratio of spending per capita in primary and secondary education between the extreme poor and the middle

class in Argentina, Bolivia, Brazil, and Peru is, respectively, 4.3, 1.8, 2.7, and 3.0.

These figures, however, may be as much the result of past successes as the source of future challenges. They indeed hide a high degree of fragmentation of service provision.

Even within the education sector, the picture almost reverses in all countries for tertiary education. In the four countries analyzed by Lustig (2011), the middle classes benefit disproportionately from public tertiary education spending (see figure 6.4). A distributional distortion may have emerged in some Latin American and Caribbean countries, where poor children who attend low-quality public schools cannot access high-quality public universities, which generally establish high standards for admission. The poor—whose willingness to pay for education is high and whose capacity to pay has increased in recent years—may end up paying tuition in low-quality tertiary education institutions, which have expanded dramatically in the past 15 years (UNESCO 2008). At the same time, better-educated middle-class children may receive free higher education in the best public universities. Not surprisingly, political movements related to public higher education in Brazil, Chile, Mexico, and other Latin American countries have been led and supported by the middle classes (Arocena and Sutz 2005; Lustig, Mizala, and Silva 2012).

To add to the fragmentation, the middle and upper classes seem to opt out disproportionately from publicly provided primary and secondary education. Figure 6.5 shows the percentage of students 6 to 12 years old who are enrolled in private schools, by income group. In most countries, with the exception of Chile (which has fostered private school enrollment through vouchers), the figure shows a sharp contrast between enrollment in private schools of the poor and vulnerable and such enrollment of the middle and upper classes: in Brazil, for instance, only 13 percent of children in the vulnerable class attend private schools at primary-school age, while the proportion for the middle class is almost half (45 percent). And even in Costa Rica, one of the countries with the highest educational achievements in Latin America and the Caribbean, only 2 percent of vulnerable children attend private schools at primary-school age, while the proportion jumps to 25.3 percent for the middle class. The picture does not change much at the secondary level.

FIGURE 6.4 Incidence of tertiary public education spending, selected Latin American countries

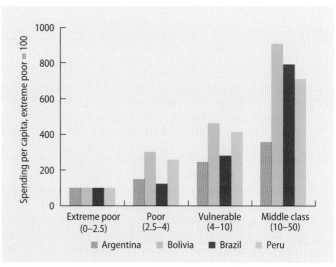

Source: Lustig 2011.
Note: Class status is based on net market income. Upper class is omitted. "Extreme poor" = per capita income of US$0–US$2.50. "Poor" = per capita income of US$2.50–US$4. "Vulnerable" = per capita income of US$4–US$10. "Middle Class" = per capita income of US$10–US$50. Poverty lines and incomes are expressed in 2005 US$ PPP per day. PPP = purchasing power parity.

FIGURE 6.5 Percentage of students 6–12 years old enrolled in private schools, by income group, selected Latin American countries

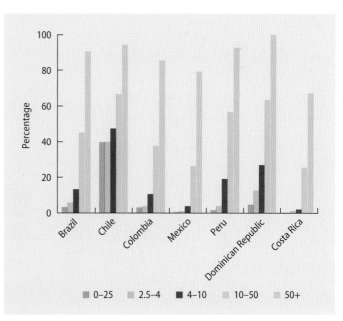

Source: Data from SEDLAC.
Note: "Extreme poor" = per capita income of US$0–US$2.50. "Poor" = per capita income of US$2.50–US$4 per day. "Vulnerable" = per capita income of US$4–US$10 per day. "Middle Class" = per capita income of US$10–US$50 per day. "Upper class" = per capita income exceeding US$50 per day. Poverty lines and incomes are expressed in 2005 US$ PPP per day. PPP = purchasing power parity. SEDLAC = Socio-Economic Database for Latin America and the Caribbean.

BOX 6.4 Individualization of public goods and lack of institutional trust in the Dominican Republic

Sánchez and Senderowitsch (2011) study how the middle class in the Dominican Republic has resorted to individualized solutions to substitute for faulty public goods. Examples of this "adaptive behavior" include the heavy reliance on domestic generation of electricity, the digging of wells to get running water at home, the use of private companies to report car accidents (instead of doing it at the police station), and the use of private services for education and health—these last two also common in other countries of the region.

Consider the electricity sector, for instance. In the Dominican Republic, it has been characterized by large energy losses caused by deficient infrastructures and maintenance, poorly targeted subsidies, and widespread nonpayment of bills. Reforms have proven to be slow and not always successful: for instance, the privatization process of the distribution companies had to be partially reversed because the mentioned inefficiencies resulted in persistent losses for private operators (Reinstein and Cayo 2010). To cope with unstable provision of electricity, the mid-

dle classes now have electrical inverters and generators at home (figure B6.4), much more so than the poor and vulnerable. The charge needs of the inverters' batteries represent 63 percent of the average electricity consumption by a middle-income household (453 kilowatt-hours a month), and approximately 246 gigawatts-hours a month are consumed just to support individual private autogeneration capacity. This inefficiency in the system is a significant opportunity cost, which burdens both the state and final consumers, who pay around US$240 million of their annual electricity bill to keep the inverters working.

The authors also provide suggestive evidence that low levels of institutional trust tend to reinforce the individualization of services and weaken the demand for better services. This may have generated a vicious cycle of poor service delivery, which self-reinforces low trust in institutions because "weak spending institutions and low quality services . . . spawn dissatisfaction and may underpin . . . low level of trust in public institutions" (Ferroni, Mateo, and Payne 2008)

FIGURE B6.4 **Ownership of electrical inverters in the Dominican Republic, 2010**

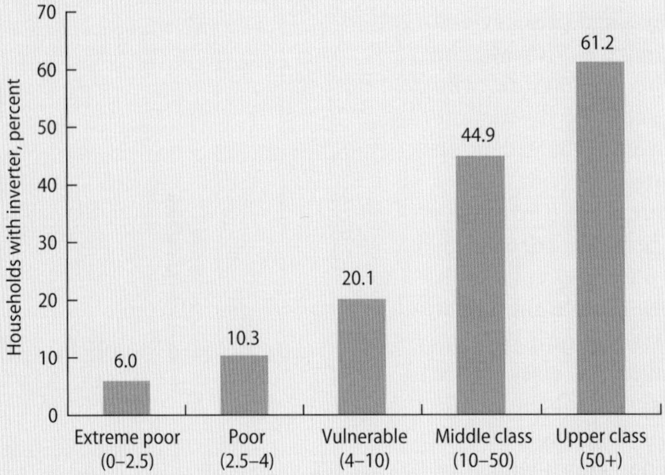

Source: Data from Sánchez and Senderowitsch 2011.

Although significant investments have been put forward to improve coverage of services, quality issues may lie behind the opting out of the middle and upper classes.

Consider, for instance, the evidence emerging from evaluations of conditional cash transfers (CCTs), reviewed in chapter 3. Although cash transfers have improved the lives of poor people and positively affected the schooling of beneficiaries, the impact on educational achievements remains limited, and gains in employment, wages, and intergenerational occupational mobility may not be sufficient to break, by themselves, the intergenerational cycle of poverty (Rodríguez-Oreggia and Freije 2012). The latter result (or lack thereof), however, is not a flaw of the CCT programs themselves, which have achieved their purpose—increasing school enrollment and attainment. Complementary policies related to quality on the supply side and employment generation seem to be missing in many cases (Fiszbein and Schady 2009).

In education, for instance, despite improved attendance from the lower quintiles, there remain marked differences in learning achievements across classes. Figure 6.6 shows reading test scores of sixth-grade children by income group (based on the nationally representative 2006 Second Regional Comparative and Explanatory Study [SERCE] assessments). The "bounds" in figure 6.6 attempt to correct for the fact that, in some countries, dropout rates remain significant and may bias the observed estimates upward (see focus note 3.1 at the end of chapter 3).

Figure 6.6 shows that there is almost as much variation across classes as across countries: for instance, children from poor and vulnerable families in Chile (the second-best-performing country in the sample after Costa Rica) appear to perform as poorly as children from the middle and upper classes in Panama (the fifth-worst-performing country). And the difference between test scores of poor and middle-class children in Uruguay (the third-best-performing country) is almost as wide as the difference between test scores of middle-class children in Uruguay and Ecuador (the second-worst-performing country). Unless quality is improved, greater demand for services will serve little to improve mobility and the cohesiveness of the social contract.

FIGURE 6.6 **Sixth-grade reading test scores, by income group, selected Latin American countries, 2006**

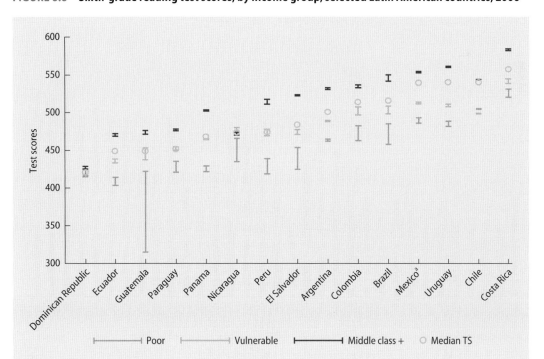

Source: Data from SERCE 2006 and household surveys.
Note: SERCE = Second Regional Comparative and Explanatory Study. TS = test score. The bounds stem from estimated biases caused by missing observations. "Poor" = per capita income of US$0–US$4 per day. "Vulnerable" = per capita income of US$4–US$10 per day. "Middle Class" = per capita income of US$10–US$50 per day. NLE = State of Nuevo Leon, Mexico. Poverty lines and incomes are expressed in 2005 US$ PPP per day. PPP = purchasing power parity.
a. For Mexico, the data is from the state of Nuevo León.

However, improving quality is not an easy task. And apart from a few countries—such as Brazil, where revenues have been historically high, or Argentina, which achieved a dramatic increase in revenues—fiscal revenues tend to be low in the region, as shown in figure 6.7. In many cases, low revenues do not stem from low tax rates (according to the 2009 U.S. Agency for International Development [USAID] Fiscal Reform and Economic Governance Project, the top marginal tax rates of personal income in Colombia and Chile, for instance, are close to Organisation for Economic Co-operation and Development [OECD] levels) but rather from evasion and narrow tax bases because many firms and workers operate informally.

Low fiscal revenues limit the ability of governments to improve quality of services. They also make it more difficult to expand coverage of more inclusive programs financed out of general taxation. The lower the revenues, the more likely that expansion of a program must come at the expense of another one, generating tensions across groups and classes that may undermine the social contract.

The good news is that low revenues stem mostly from a compliance challenge. Technically, it would thus be possible to increase revenues through administrative reforms. Data from USAID's Fiscal Reform and Economic Governance Project suggest that in Ecuador, for instance, value added tax (VAT) receipts out of each VAT percentage point increased from 0.22 percent of GDP in 2004 to 0.53 percent in 2009, mostly thanks to administrative reforms.

The main challenge in raising revenues, however, may not be technical. To enforce taxation, there must be the political will

FIGURE 6.7   Tax revenues by type, selected Latin American and other countries, 1990–2010

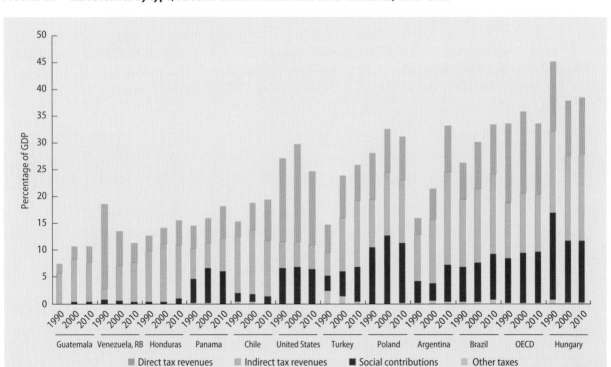

Sources: OECD.Stat (stats.oecd.org) and ECLACSTAT (www.eclac.org) databases.
Note: ECLAC = Economic Commission for Latin America and the Caribbean; OECD = Organisation for Economic Co-operation and Development.

to do so, and unless the middle and upper classes (which contribute the largest share of revenues) benefit from the increase in spending, it may be difficult to gain their support for higher taxation.

We end the section—and the chapter—on a positive note. We see two ways out of this vicious cycle in which some countries may be trapped:

- First, it is not all about money. In many countries, the design of social policies presents serious flaws, and redressing institutional and individual incentives in a flat budgetary environment may go a long way toward improving quality. A recent study about teaching practices in the region, for instance, suggests that learning achievements can be raised by providing the right incentives to teachers to improve their mastery of content and teaching practices (Bruns, Evans, and Luque 2012). In Mexico, a low-cost intervention to empower parents in the management of schools in disadvantaged rural areas has had an impact on grade failure and grade repetition (Gertler, Patrinos, and Rubio-Codina 2012).

- Second, the recent boom in commodity prices, coupled with new oil and commodities discoveries, and improved macroeconomic management has given to many countries the fiscal space necessary to invest in the quality of services without engaging into a zero-sum competition for a limited pool of resources between the poorer and the wealthier segments of society.

If the middle classes are more pragmatic, rather than particularly value-oriented, as this chapter suggests, building coalitions around the right policies may require less of a normative discussion and more of an effort to design the right incentive-compatible political platform. In any case, how to improve services and achieve greater buy-in of the wealthier segments of society is likely to remain at the center of the social policy debate for the foreseeable future.

Notes

1. See, among many others, Weber (1905), Adelman and Morris (1967), and Landes (1998) for Western Europe, and Pike (1963), Parker (1998), Barr-Melej (2001), and Adamovsky (2009) for Latin America.

2. These arguments have mostly been studied in the context of the literature on inequality and growth (Banerjee and Newman 1993; Galor and Zeira 1993), but they also apply to the middle classes. See also Galor and Moav (2004), Voitchovsky (2005), and Foellmi and Oechslin (2008).

References

Adamovski, Ezequiel. 2009. *Historia de la Clase Media Argentina: Apogeo y Decadencia de una Ilusión, 1919–2003*. Buenos Aires: Planeta.

Acemoglu, Daron, Simon Johnson, James A. Robinson, and Pierre Yared. 2008. "Income and Democracy." *American Economic Review* 98 (3): 808–42.

———. 2009. "Reevaluating the Modernization Hypothesis." *Journal of Monetary Economics* 56 (8): 1043–58.

ADB (Asian Development Bank). 2010. *Annual Report 2010*. Manila: ADB.

Adelman, Irma, and Cynthia T. Morris. 1967. *Society, Politics, and Economic Development: A Quantitative Approach*. Baltimore, MD: Johns Hopkins University Press.

AfDB (African Development Bank). 2011. *The Africa Competitiveness Report 2011*. Geneva: The World Economic Forum.

Alesina, Alberto, and Roberto Perotti. 1996. "Income Distribution, Political Instability and Investment." *European Economic Review* 40 (6): 1203–28.

Alesina, Alberto, and Dani Rodrik. 1994. "Distributive Politics and Economic Growth." *Quarterly Journal of Economics* 109 (2): 465–90.

Amoranto, Glenita, Natalie Chun, and Anil Deolalikar. 2010. "Who Are the Middle Class and What Values Do They Hold? Evidence from the World Values Survey." Economics Working Paper 229, Asian Development Bank, Manila.

Antón, Arturo, Fausto Hernández, and Santiago Levy. 2012. "The End of Informality in

Mexico? Fiscal Reform for Universal Social Insurance." Working paper, Centro de Investigación y Docencia Económicas, Mexico City; Inter-American Development Bank, Washington, DC.

Arellano, Manuel, and Stephen Bond. 1991. "Some Tests of Specification for Panel Data: Monte Carlo Evidence and an Application to Employment Equations." *Review of Economic Studies*, 58 (2): 277–97.

Arellano, Manuel, and Olympia Bover. 1995. "Another Look at the Instrumental-Variable Estimation of Error-Components Models." *Journal of Econometrics* 68 (1): 29–52.

Arocena, R., and J. Sutz. 2005. "Latin American Universities: From an Original Revolution to an Uncertain Transition." *Higher Education* 50 (4): 573–92.

Banerjee, Abhijit V., and Esther Duflo. 2003. "Inequality and Growth: What Can the Data Say?" *Journal of Economic Growth* 8 (3): 267–99.

Banerjee, Abhijit V., and Andrew F. Newman. 1993. "Occupational Choice and the Process of Development." *Journal of Political Economy* 101 (2): 274–98.

Barr-Melej, Patrick. 2001. *Reforming Chile: Cultural Politics, Nationalism and the Rise of the Middle Class*. Chapel Hill: University of North Carolina Press.

Barro, Robert J. 1999. "Determinants of Democracy." *Journal of Political Economy* 107 (6): 158–83.

———. 2000. "Inequality and Growth in a Panel of Countries." *Journal of Economic Growth* 5 (1): 5–32.

———. 2008. "Inequality and Growth Revisited." Working Paper on Regional Economic Integration 11, Asian Development Bank, Manila.

Benhabib, Jess, Alejandro Corvalan, and Mark M. Spiegel. 2011. "Reestablishing the Income-Democracy Nexus." Working Paper 16832, National Bureau of Economic Research, Cambridge, MA.

Benhabib, Jess, and Adam Przeworski. 2006. "The Political Economy of Redistribution under Democracy." *Economic Theory* 29 (2): 271–90.

Benhabib, Jess, and Aldo Rustichini. 1996. "Social Conflict and Growth." *Journal of Economic Growth* 1 (1): 125–42.

Benhabib, Jess, and Mark M. Spiegel. 1994. "The Role of Human Capital in Economic Development: Evidence from Aggregate Cross-Country Data." *Journal of Monetary Economics* 34 (2): 143–73.

Birdsall, Nancy. 2010. "The (Indispensable) Middle Class in Developing Countries; Or, the Rich and the Rest, Not the Poor and the Rest." Working Paper 207, Center for Global Development, Washington, DC.

Bruns, Barbara, Dave Evans, and Javier Luque. 2012. *Building Better Teachers in Latin America and the Caribbean*. Washington, DC: World Bank.

Cárdenas, Mauricio, Homi Kharas, and Camila Henao. 2011. "Latin America's Global Middle Class." Working Paper, Global Economy and Development, Brookings Institution, Washington, DC.

Doepke, Matthias, and Fabrizio Zilibotti. 2008. "Occupational Choice and the Spirit of Capitalism." *Quarterly Journal of Economics* 123 (2): 747–93.

Downs, Anthony. 1957. "An Economic Theory of Political Action in a Democracy." *Journal of Political Economy* 65 (2): 135–50.

Easterly, William. 2001. "The Middle Class Consensus and Economic Development." *Journal of Economic Growth* 6 (4): 317–35.

Easterly, William, Jozef Ritzen, and Michael Woolcock. 2006. "Social Cohesion, Institutions, and Growth." *Economics and Politics* 18 (2): 103–20.

ECLACSTAT (database). Statistics of the Economic Commission for Latin America and the Caribbean (ECLAC; in Spanish, CEPAL) of the United Nations. http://www.eclac.org/esta disticas/default.asp.

Epstein, David, Robert Bates, Jack A. Goldstone, Ida Kristensen, and Sharyn O'Halloran. 2006. "Democratic Transitions." *American Journal of Political Science* 50 (3): 551–69.

Esteban, Joan, and Debraj Ray. 2008. "Polarization, Fractionalization and Conflict." *Journal of Peace Research* 45 (2): 163–82.

Esteban, Joan, and Gerald Schneider. 2008. "Polarization and Conflict: Theoretical and Empirical Issues." *Journal of Peace Research* 45 (2): 131–41.

Ferroni, Marco, Mercedes Mateo, and Mark Payne. 2008. "Development under Conditions of Inequality and Distrust." Discussion paper 777, International Food Policy Research Institute, Washington, DC.

Fischer, Justina A. V., and Benno Torgler. 2007. "Social Capital and Relative Income Concerns: Evidence from 26 Countries." Working Paper

Serics, Berkeley Olin Program in Law & Economics, University of California–Berkeley.

Fiszbein, Ariel, and Norbert Schady. 2009. *Conditional Cash Transfers: Reducing Present and Future Poverty.* Washington, DC: World Bank.

Foellmi, Reto, and Manuel Oechslin. 2008. "Why Progressive Redistribution Can Hurt the Poor." *Journal of Public Economics* 92 (3–4): 738–47.

Forbes, Kristin J. 2000. "A Reassessment of the Relationship between Inequality and Growth." *American Economic Review* 90 (4): 869–87.

Fukuyama, Francis. 2012. "The Politics of Latin America's New Middle Class." Remarks at 2012 Sol M. Linowitz Forum, The Inter-American Dialogue, Washington, DC, June 8–9.

Galor, Oded, and Omer Moav. 2004. "From Physical to Human Capital Accumulation: Inequality and the Process of Development." *Review of Economic Studies* 71 (4): 1001–26.

Galor, Oded, and Joseph Zeira. 1993. "Income Distribution and Macroeconomics." *Review of Economic Studies* 60 (1): 35–52.

Gertler, Paul, Harry Patrinos, and Marta Rubio-Codina. 2012. "Empowering Parents to Improve Education: Evidence from Rural Mexico." *Journal of Development Economics* 99 (1): 68–79.

Glaeser, Edward L., Rafael La Porta, Florencio López-de-Silanes, and Andrei Shleifer. 2004. "Do Institutions Cause Growth?" *Journal of Economic Growth* 9 (3): 271–303.

Kaplan, David S., and Santiago Levy. 2012. "The Evolution of Social Security Systems in Latin America." Working paper, Inter-American Development Bank, Washington, DC.

Kharas, Homi. 2010. "The Emerging Middle Class in Developing Countries." Working Paper 285, Development Centre, Organisation for Economic Co-operation and Development, Paris.

Landes, David S. 1998. *The Wealth and Poverty of Nations.* New York, London: W. W. Norton & Company.

Levy, Santiago. 2008. *Good Intentions, Bad Outcomes: Social Policy, Informality, and Economic Growth in Mexico.* Washington, DC: Brookings Institution Press.

Lipset, Seymour M. 1959. "Some Social Requisites of Democracy: Economic Development and Political Legitimacy." *American Political Science Review* 53 (1): 69–105.

Loayza, Norman, Jamele Rigolini, and Gonzalo Llorente. 2012. "Do Middle Classes Bring Institutional Reforms?" Policy Research Working Paper 6015, World Bank, Washington, DC.

López-Calva, Luis F., and Nora Lustig, eds. 2010. *Declining Inequality in Latin America: A Decade of Progress?* Washington, DC: Brookings Institution Press.

López-Calva, Luis F., Jamele Rigolini, and Florencia Torche. 2011. "Is There Such a Thing as Middle Class Values? Class Differences, Values, and Political Orientations in Latin America." Policy Research Working Paper 5874, World Bank, Washington, DC.

Lustig, Nora. 2011. "Fiscal Policy, 'Fiscal Mobility,' the Poor, the Vulnerable and the Middle Class in Latin America." Background paper prepared for this volume, The Inter-American Dialogue, Washington, DC; Tulane University, New Orleans.

Lustig, N., A. Mizala, and G. E. Silva. 2012. "¡Basta YA! Chilean Students Say 'Enough'." In *The Occupy Handbook*, ed. J. Byrne. Back Bay, MA: Little, Brown & Company.

Matsuyama, Kiminori. 2002. "The Rise of Mass Consumption Societies." *Journal of Political Economy* 110 (5): 1035–70.

Meltzer, Allan H., and Scott F. Richard. 1981. "A Rational Theory of the Size of Government." *Journal of Political Economy* 89 (5): 914–27.

Murphy, Kevin M., Andrei Shleifer, and Robert W. Vishny. 1989. "Income Distribution, Market Size, and Industrialization." *Quarterly Journal of Economics* 104 (3): 537–64.

Nun, José. 1967. "The Middle-Class Military Coup." In *The Politics of Conformity in Latin America*, ed. Claudio Veliz, 66-118. London: Oxford University Press.

OECD (Organisation for Economic Co-operation and Development). 2011. *Latin American Economic Outlook 2011: How Middle-Class Is Latin America?* Paris: OECD.

OECD.Stat (database). Data and metadata for Organisation for Economic Co-operation and Development countries and selected non-member economies. stats.oecd.org.

Parker, Danny S. 1998. *The Idea of the Middle Class: White-Collar Workers and Peruvian Society, 1900–1950.* University Park: Pennsylvania State University Press.

Perotti, Roberto. 1996. "Growth, Income Distribution, and Democracy: What the Data Say." *Journal of Economic Growth* 1 (2): 149–87.

Persson, Torsten, and Guido Tabellini. 1991. "Is Inequality Harmful for Growth? Theory and

Evidence." Discussion Paper 581, Centre for Economic Policy Research, London.

Pike, Fredrick B. 1963. "Aspects of Class Relations in Chile, 1850–1960." *Hispanic American Historical Review* 43 (1): 14–33.

PovcalNet. Online poverty analysis tool. World Bank, Washington, DC. http://iresearch.world bank.org/povcalnet.

PRC (Pew Research Center). 2008. *Inside the Middle Class: Bad Times Hit the Good Life.* Washington, DC: PRC.

Przeworksi, Adam, Michael E. Alvarez, Jose A. Cheibub, and Fernando Limongi. 2000. *Democracy and Development: Political Institutions and Well-Being in the World: 1950–1990.* New York: Cambridge University Press.

Reinstein, David, and Juan M. Cayo. 2010. "El Sector Eléctrico." In *República Dominicana: de la crisis financiera internacional al crecimiento para todos,* ed. Roby Senderowitsch and Yvonne M. Tsikata, 77–87. Dominican Republic: World Bank.

Ribe, Helena, David Robalino, and Ian Walker. 2010. *From Right to Reality: Achieving Social Protection for All in Latin America and the Caribbean.* Washington, DC: World Bank.

Roberts, Kevin, W.S., 1977. "Voting Over Income Tax Schedules." *Journal of Public Economics* vol 8 (3): 329–40.

Rodríguez-Oreggia, Eduardo, and Samuel Freije. 2012. "Long-Term Impact of a Cash-Transfers Program on Labor Outcomes of the Rural Youth." Working Paper 230, Center for International Development, Harvard University, Cambridge, MA.

Sánchez, Miguel E., and Roby Senderowitsch. 2011. "The Political Economy of the Middle Class in the Dominican Republic: Individualization of Public Goods, Lack of Institutional Trust, and Weak Collective Action." Policy Research Working Paper 6049, World Bank, Washington, DC.

SEDLAC (Socio-Economic Database for Latin America and the Caribbean). 2011. Center for Distributive, Labor and Social Studies, Argentina, and World Bank, Washington, DC. http://sedlac.econo.unlp.edu.ar/eng.

SERCE (Segundo Estudio Regional Comparativo y Explicativo (UNESCO)).

Torche, Florencia. 2009. "Sociological and Economic Approaches to the Intergenerational Transmission of Inequality in Latin America." Working Paper HD-09-2009-UNDP, United Nations Development Programme, New York.

UNESCO (United Nations Educational, Scientific, and Cultural Organization). 2008. *Trends in Higher Education in Latin America and the Caribbean,* ed. Lúcia Gazzola and Axel Didriksson. Bogotá: Panamericana.

Voitchovsky, Sarah. 2005. "Does the Profile of Income Inequality Matter for Economic Growth? Distinguishing Between the Effects of Inequality in Different Parts of the Income Distribution." *Journal of Economic Growth* 10 (3): 273–96.

Weber, Max. (1905) 2003. *The Protestant Ethic and the Spirit of Capitalism.* Mineola, NY: Dover.

World Bank. 2010. *Did Latin America Learn to Shield Its Poor from Economic Shocks?* Washington, DC: World Bank.

Wright, Erik O. 2005. *Approaches to Class Analysis.* Cambridge, U.K.: Cambridge University Press.

You, Jong-Sung, and Sanjeev Khagram. 2005. "A Comparative Study of Inequality and Corruption." *American Sociological Review* 70 (1): 136–57.